Tracings

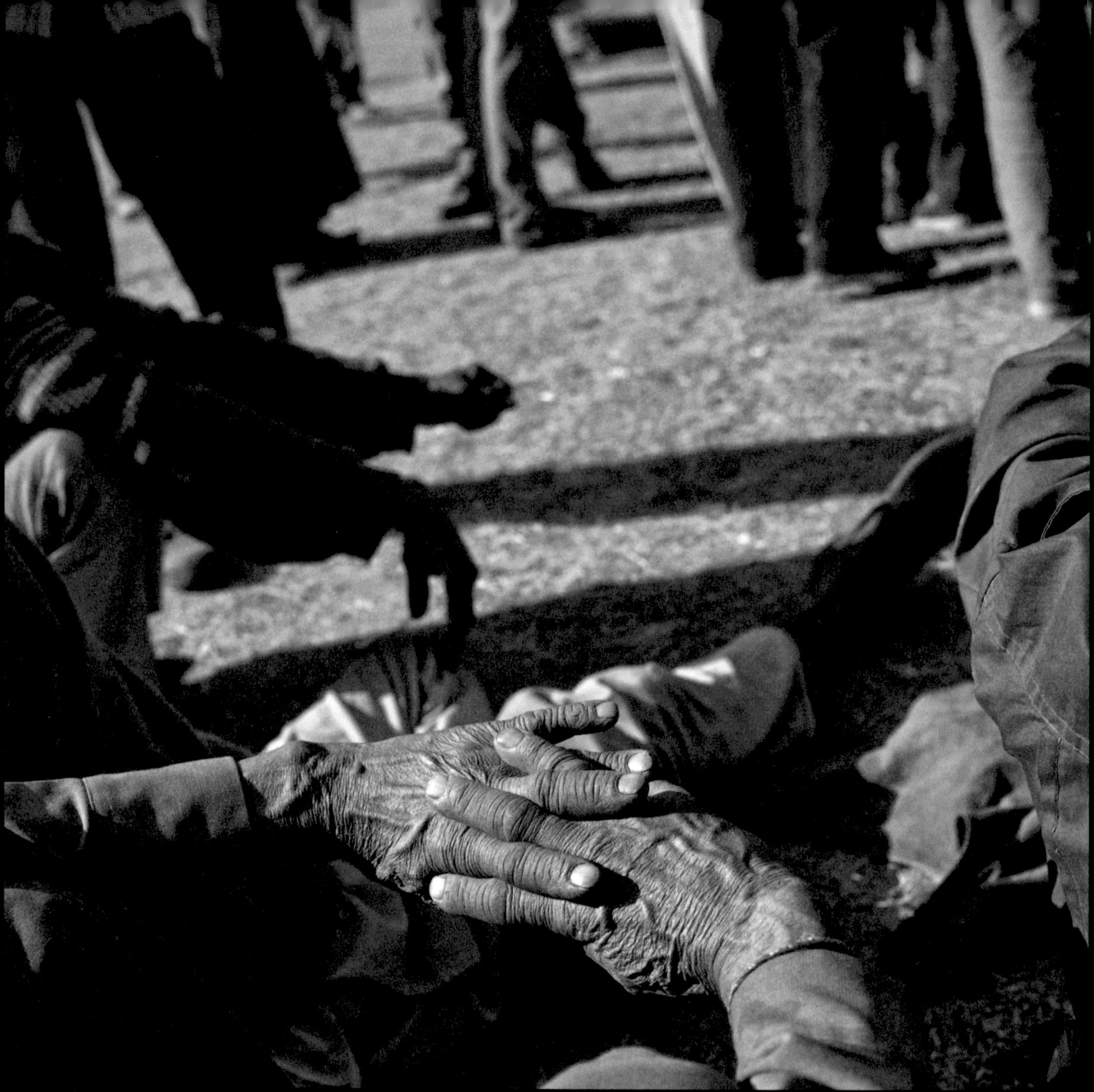

1

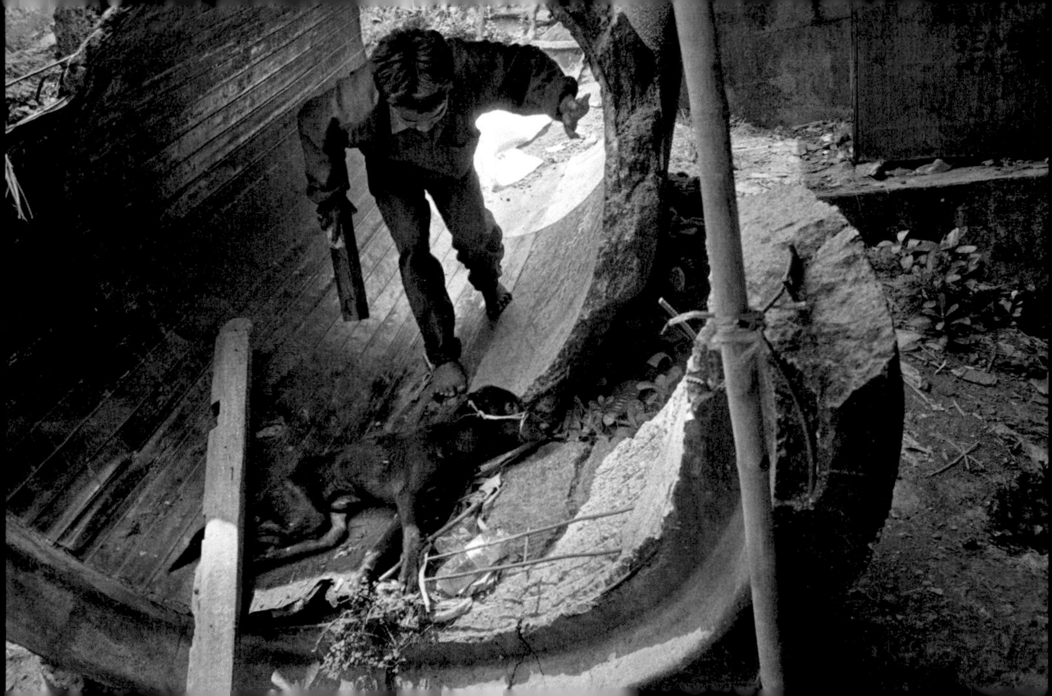

2

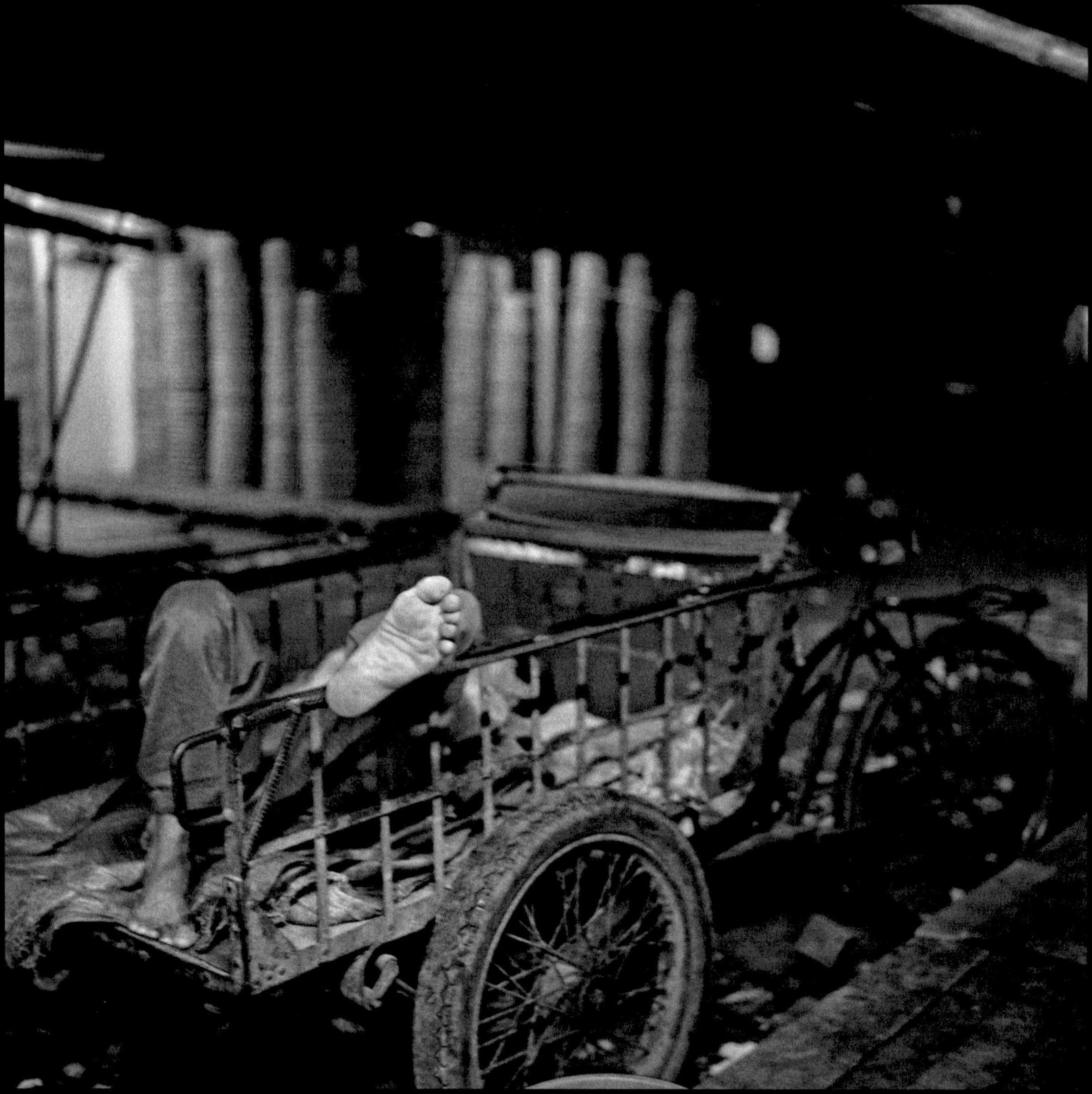

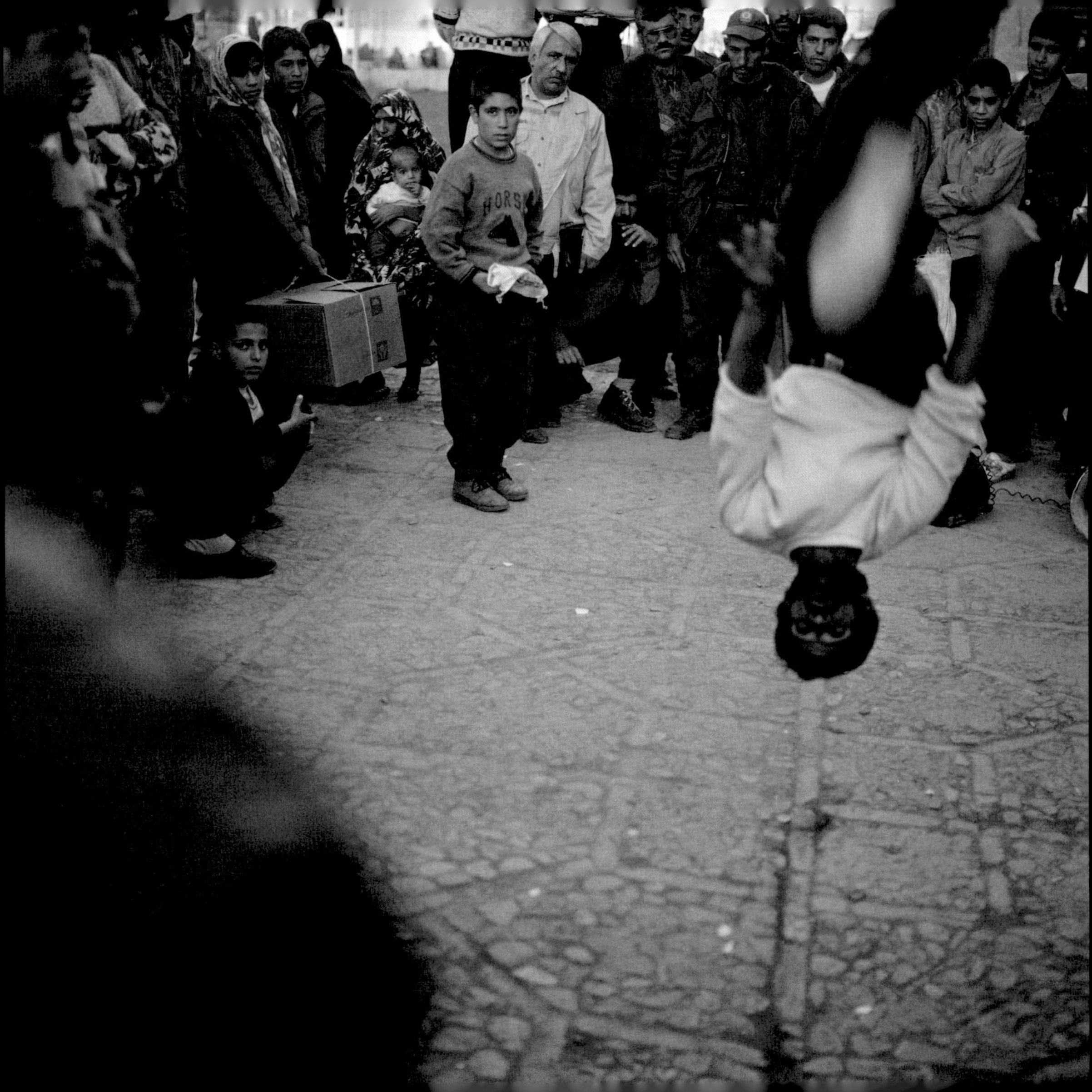

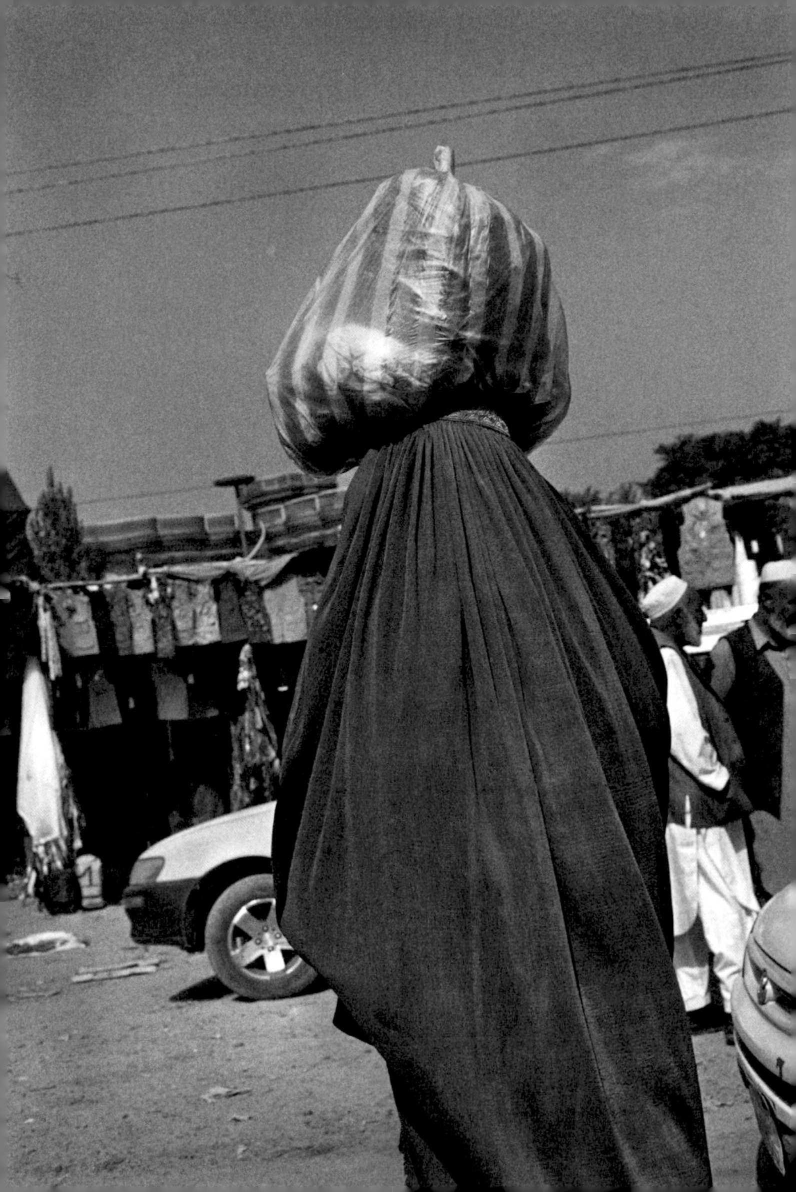

6

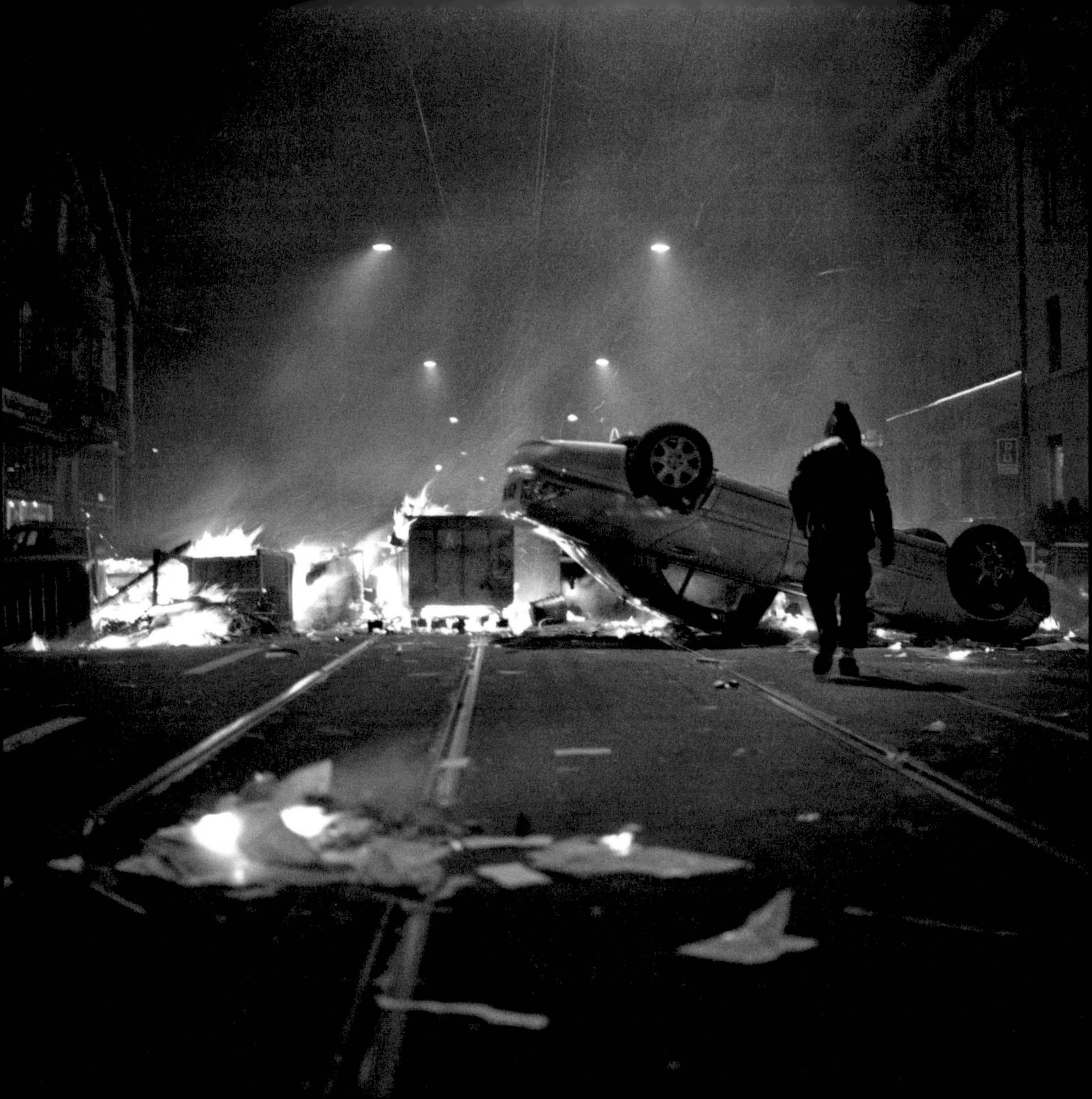

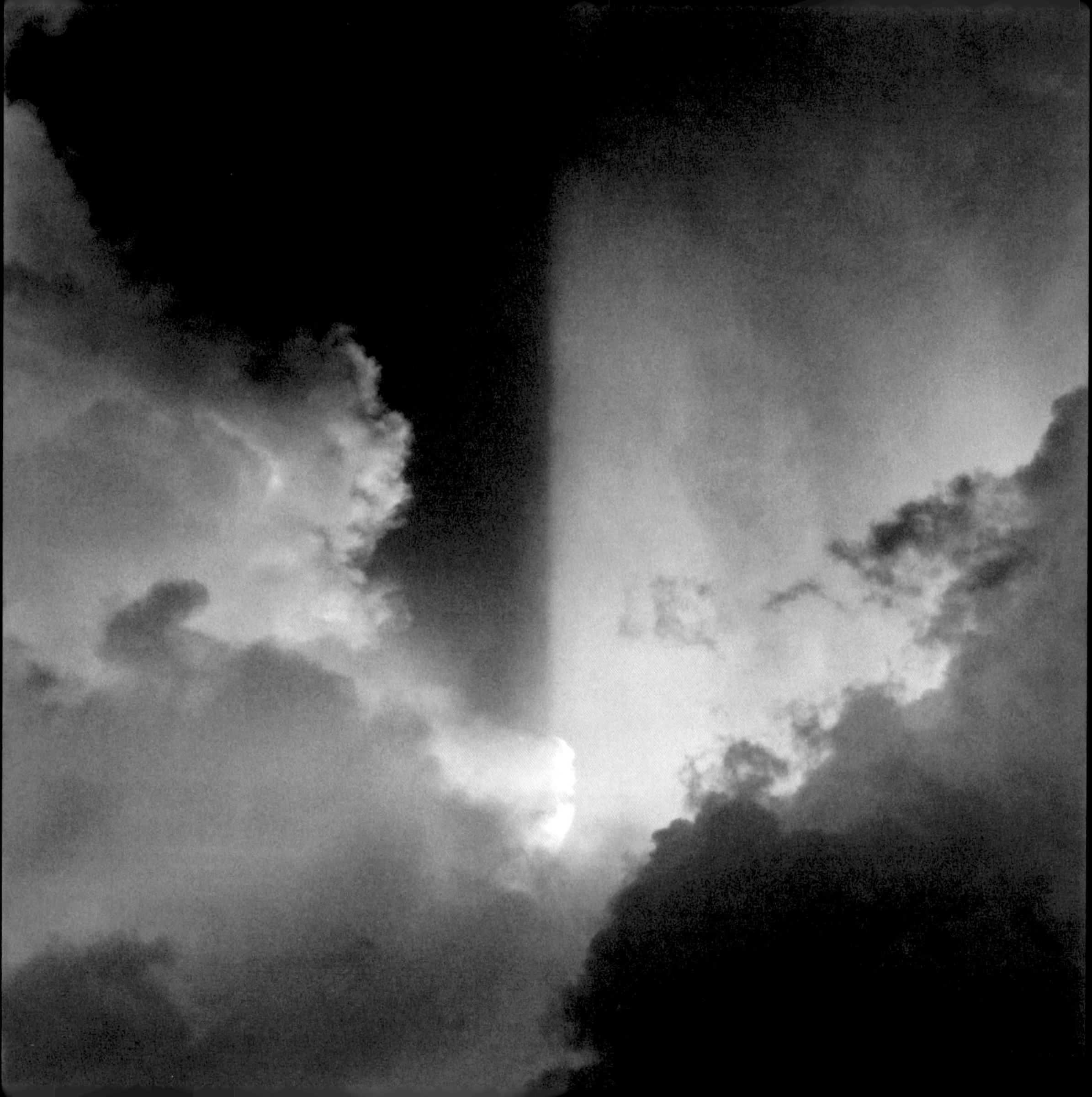

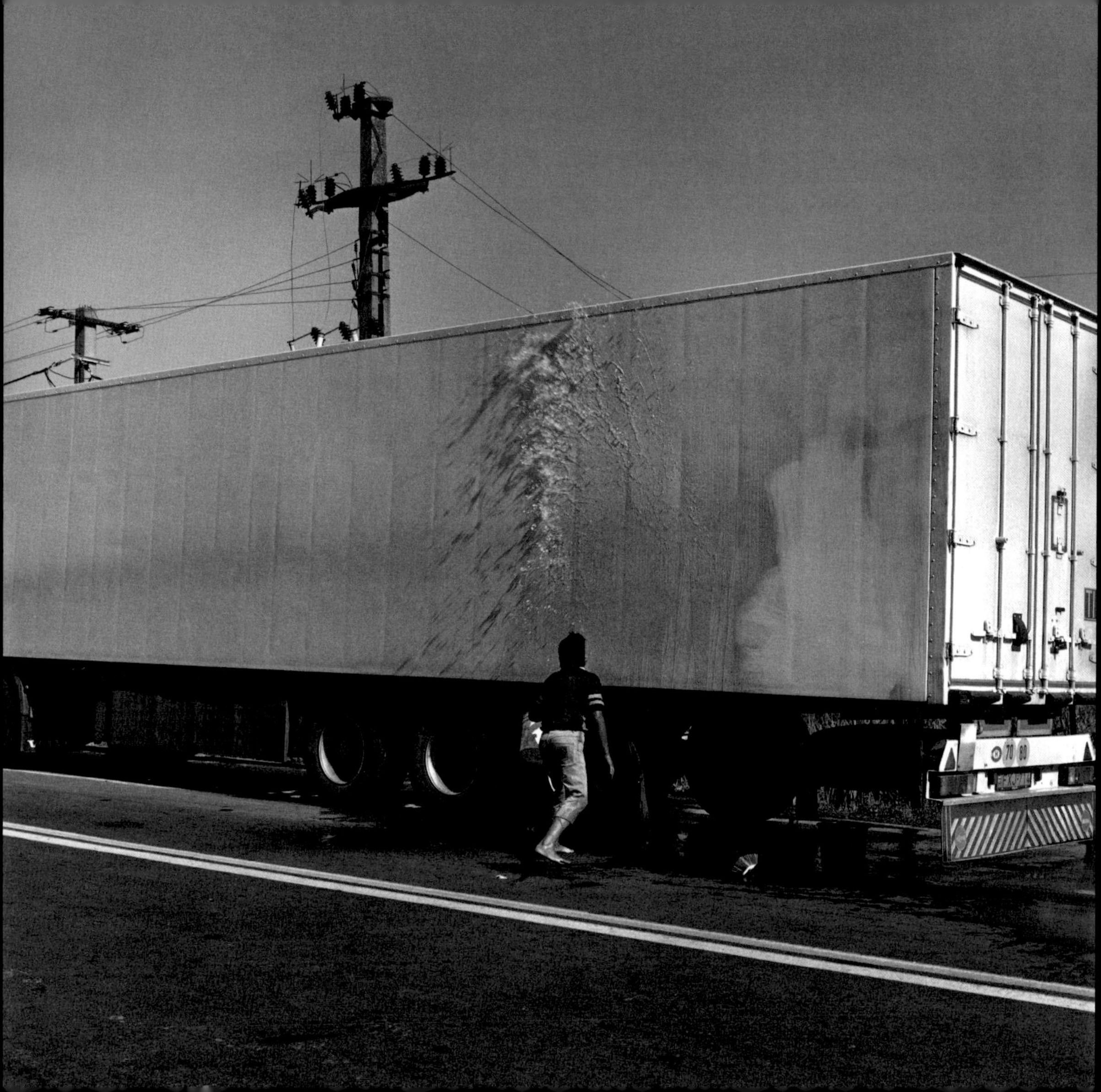

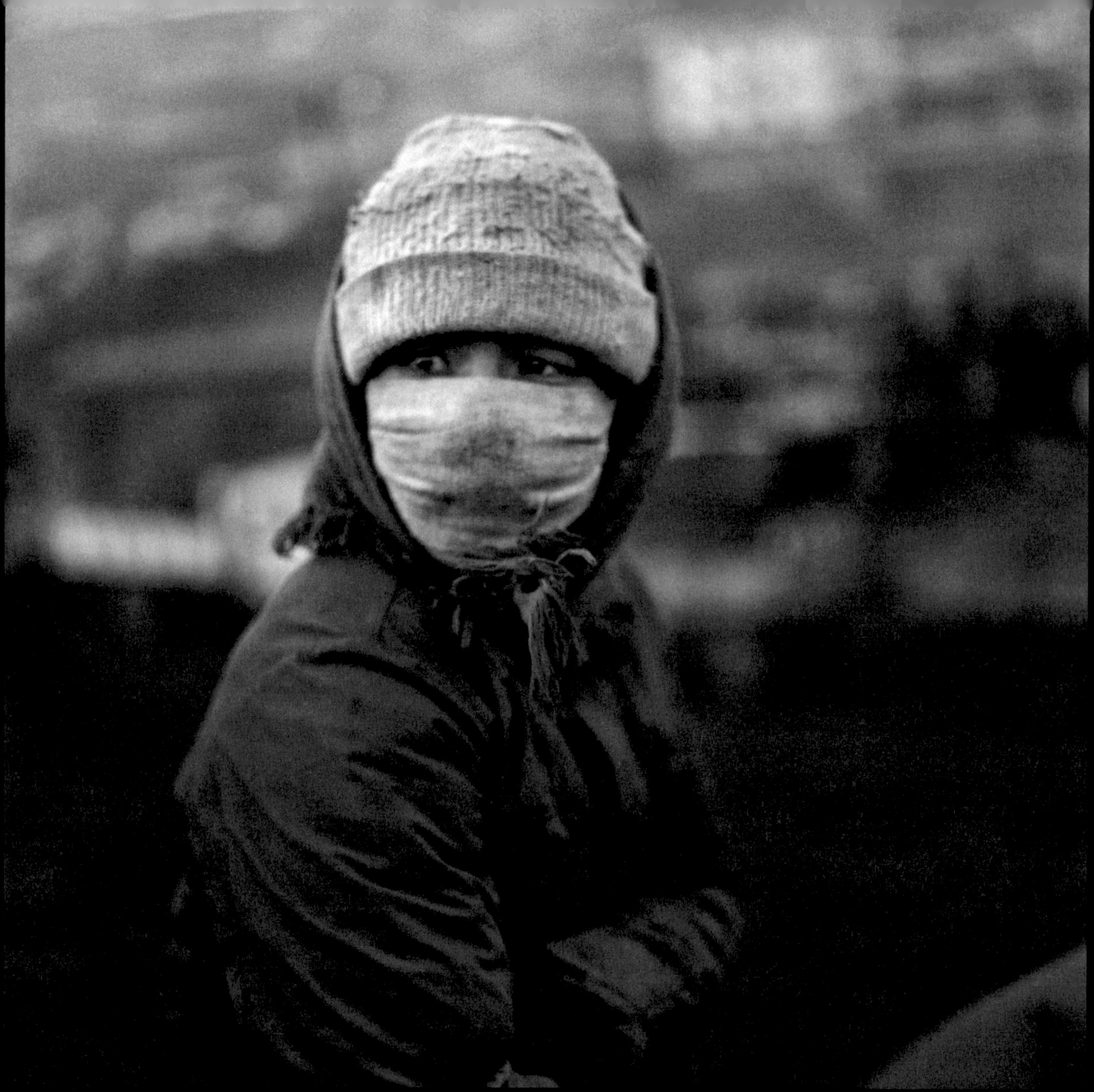

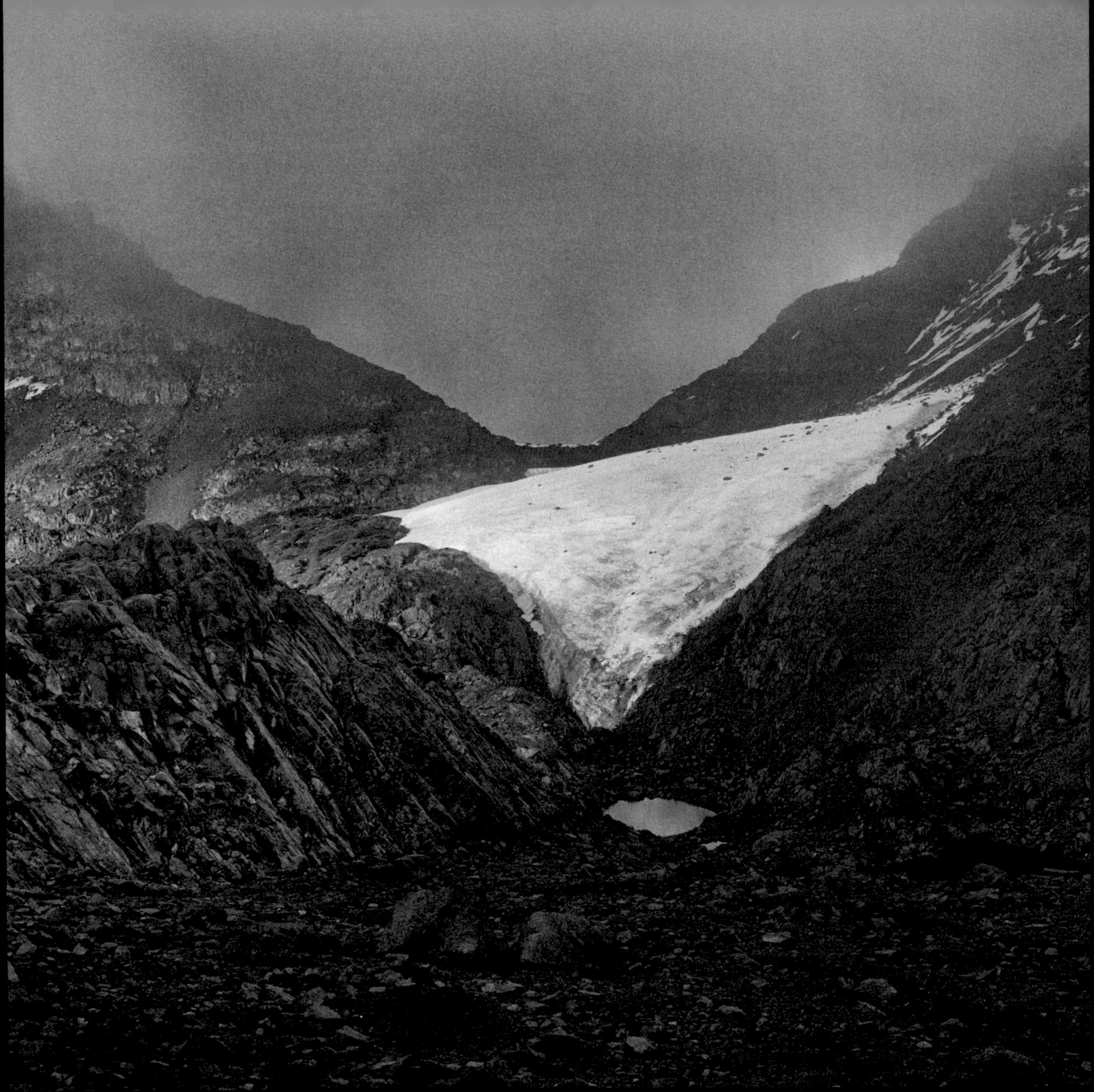

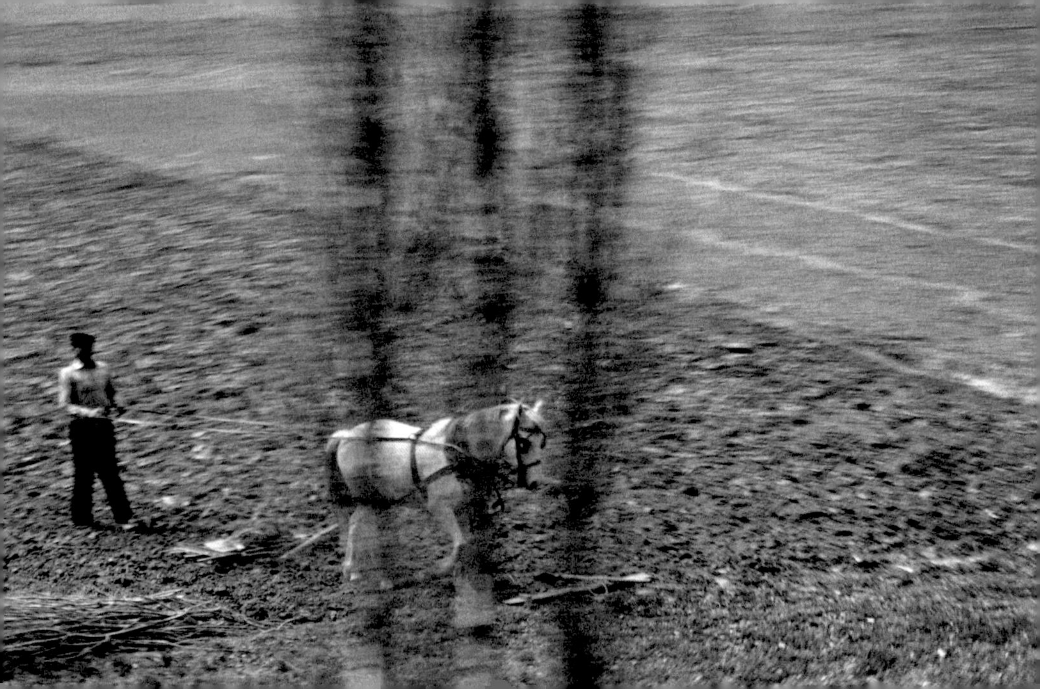

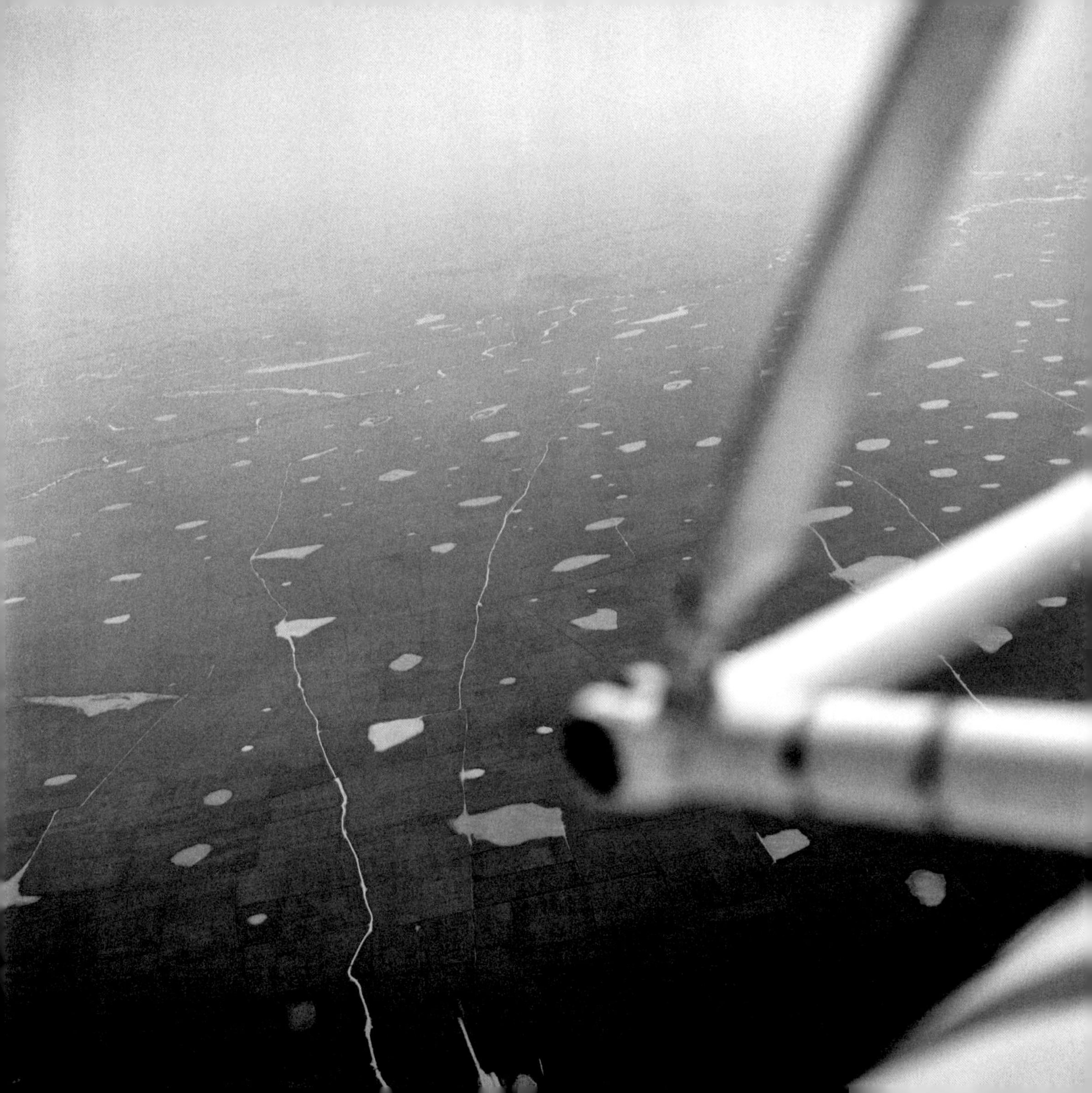

Preceding pages

Plate 1
After the Gharwal earthquake of 20 October 1991
Maneri, Uttarkashi, Uttarakhand state (then part of Uttar Pradesh), India
2 November 1991

Plate 2
Killing a captured stray dog for food
Jakarta, Indonesia
14 November 1994

Plate 3
Night market
Cholon, Ho Chi Minh City, Vietnam
18 February 2001

Plate 4
Street performer
Kerman, Iran
25 November 1995

Plate 5
On an ordinary day
Kabul, Afghanistan
12 September 2012

Plate 6 – commentary on p. 172
Riots after anti-World Economic Forum (WEF) demonstrations
Zürich, Switzerland
27 January 2001

Plate 7
Sky at dusk
Twante Canal, Myanmar
4 October 2019

Plate 8
Truck wash
Nădlac, Romania
6 June 2000

Plate 9
Coal worker
Yungang Zhuo Yun loading station, Datong, Shanxi province, China
20 November 1987

Plate 10
Lewis Glacier (4800 MASL)
Kirinyaga (Mt Kenya), Kenya
18 December 2021

Plate 11 – commentary on p. 172
View from the *Orient Express*
Former Yugoslavia
10 April 1976

Plate 12 – commentary on p. 172
Bomb craters used as fish ponds
Prêy Veng province, Cambodia
27 November 1992

Daniel Schwartz

Tracings Photography and Thought

Edited by Beat Wismer

Contributions by Giovanna Calvenzi, Carolin Emcke and Fanni Fetzer

T&H

Published on the occasion of the exhibition 'Daniel Schwarz, Tracings', curated by Beat Wismer,
at Kunstmuseum Luzern, Europaplatz 1, 6002 Lucerne, 30 September 2023 – 4 February 2024

Kunstmuseum
Luzern

First published in the United Kingdom in 2023 by
Thames & Hudson Ltd, 181A High Holborn, London WC1V 7QX

Concept by Daniel Schwartz and Beat Wismer

Scans: Laboratorium. Labor für Fotografie, Zürich, Switzerland

Designed by Martin Andersen / Andersen M Studio
www.andersenm.com

Text by Giovanna Calvenzi translated from the Italian by Gabriela Zehnder
Texts by Giovanna Calvenzi, Carolin Emcke, Fanni Fetzer and Beat Wismer
translated from the German by Isabel Adey

British Library Cataloguing-in-Publication Data
A catalogue record for this book is available from the British Library

ISBN 978-0-500-02634-2

Binding
Sélection d'Artistes
N° 105

Printed & bound in Italy by Editoriale Bortolazzi-Stei srl

FSC www.fsc.org MIX Paper from responsible sources FSC® C163211

Contents

Carolin Emcke: The Void

'Both [work and consumption] are devouring processes that seize and destroy matter, and the "work" done by labour upon its material is only the preparation for its eventual destruction.'
Hannah Arendt, *The Human Condition* (1958)

It is not a single image, nor a particular region, nor a specific moment in time caught on film that captivates me; rather it is a question that presents itself in ever-changing guises in these pictures and will not let go: the question of labour, of humankind as *animal laborans*, the question of what we are really doing. The way Daniel Schwartz homes in on what we call labour, the way he shows us, tells us, illuminates and exposes what labour as a 'devouring process' means. This is more than merely a motif; it is like a *basso continuo* running through the whole composition, the entire work. And it is a lesson in visual thinking.

In Daniel Schwartz's photography, labour is stripped of any element of the romanticizing abstract. What we see is not labour in the singular but in the plural. These are real people working on the field, in the mine, on an oil rig, at war or in the middle of nowhere; these are their bodies, old or young – too old or too young, even – often vulnerable and exposed, weighed-down bodies, people whose hands, feet or backs serve merely as vehicles; they carry goods on their heads, they pull handcarts or a plough. These are bodies that freeze or sweat; gaunt bodies on which there is nothing superfluous, nothing incidental, to be seen.

Schwartz's photographs clearly depict labour as a process of consumption. Bodies are devoured as they toil; they become material, merge into the material they are working on or transporting, like the faceless woman in Kabul 'on an ordinary day' in 2012, beneath a burka, carrying a bag on her head (plate 5) – everything combines to form a single entity. Or the images of bodies pushing or pulling handcarts in Kolkata in 1993 (plates 20, 21) : what we see are less subjects manufacturing something – a product – or transforming material, these are people who are exploiting and devouring themselves. This is the first thing Daniel Schwartz tells us in this book, with calm incorruptibility.

Still, the people in the images remain autonomous. The bodies toiling here, the bodies being maltreated here, remain individual; in Daniel Schwartz's photographs, they are almost always depicted alone in their work. This is not only an aesthetic statement but an ethical one, too. The working people are never shown in series, never collectively, never as part of a crowd. They are not dehumanized, they never appear animalistic or mechanical; there is no way to distance oneself from them. The observer is never, really never, excused from the task of engaging with what they see, because it is always another lone individual in the scene.

Daniel Schwartz's quiet, refined artistry lies in his unerring eye for the right distance: he never gets too close, but nor is he ever too far removed. I can think of hardly any photographer as adept at calibrating distance. He never crowds the people in his images, never pressures them, never with quiet excitement puts injuries, pain or suffering on display. If one of his subjects is injured, the bandaged leg stump is all he needs to show; there is no place for sombre expressions. And he never removes himself to the extent that all the brutality, all the severity, all the poverty is lost in a scene of picturesque beauty. He is never so distanced from the misery and destitution that his images can be savoured merely for their aesthetic qualities. Schwartz's photographs are always discreet but never innocuous; they are always approachable but never encroaching.

As the reader is confronted with more and more diverse scenes of labour as a devouring process, we gain a greater understanding of the merciless, manic way in which nature is exploited and destroyed; we see how this ideology of appropriating everything, of assimilating and consuming everything, repeatedly violates itself. It isn't just raw materials being consumed, it isn't just bodies; people's lives are being destroyed. Daniel Schwartz gradually maps out this destruction with each additional image of the working human being; he pieces together the knowledge of disaster gradually on these pages, very slowly, without reproach, without fuss, but uncompromisingly all the same.

Finally, we happen upon the other photographs in this collection, depicting the counter-narrative in which there are no human beings at work: the images of nature. And suddenly these scenes have lost their innocence; they can no longer be viewed innocuously: Schwartz's glacier photographs become archives of loss, his photographs of the Lewis Glacier, Mount Kenya (plate 10) and the Findel Glacier (plate 57) hit hard. Nothing is happening in these pictures, there is no one to be seen here, but as observers, we must try to understand in this void the space between what is and is not depicted. As these photographs make abundantly clear, we are the void; we, the people who refused to see what we are destroying, what we wanted to exploit and consume as if there were no price to pay.

These photographs do not show us mountains of plastic, industrial slag heaps, blazing forests; that would be too exculpatory. To do so would not demonstrate the connection between our own actions, our own labour as a destructive process, and the obliteration of the environment. These images contain a lesson in visual thinking. And the lesson is uncomfortable because it requires us to make connections between ourselves and the world that has been entrusted to us. We must try to understand this void and act within it, and this is precisely where Daniel Schwartz's tremendous humanitarianism lies – because he trusts that we will be willing to rise to this challenge.

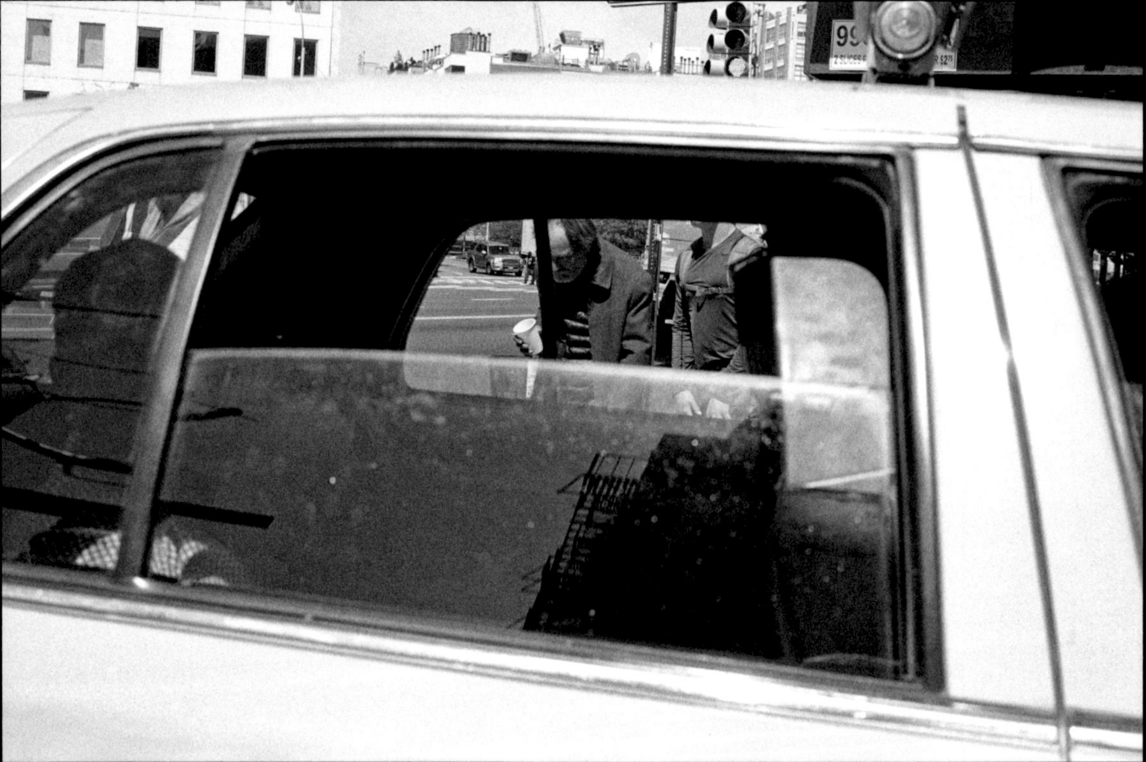

I Motif

Looking at pictures, the motif first attracts attention to itself completely involuntarily. In this series, the term 'motif' is used to connect photographs that record various aspects of activities in which the hand and hands play an elementary role.

Even if hands are the focus of a photograph, they never become the exclusive subject. They are always pictured doing something, whether they are simply pointing or undertaking a more complex activity. *Hand*, *business* and *action* (in German, *hand*, *handel* and *handlung*) essentially belong together; the close relationship of the German words is not surprising. The situation is similar in the case of the term 'motif', which stands for the subject of the picture, but is also closely related to comprehensive and diverse 'motivation', to the sum of the 'motives' that lead to the decision to take a picture.

An intensive preoccupation with a topic, usually for years, lies behind the photographer's motivation and his (often self-imposed) assignments to travel to countries and regions that have become geopolitical crisis zones, with red-hot conflicts, or places where partly anthropogenic climate change leads to fatal transformations with catastrophic consequences. Daniel Schwartz's pictures record these precarious circumstances in a compressed form, with occasional focus on the hand. This plays a central role in two senses: first, in terms of content, starting with the basic function of gripping; and secondly, getting to grips with the complex world, both formally with its positioning as a motif and with the composition created by the intuitive certainty of the photographer's eye. Both aspects are inextricably linked.

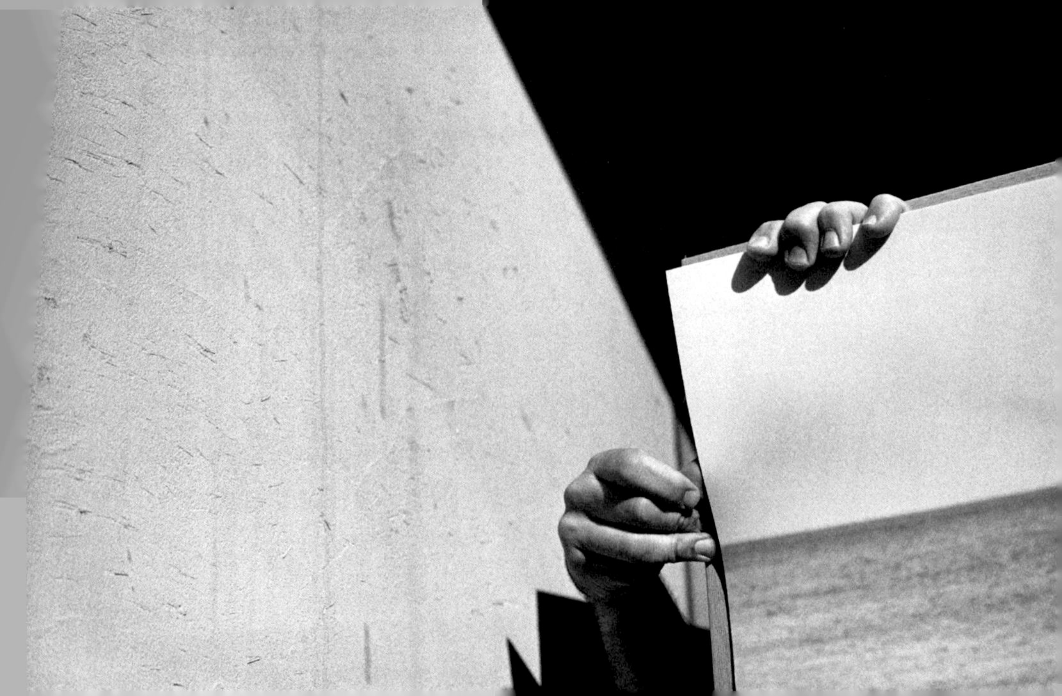

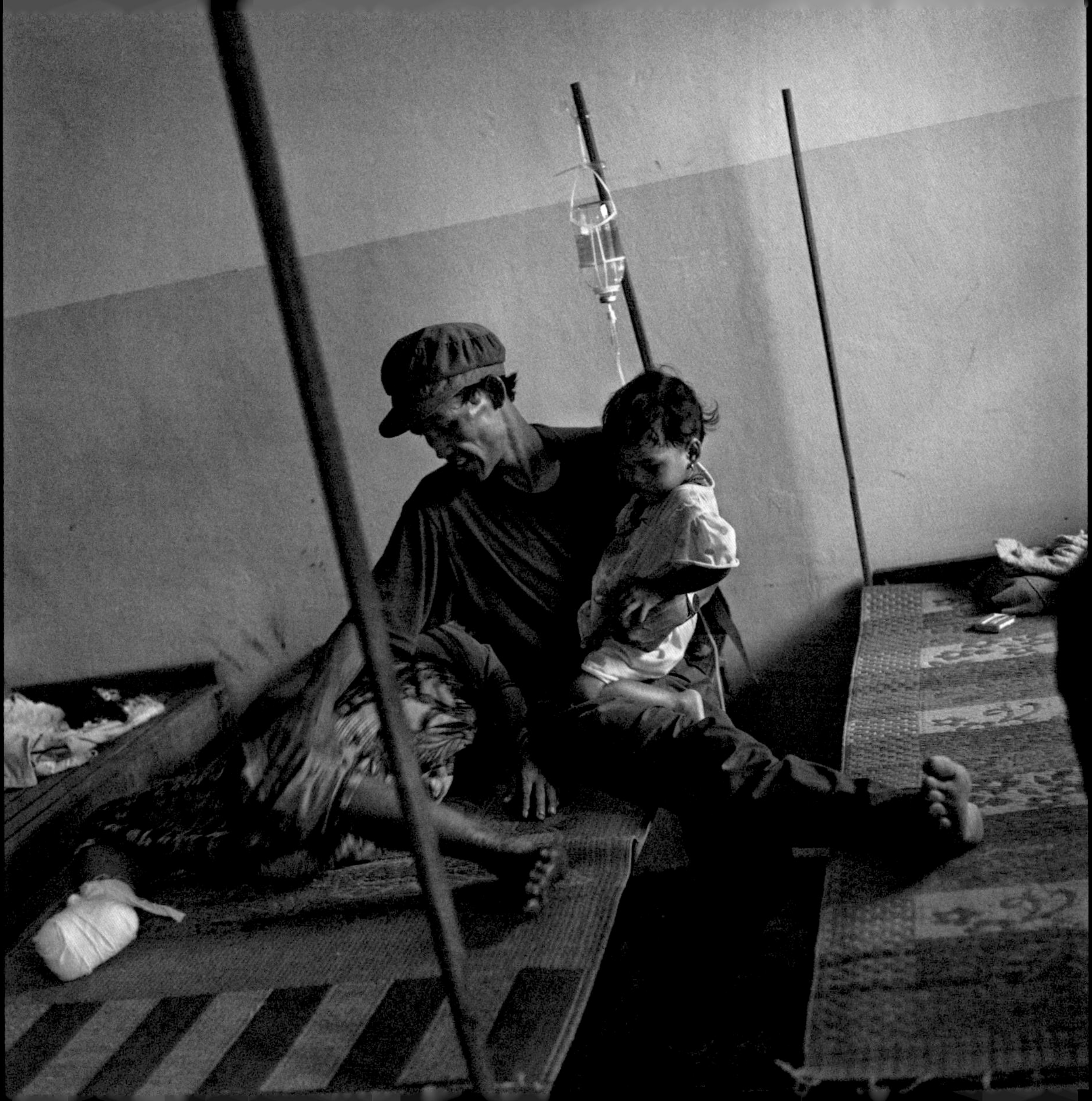

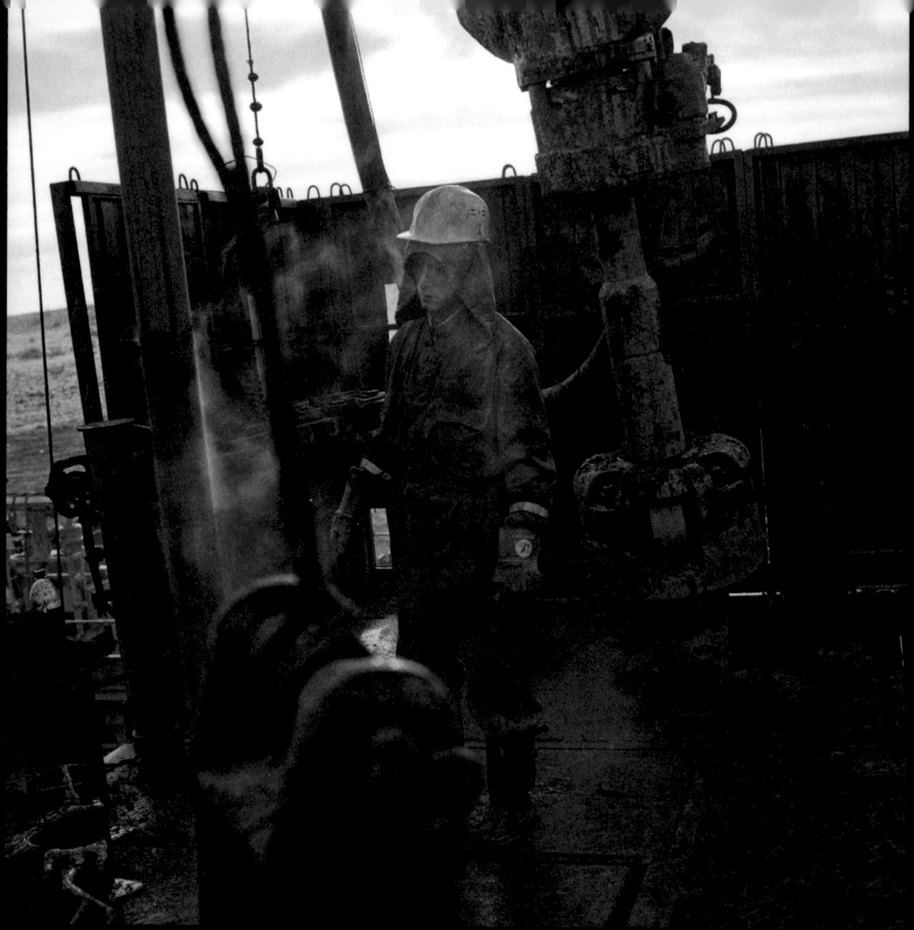

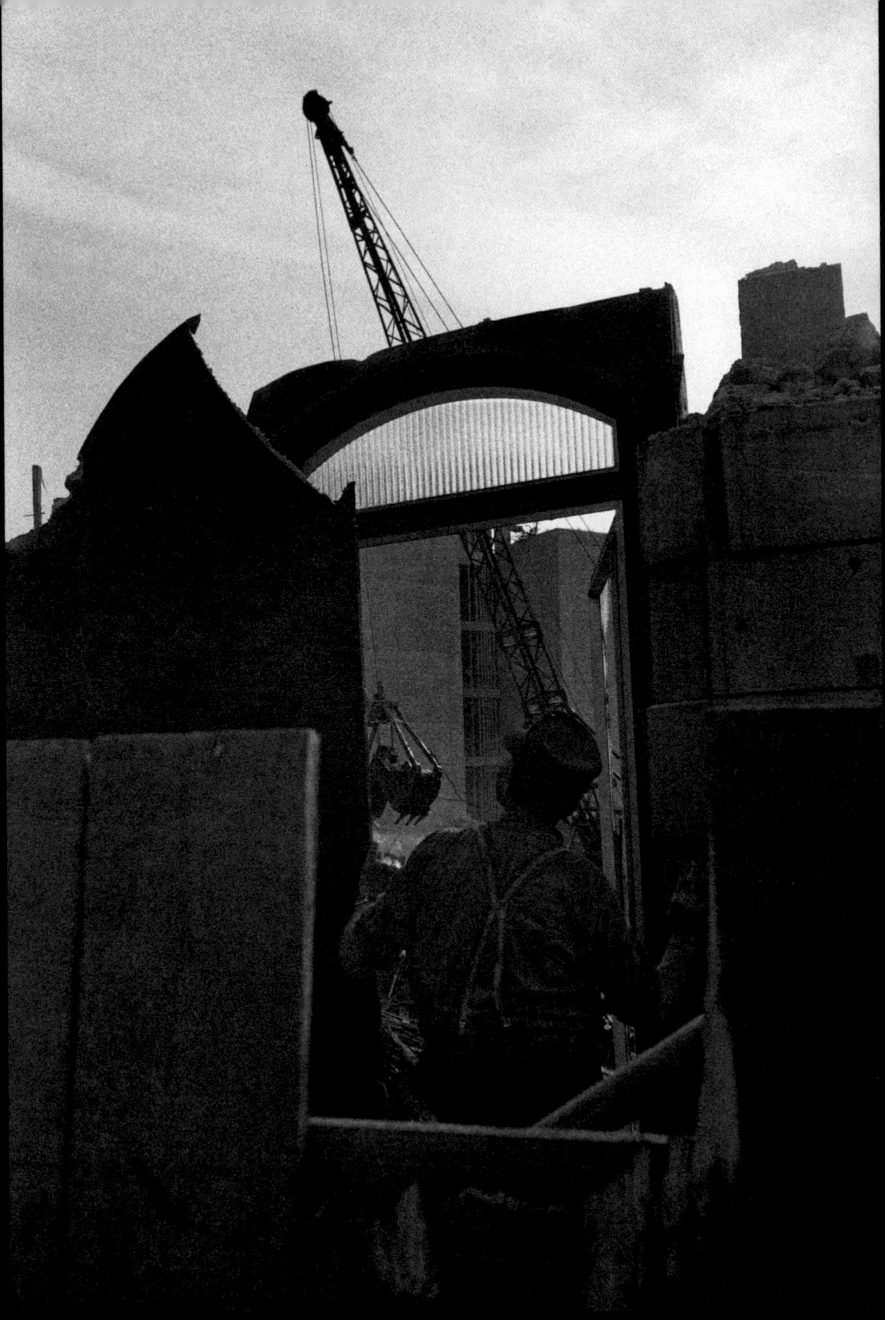

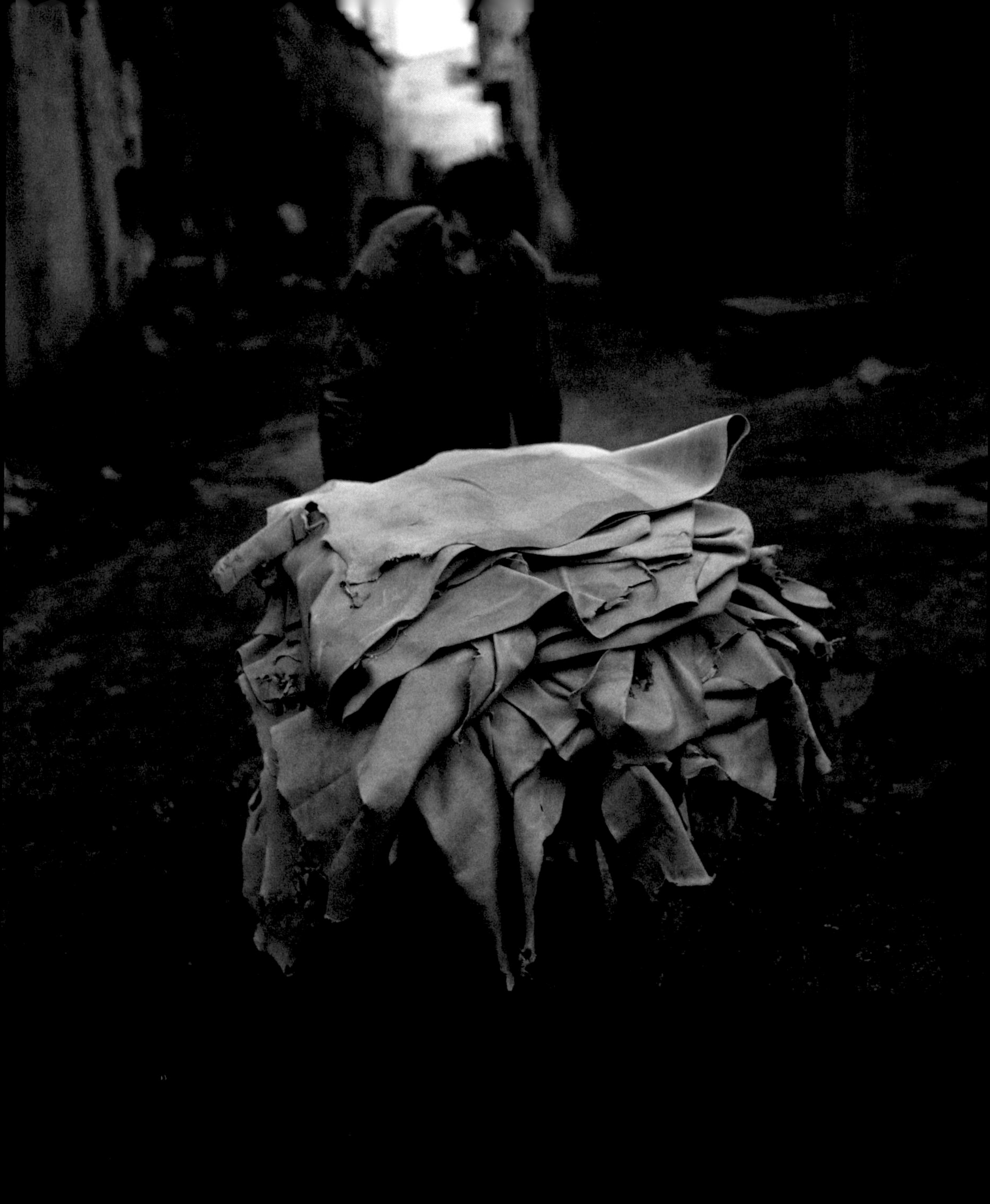

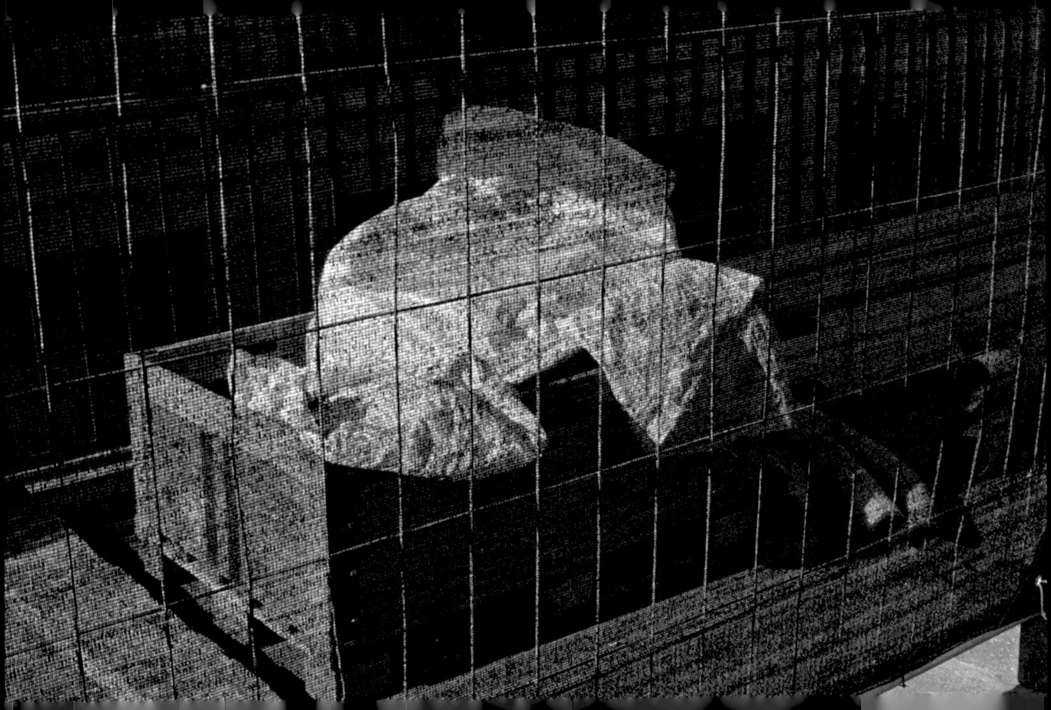

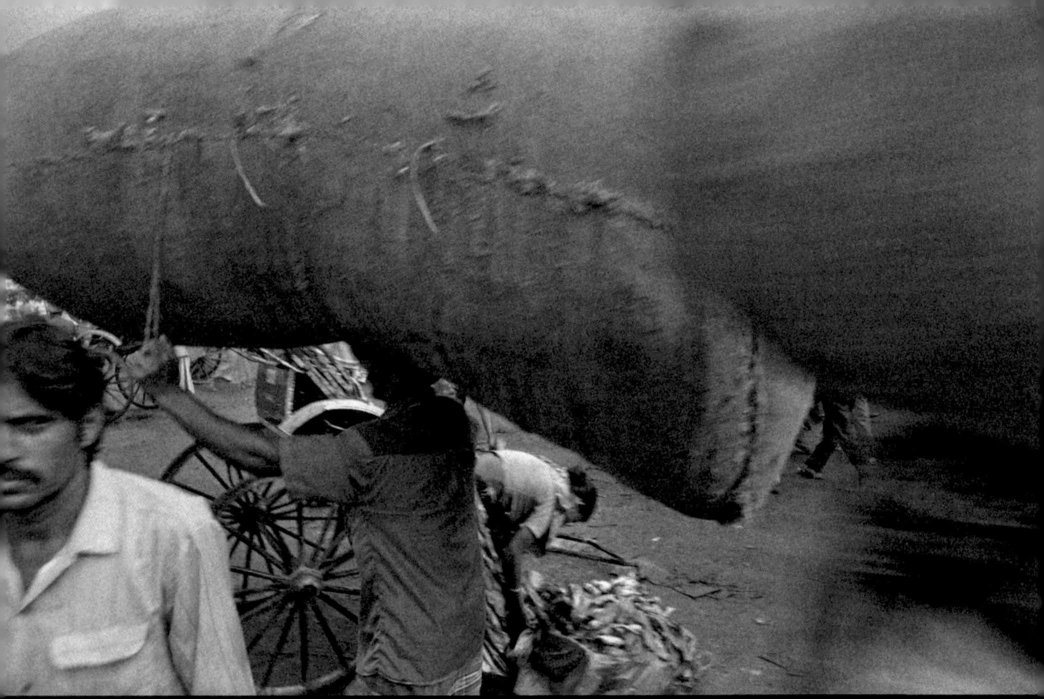

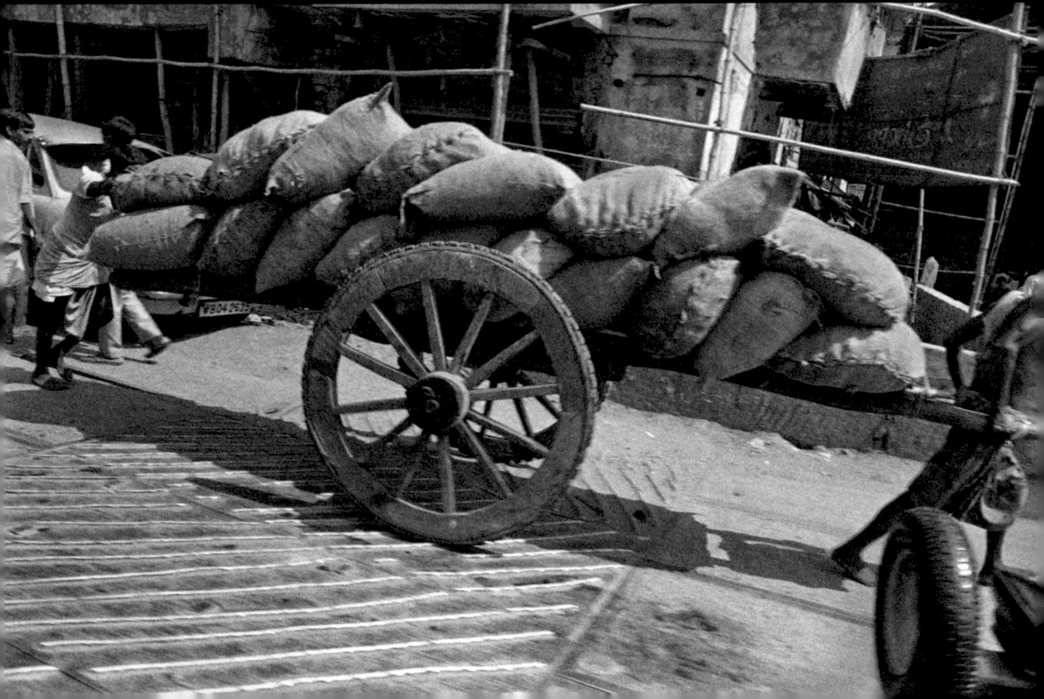

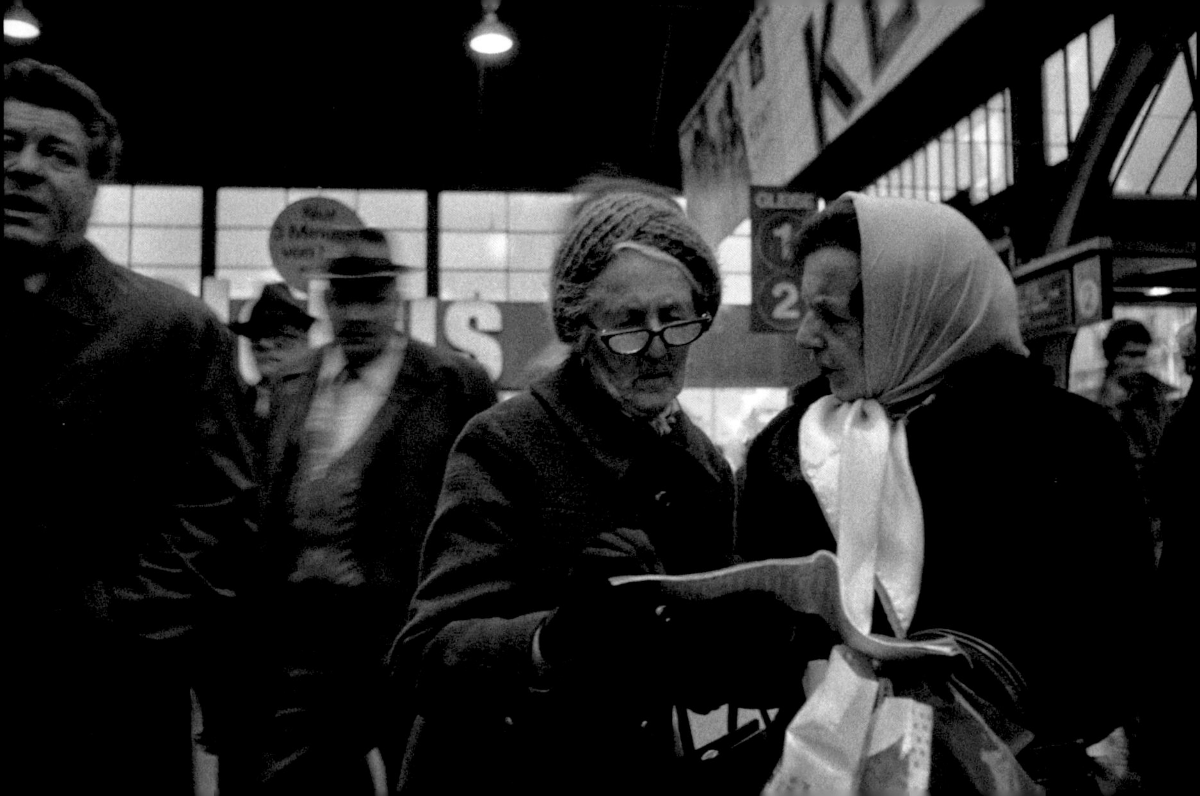

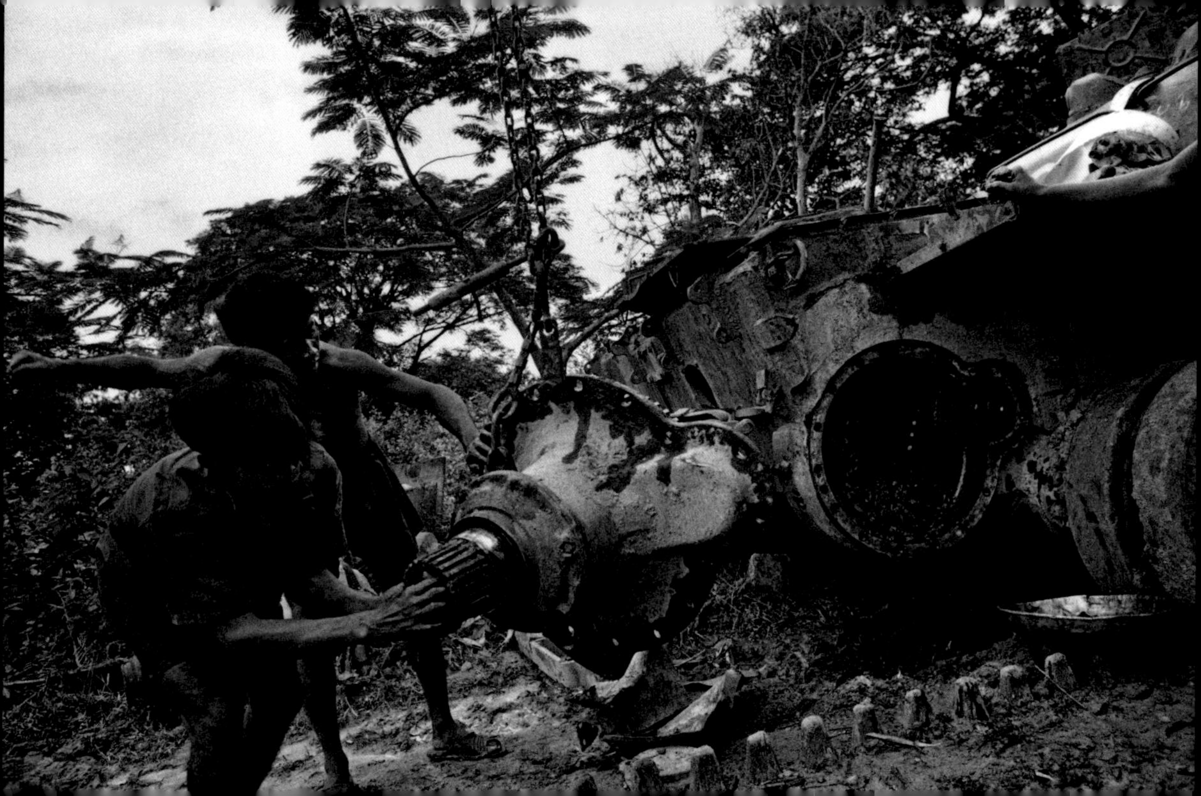

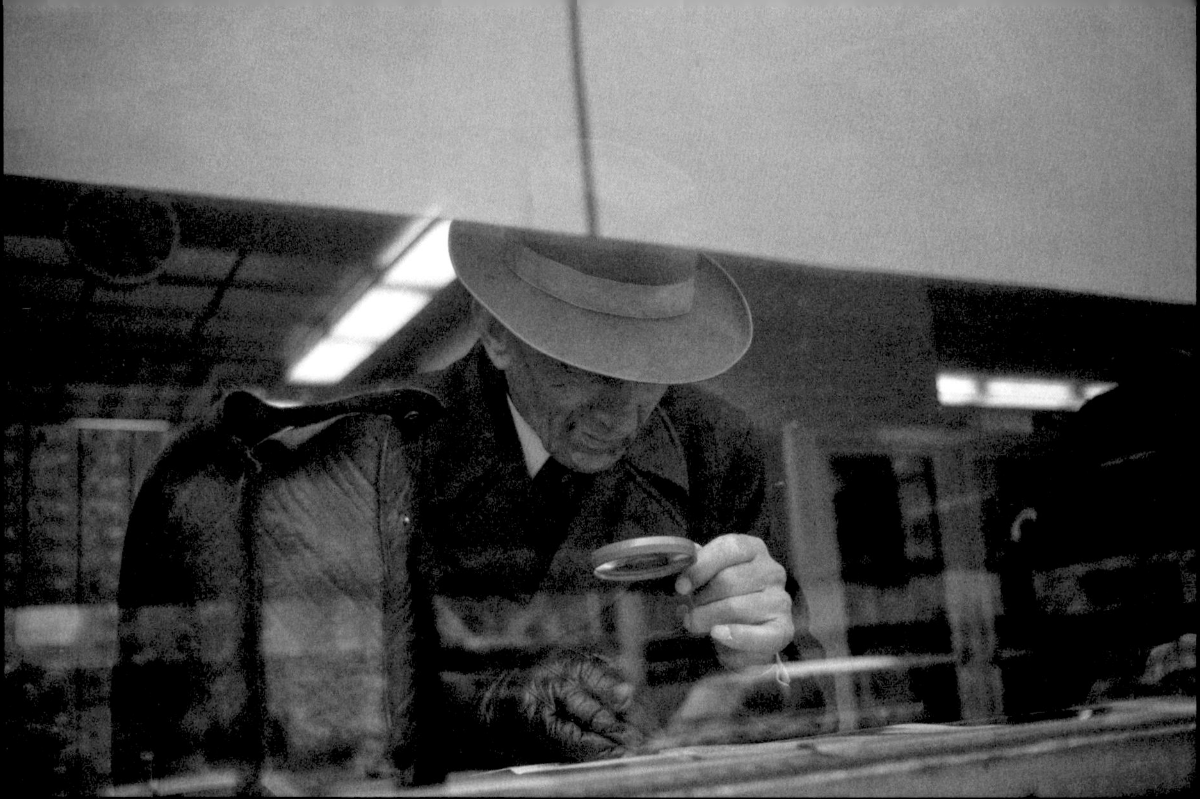

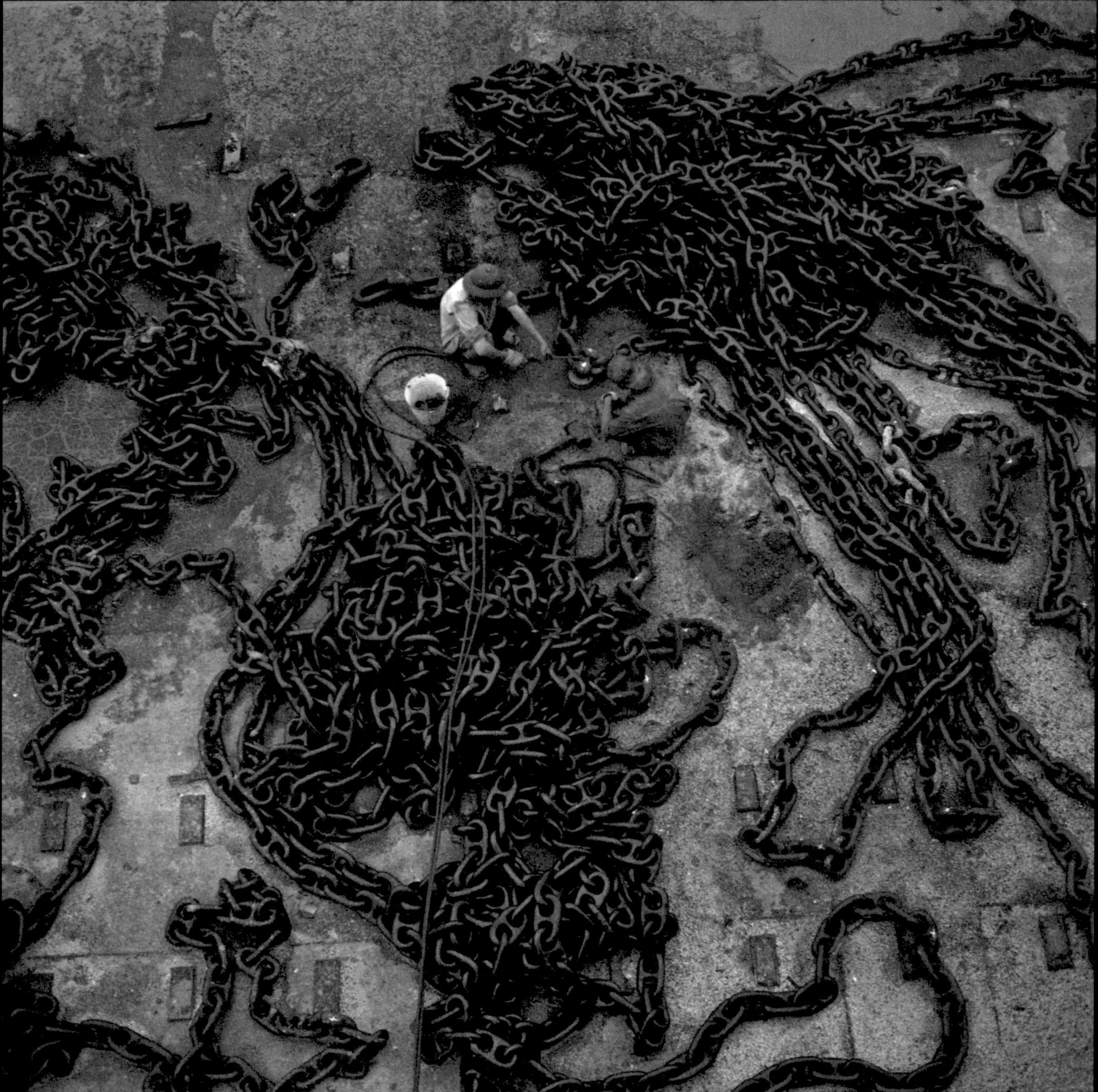

25

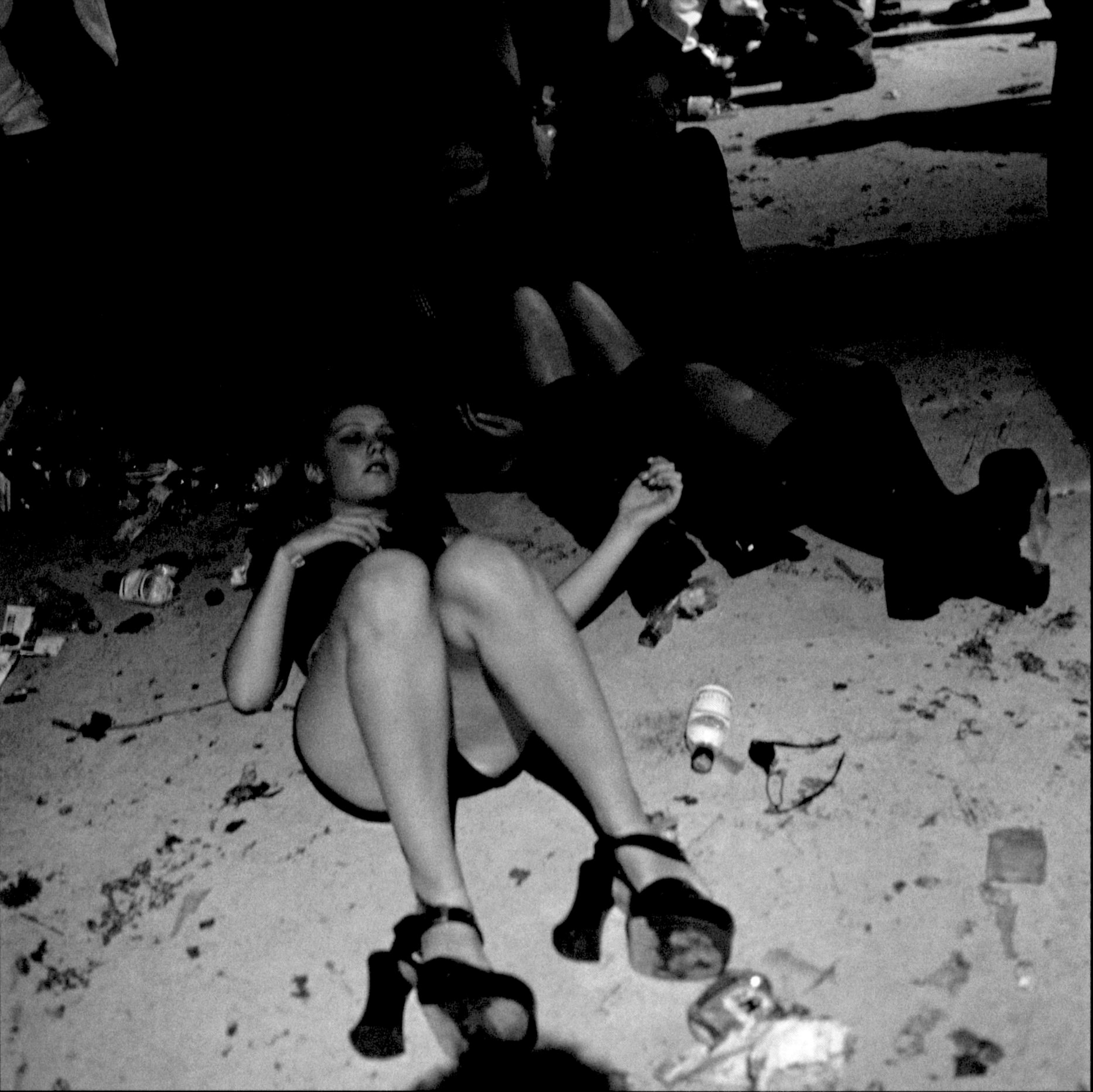

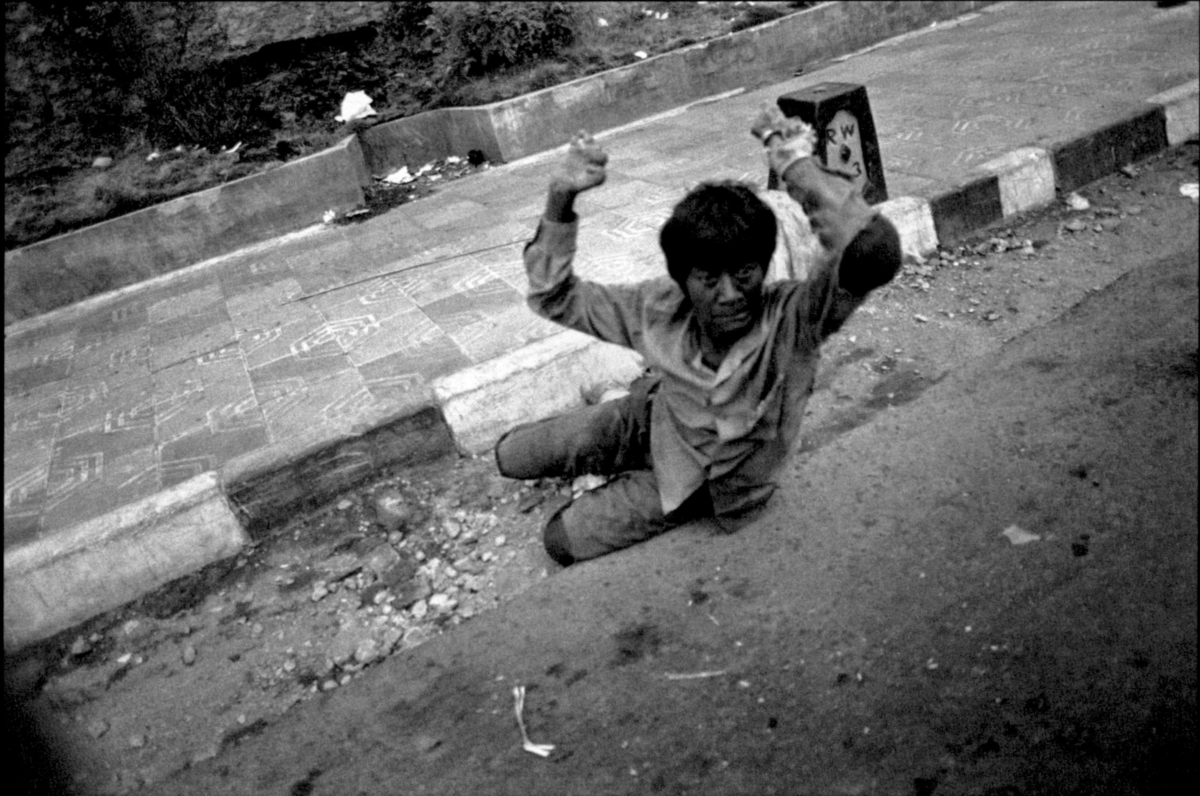
RW

Preceding pages

Plate 13
The paper cup
Soho, New York City, United States
4 May 2017

Plate 14
London, United Kingdom
22 May 2018

Plate 15 – commentary on p. 172
Pailin, Cambodia
3 October 1997

Plate 16 – commentary on p. 172
Drilling rig platform
Akshabulak oilfield, Kyzylorda, Kazakhstan
6 November 2007

Plate 17
Demolition
Schaffhausen, Switzerland
18 October 1976

Plate 18 – commentary on p. 173
Tanned cowhides
Istanbul, Turkey
14 October 1989

Plate 19
Roadworks
Bern, Switzerland
9 July 2019

Plate 20
Sealdah railway station
Kolkata, India
20 October 1993

Plate 21
Koley Market
Kolkata, India
27 October 1993

Plate 22
Main railway station
Zürich, Switzerland
29 March 1977

Plate 23
Repair work on a Soviet T54 tank
Siem Reap, Cambodia
19 July 1994

Plate 24
The magnifying glass
Post office, main railway station, Zürich, Switzerland
29 March 1977

Plate 25
The anchor chain
Bach Dang Shipyard, Haiphong, Vietnam
30 September 1993

Plate 26
Waking up from the Street Parade
Hallenstadion, Zürich, Switzerland
8 August 1999

Plate 27
Enraged for a reason
Jakarta, Indonesia
17 November 1994

Fig. 1

Commuters
Shibuya-ku railway station, Tokyo, Japan
13 May 2009

Gelatin silver double-exposure print, 2020
Sheet size 50 x 40 cm (19 3/4 x 15 3/4 in.)

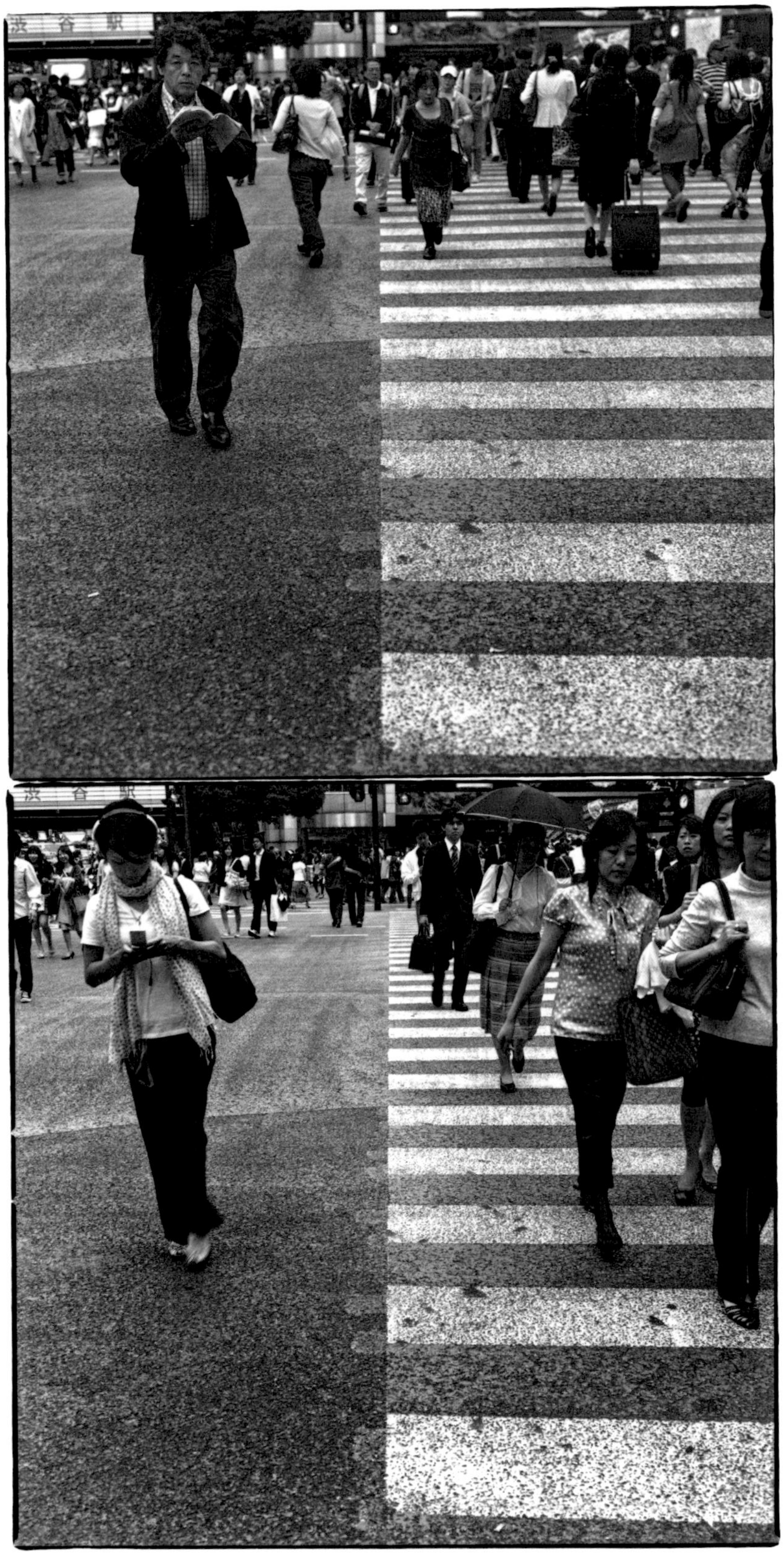

Fig. 1

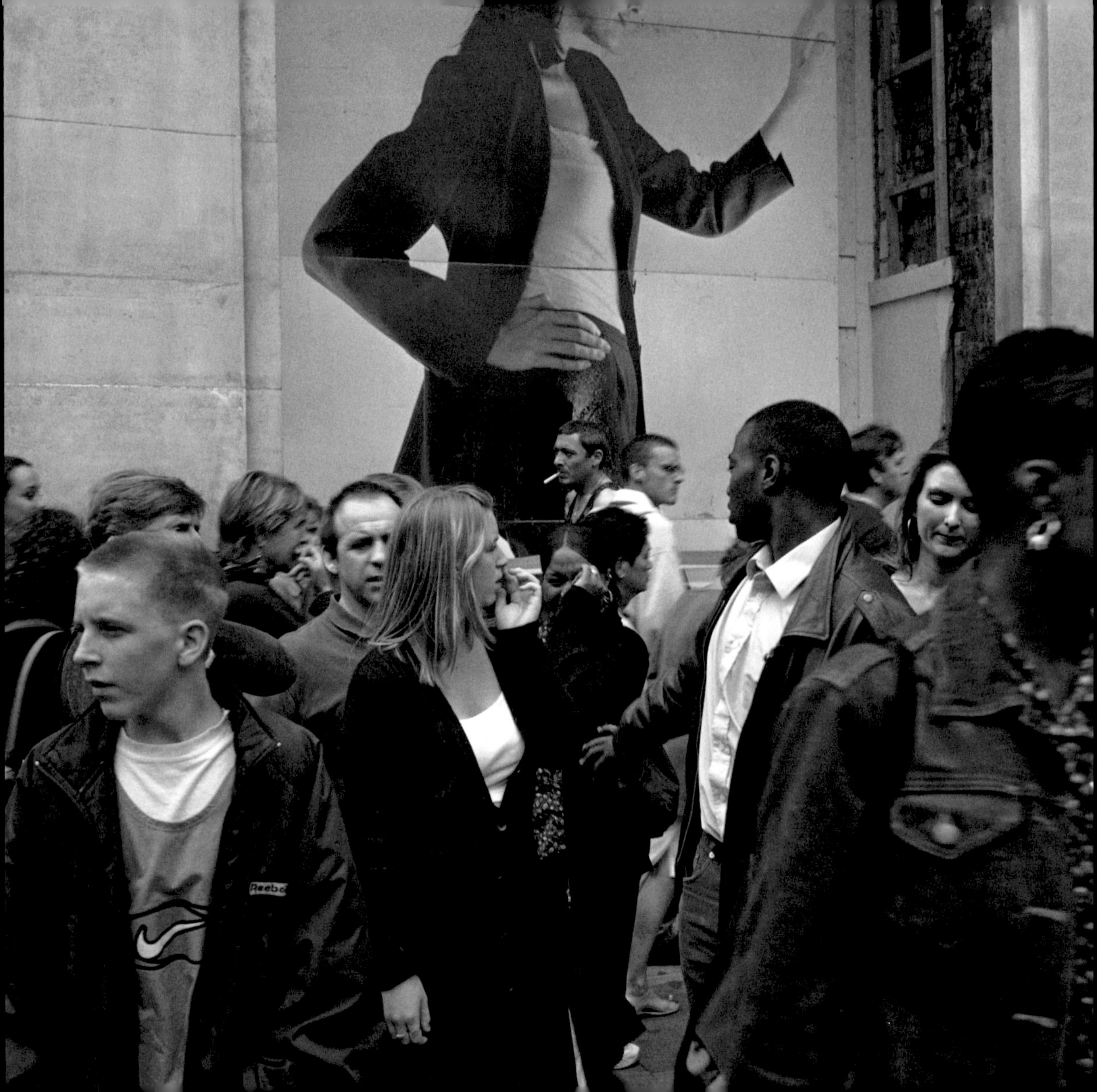

II Association

These pictures speak of the individual and a relationship to one's neighbour; to the community; to the community with a shared destiny; to society; to the masses. They indicate a person's being included and being excluded. They are about social integration and separation, about the actions of the autonomous individual and the ability to prevail in the uncontrollable flow of even the most adverse, inhumane circumstances. The key term is 'association', with two meanings: not only the bond that connects people and their destinies, but also the connection that we as viewers supposedly create between the picture and the world. Beyond that, the term also indicates the connection that exists between us and governs us, the world and its people. Here is 'a lesson in visual thinking' (Carolin Emcke, p. 19), which Daniel Schwartz offers the viewer in his pictures.

People and their precarious existence are at the centre of these images, most of which were created as part of broad investigations into clearly outlined themes. Here, they are presented for the first time independently of the context in which they were created, as individual images from an overarching point of view. But of course, they also record the journeys that Schwartz undertook as a reportage photographer. With his stupendous technique, his concentration on black and white, and above all with his incorruptible, humane attitude, Daniel Schwartz is a late representative of classic reportage photography: 'all in the best Swiss tradition', according to the legendary war photographer Tim Page.

When we stand in front of the picture, mentally we associate the person depicted with the abstract idea of their predicament. But perhaps, from a different point of view, when confronted with the picture of the Bangladesh flood victim (plate 35), evoked involuntarily in our minds is a Werner Bischof image. This association is not unreasonable, as it also signifies the respect that Schwartz pays to the tradition to which he himself would claim to belong.

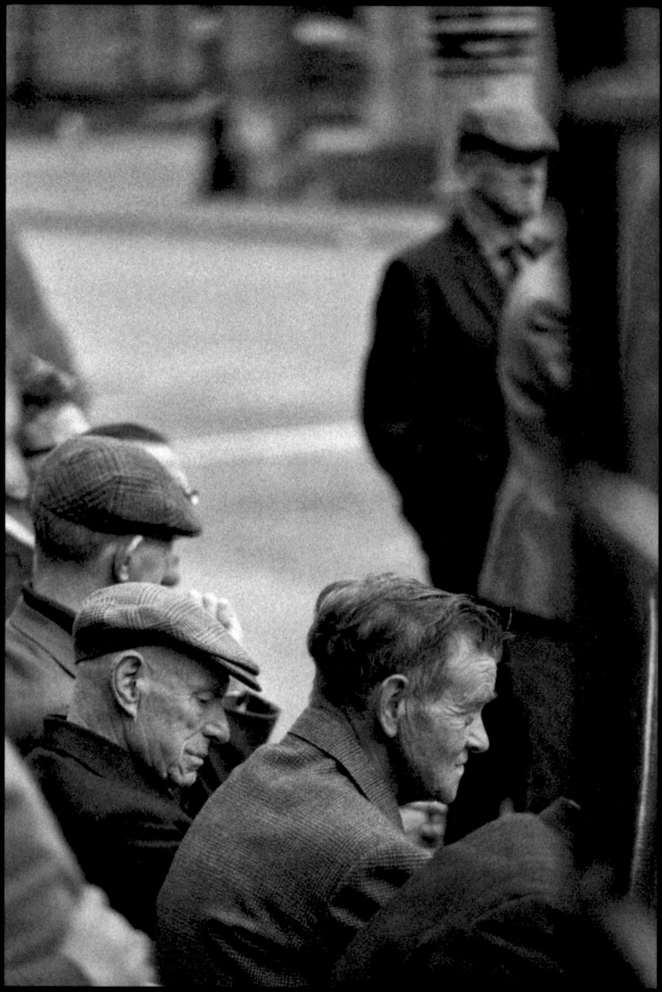

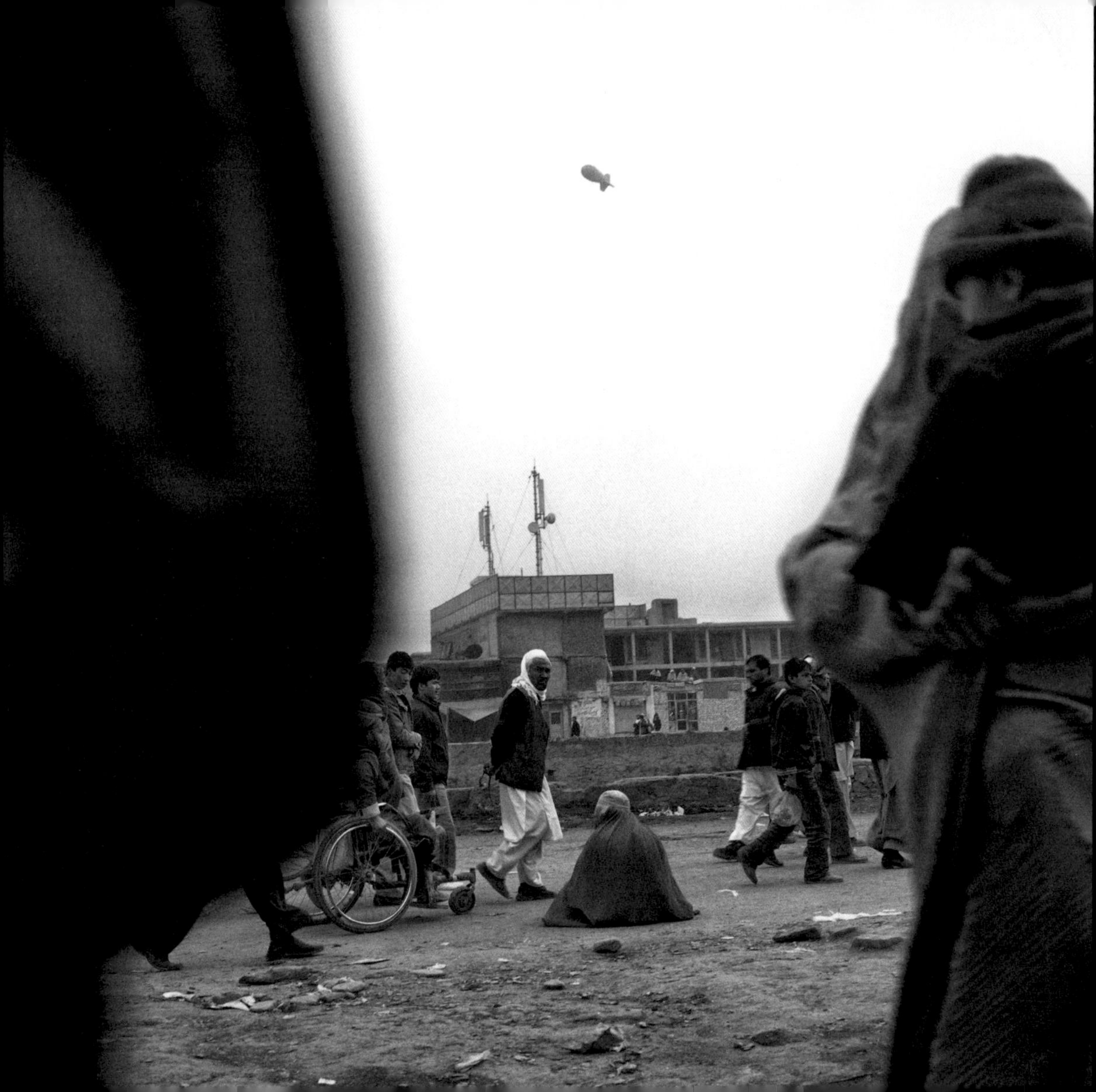

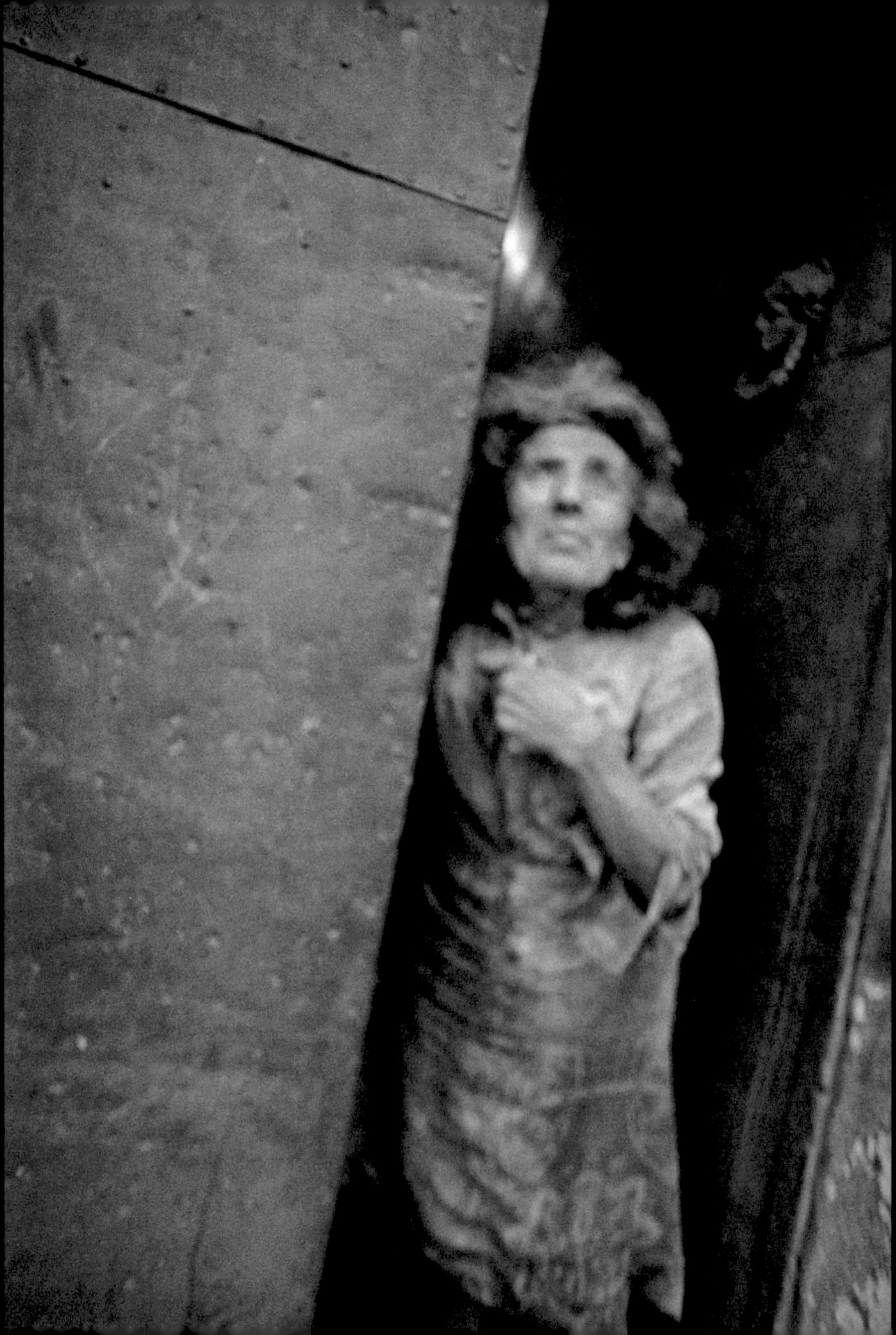

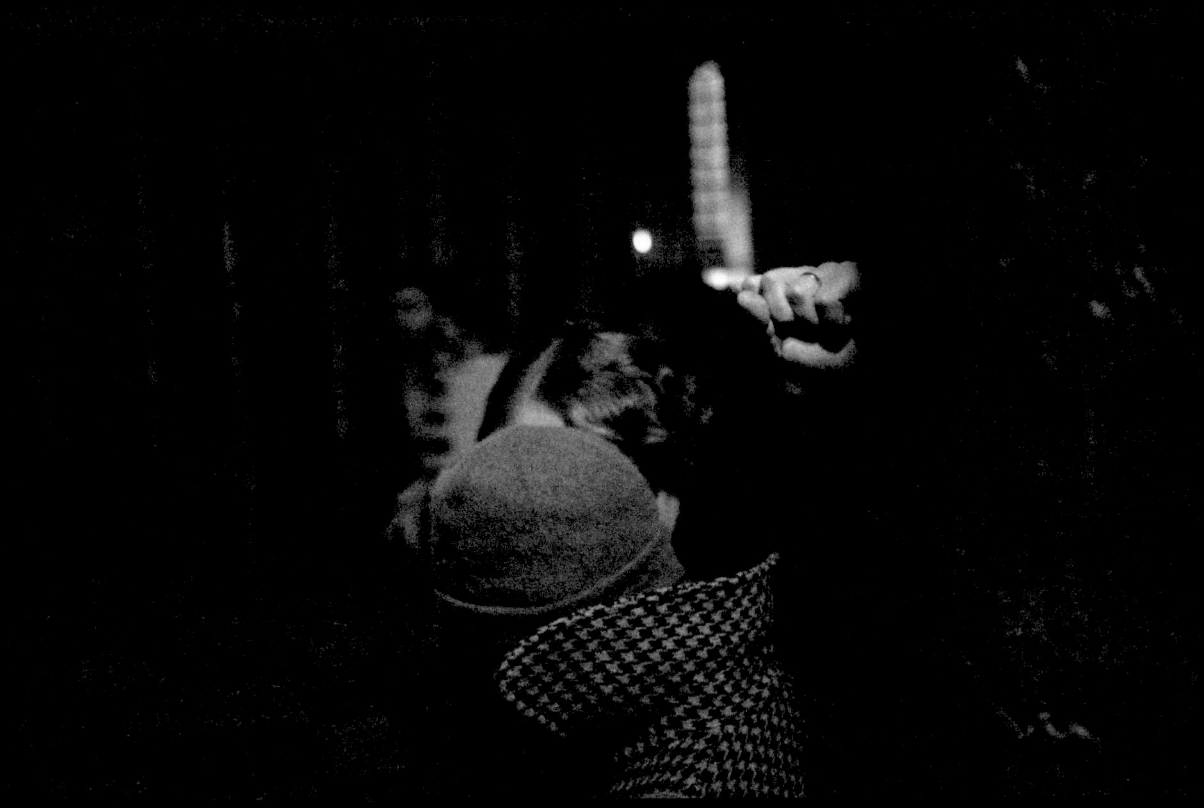

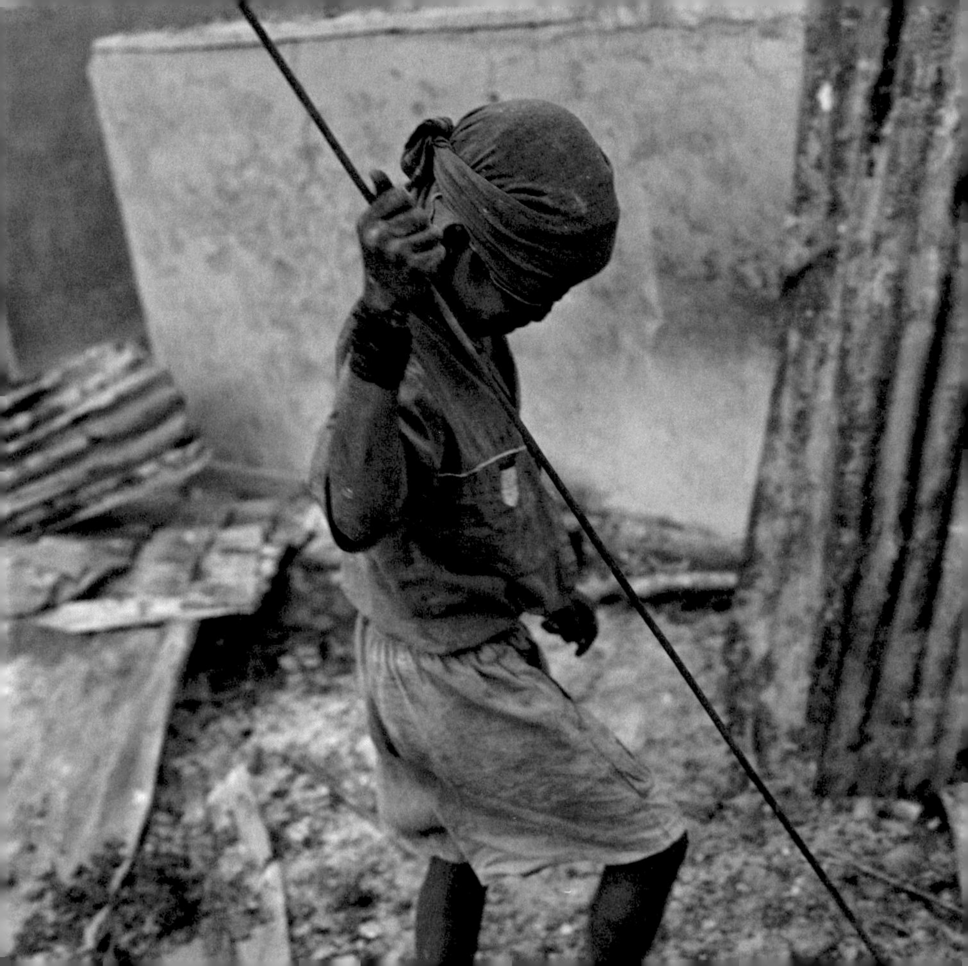

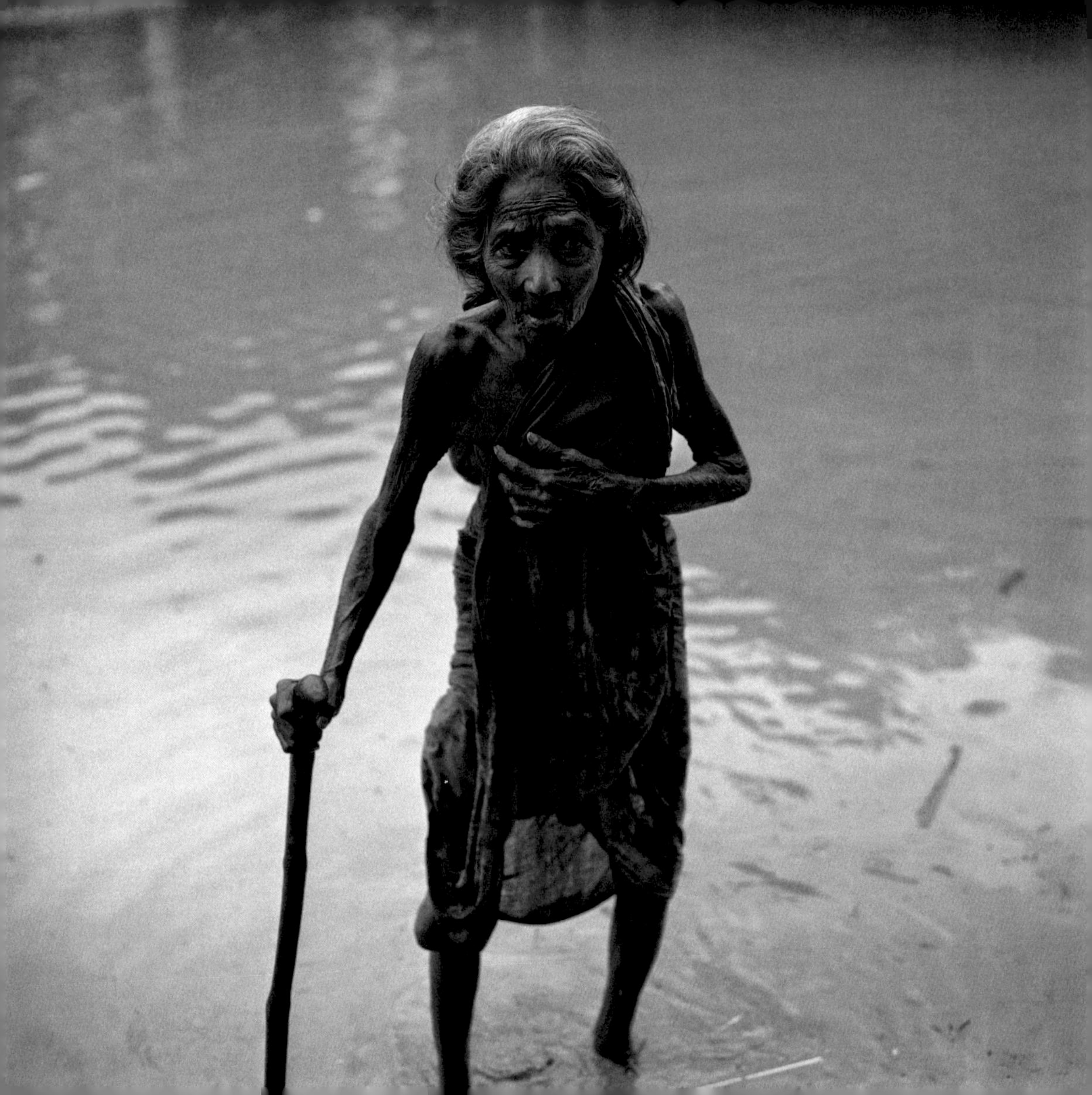

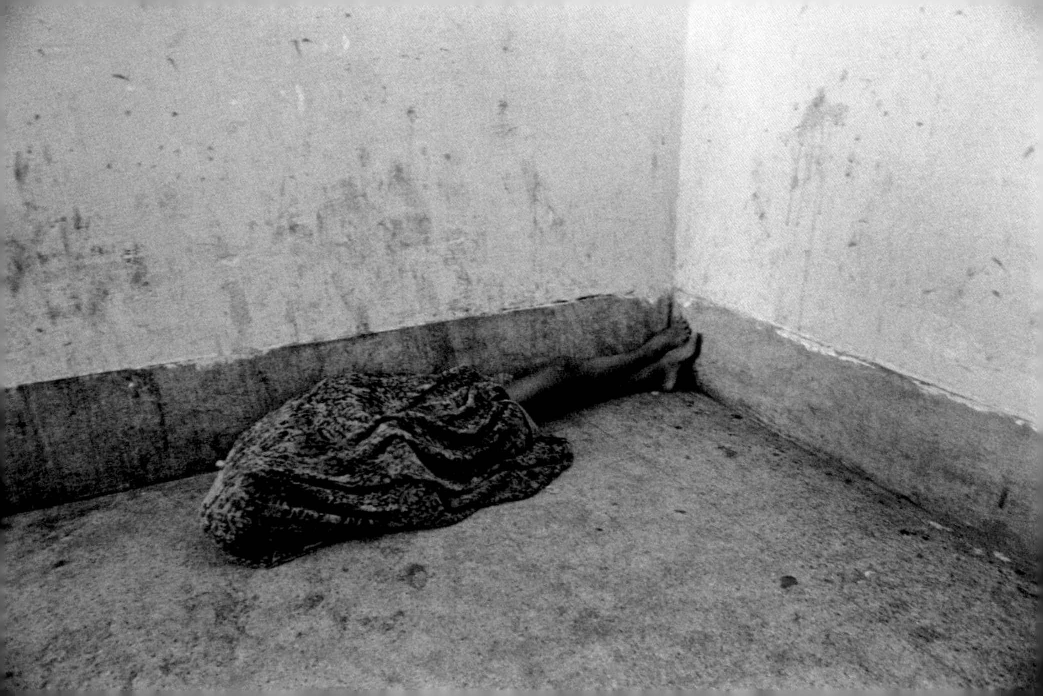

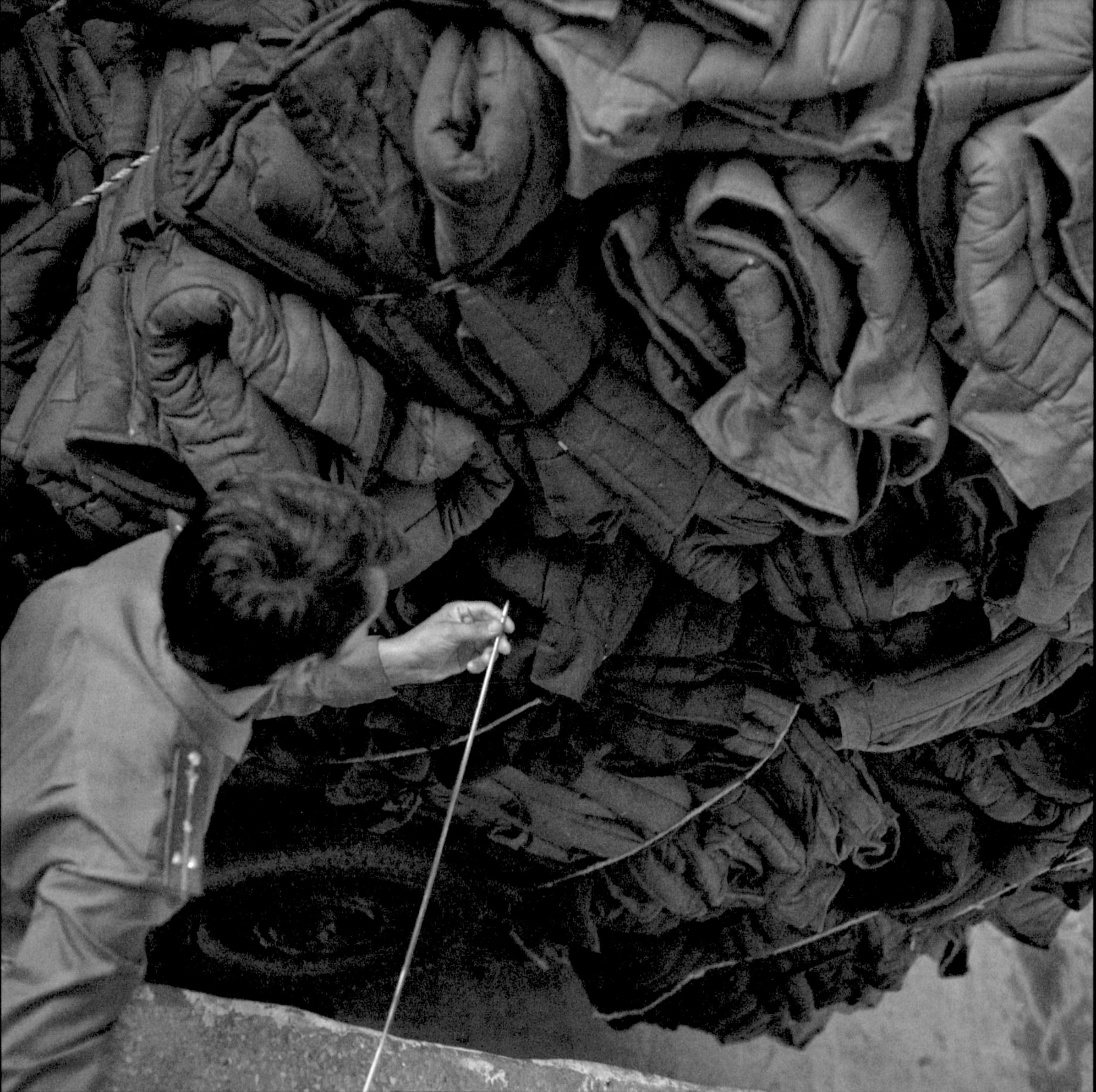

3

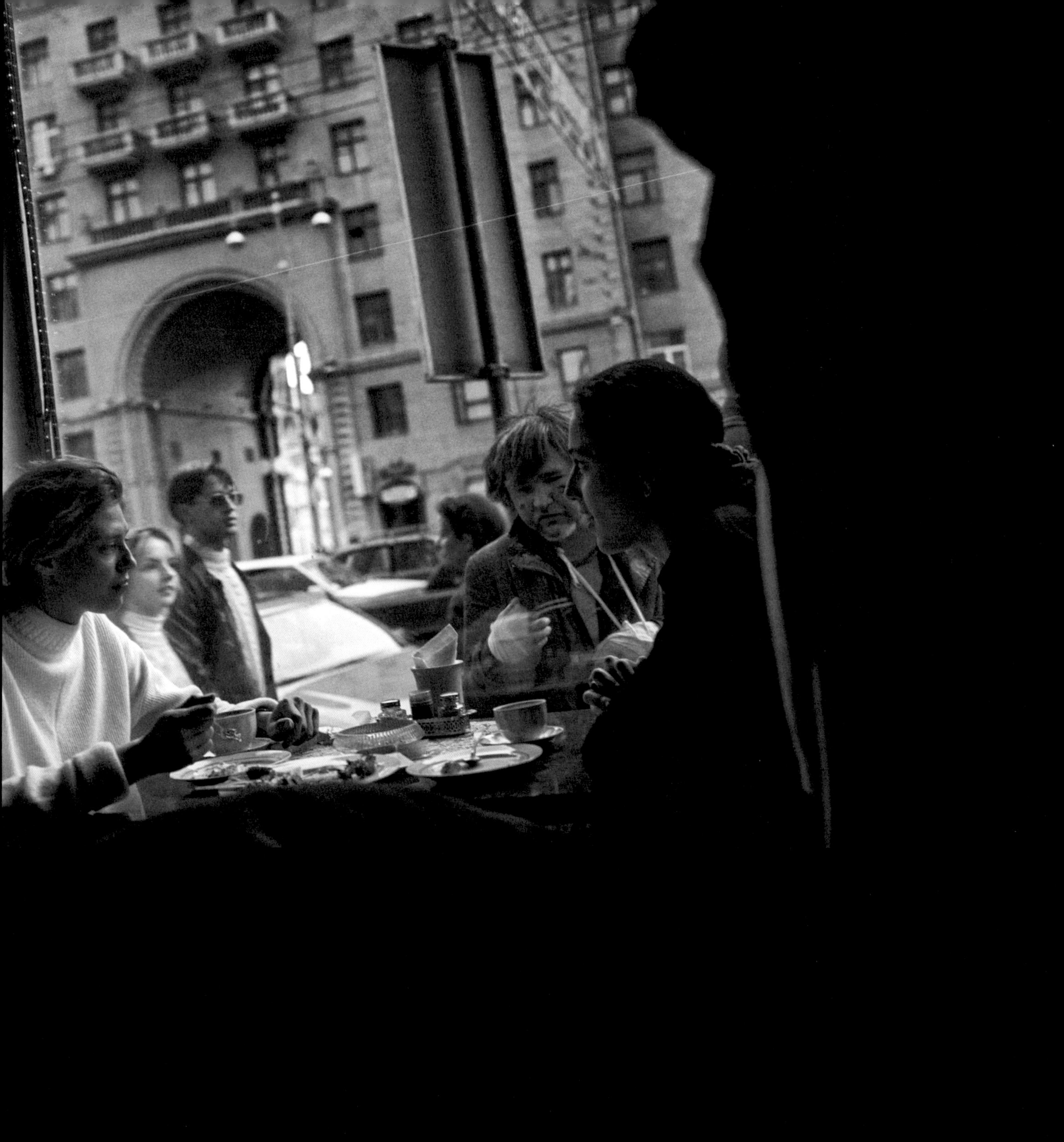

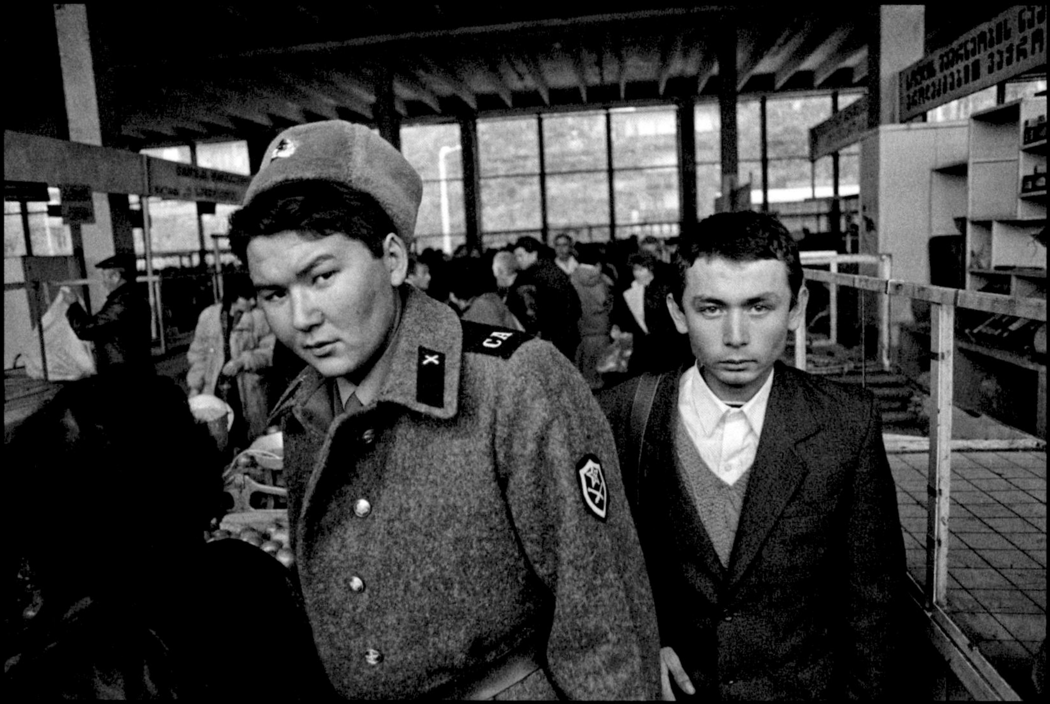
СА

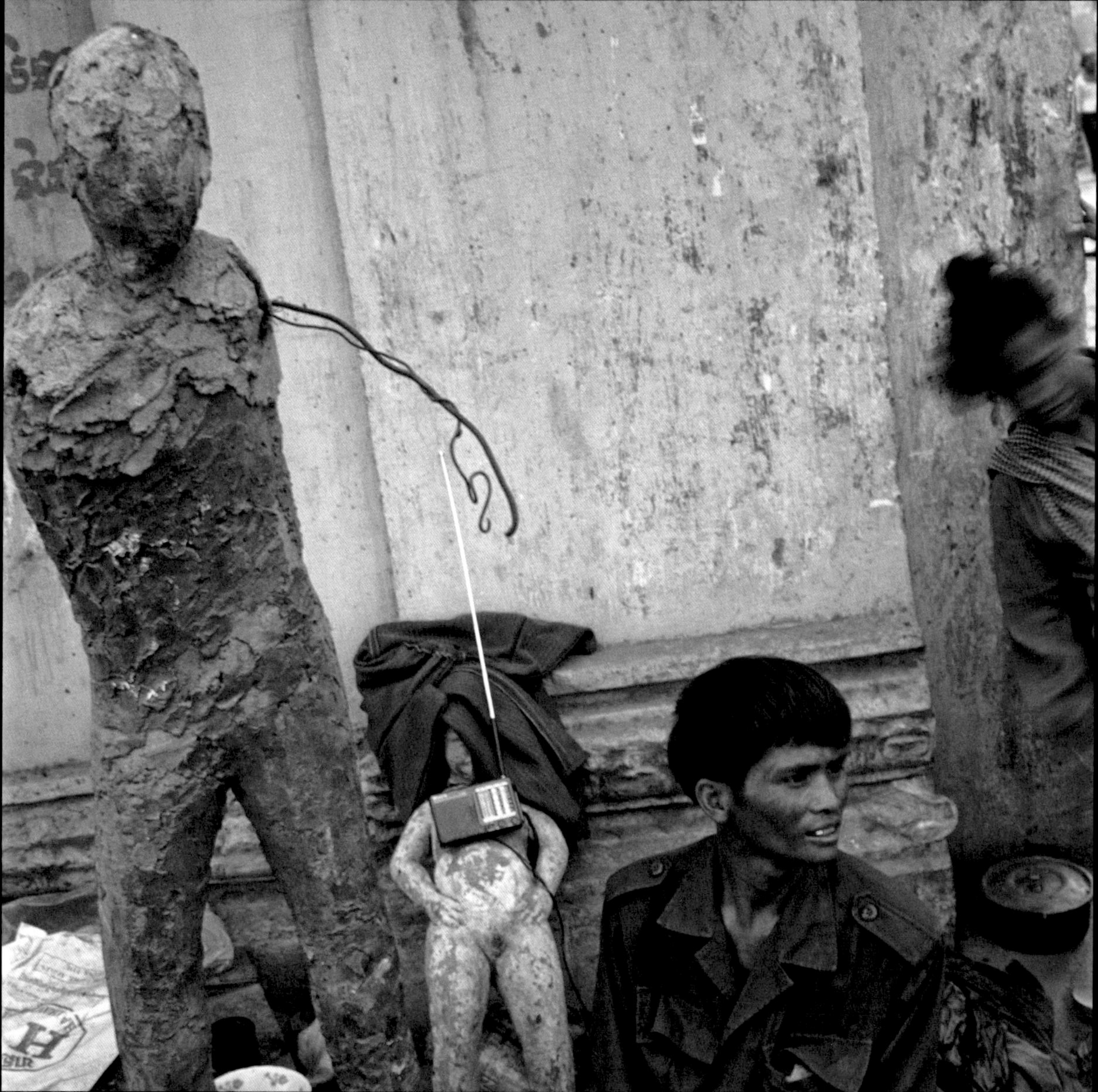

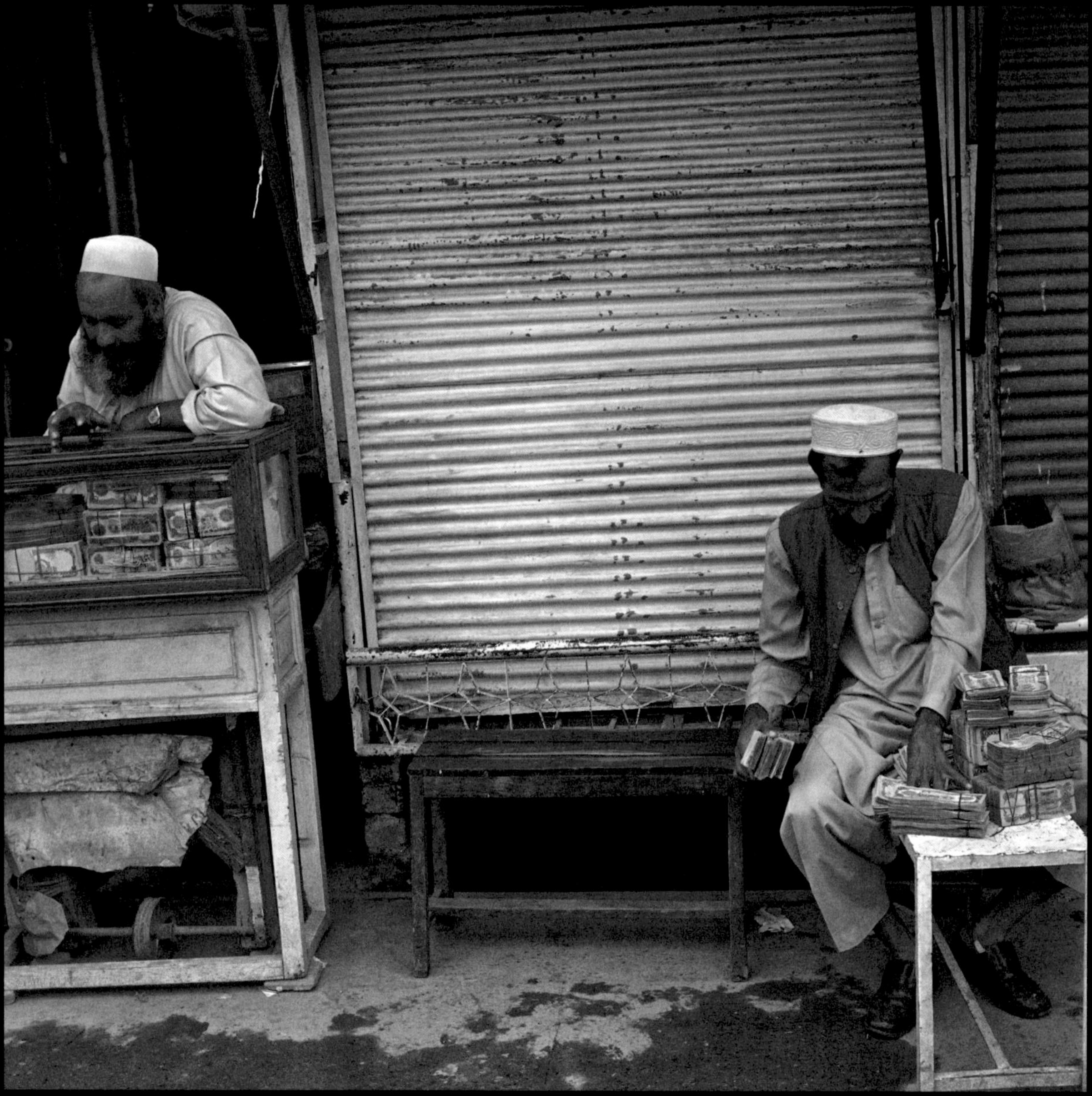

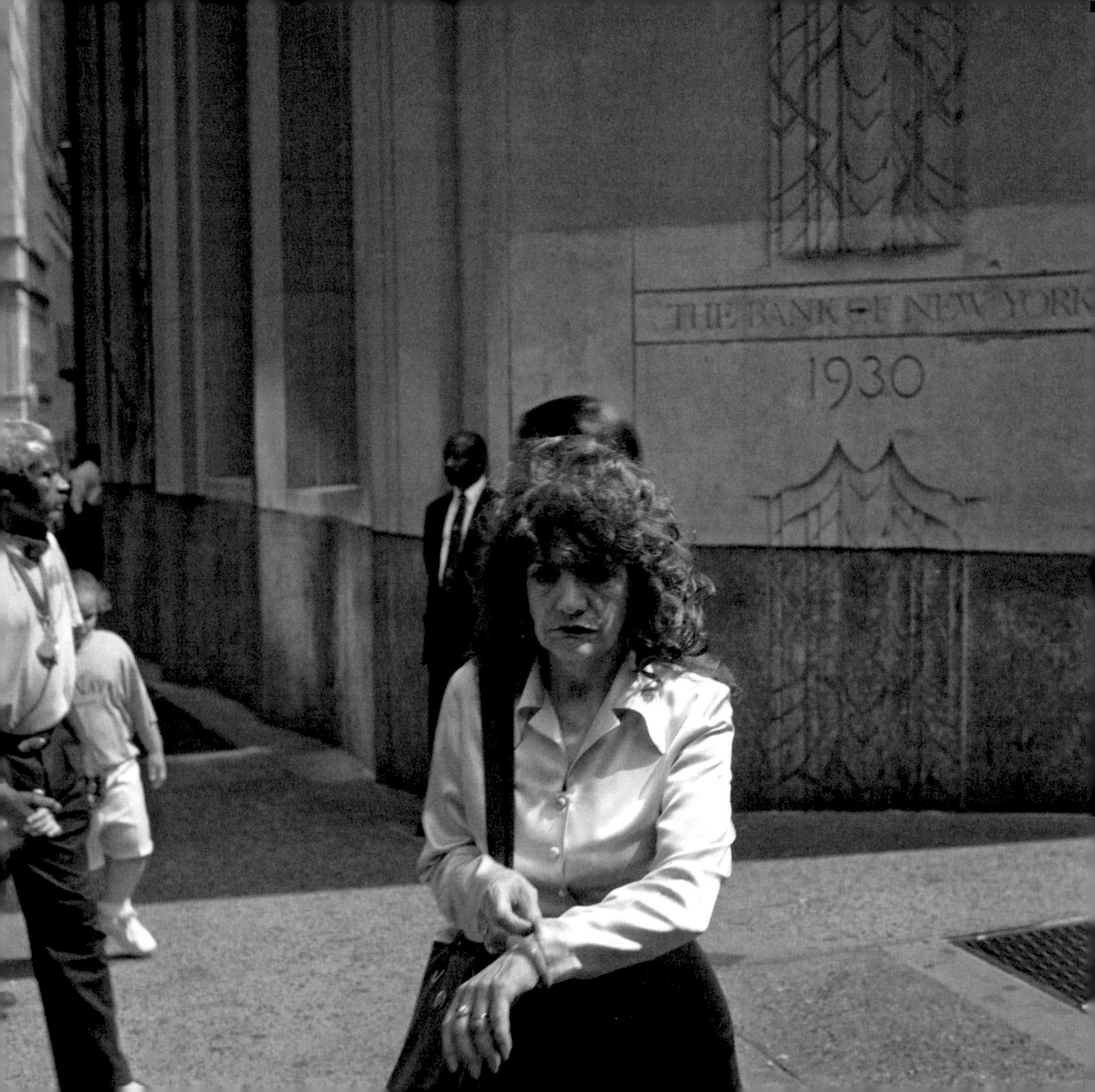
1930

Preceding pages

Plate 28
Commuters
Oxford Circus, London, United Kingdom
25 August 1998

Plate 29
Princes Street Gardens
Edinburgh, United Kingdom
July 1974

Plate 30 – commentary on p. 173
Surveillance
Kabul, Afghanistan
27 December 2009

Plate 31
The door knocker
Catania, Sicily, Italy
September 1979

Plate 32
The ring
Cathédrale Notre-Dame, Paris, France
December 1976

Plate 33 – commentary on p. 173
After an arson attack
Dili, East Timor (then Indonesia)
22 April 1999

Plate 34
Rear window
Biel, Switzerland
10 April 2012

Plate 35
From flood to shelter
Pabna district, Bangladesh
24 September 1991

Plate 36 – commentary on p. 173
A *tokai*, a homeless child
Sadarghat, Dhaka, Bangladesh
25 August 1993

Plate 37
Checking cotton coats for contraband
Gishkuprik Uzbekistan–Kazakhstan border,
Tashkent, Uzbekistan
2 October 2002

Plate 38 – commentary on p. 173
During the collapse of the ruble
Tverskaya Street, Moscow, Russia
5 September 1998

Plate 39 – commentary on p. 174
Dezerter Bazaar
Tbilisi, Georgia
13 November 1990

Plate 40
At the gates of Wat Saravan
Phnom Penh, Cambodia
27 February 1998

Plate 41
Money jobbers
Yadgar Square, Peshawar, Pakistan
12 June 1998

Plate 42
Wall Street
New York City, United States
10 August 1998

Fig. 2

The morning after 9/11
Zürich, Switzerland
12 September 2001

Gelatin silver double-exposure print, 2020.
Sheet size 50 × 40 cm (19 3/4 × 15 3/4 in.)

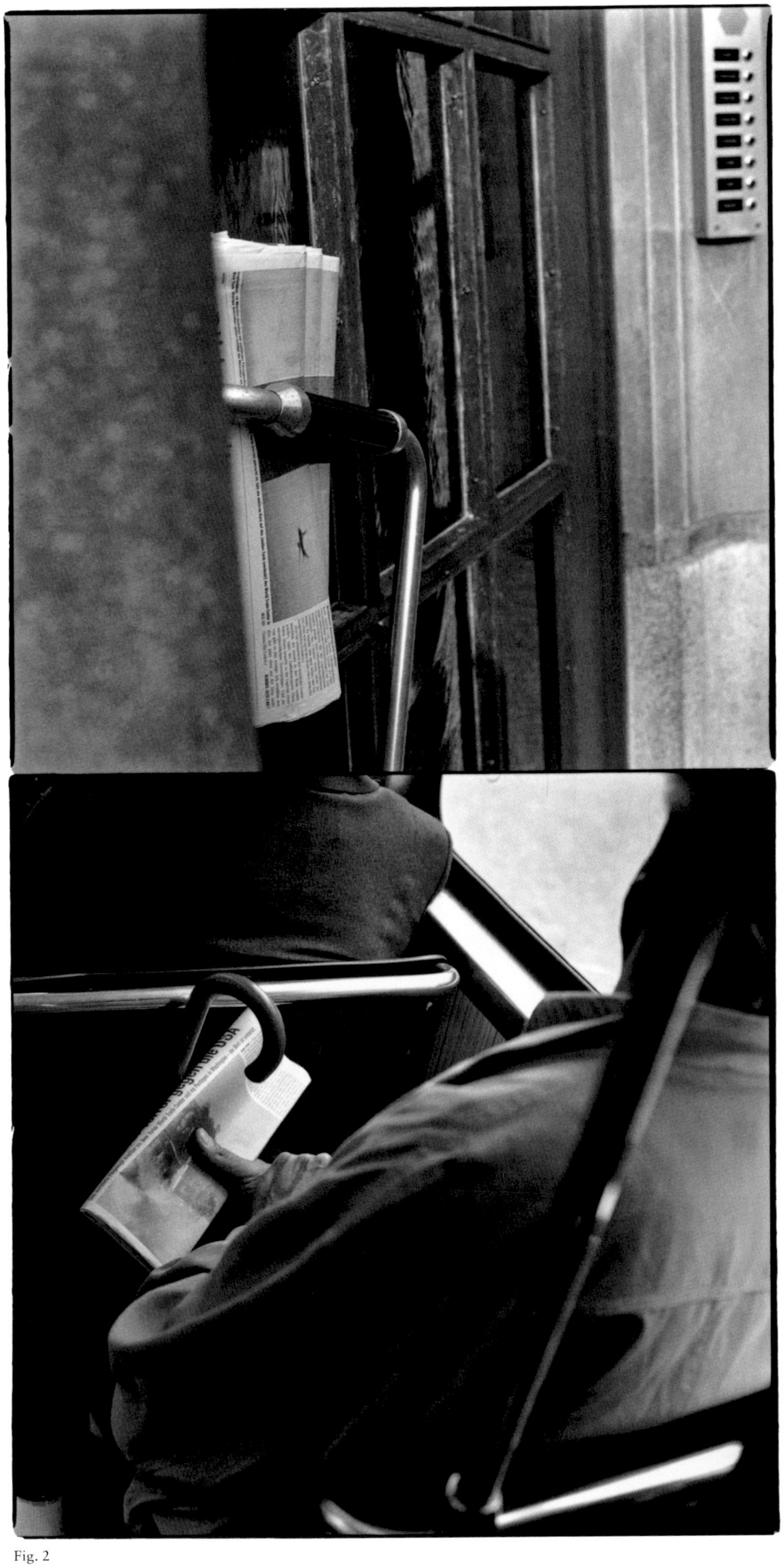

Fig. 2

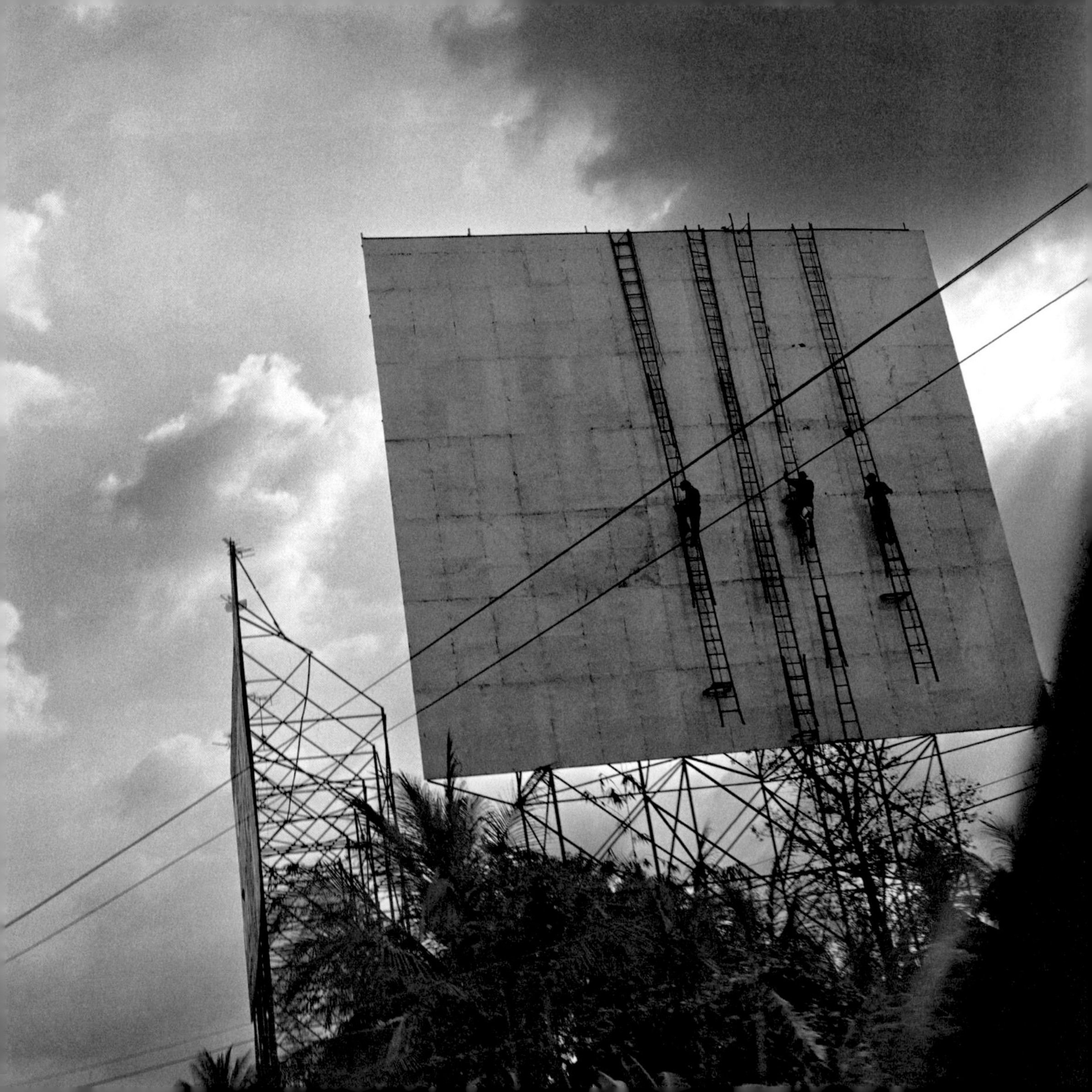

III Absence

First, the superficially very simple question: what does the huge empty billboard in Ho Chi Minh City promise, as it is being prepared by workers for the presentation of a state proclamation, while the message is not there yet? For the photographer, it provides the basis of a strong image, but the propaganda that it will convey has not yet arrived: is that an empty promise, too? Even if it provokes questions in the first place, the term ‘absence’ is eye-catching and makes us reflect when looking at Daniel Schwartz's photographs. It proves to be a multifaceted term, consistently and dialectically connected with its opposite, ‘presence’. An example of this is the image of a woman with a bundle on her head at a market in Kabul (plate 5). Her strong formal presence in the picture's composition is counteracted by the abstraction of her person, her face, beneath the bag and her burqa, by the enforced absence of women’s personhood from Afghan public life.

Where has God gone, where has he been banished to, when his house, a Byzantine church in Anatolia, is now used as a barn (plate 44)? What about the potency of Buddha's knowledge and spirit when his smiling face on thousand-year-old reliefs in Pakistan is obliterated in the hope of spiritual reward (plate 54)?

Between 2009 and 2016, Daniel Schwartz devoted systematic, thematic investigation to a drastically accelerated disappearance caused by modern humans, the death throes of glaciers on four continents. Even if this comprehensive work produces photographs that speak a more abstract visual language than those discussed above, they nevertheless confront the viewer, perhaps precisely because of this, all the more ruthlessly and urgently with the inevitable question: What will happen to our planet when the glaciers are no longer there?

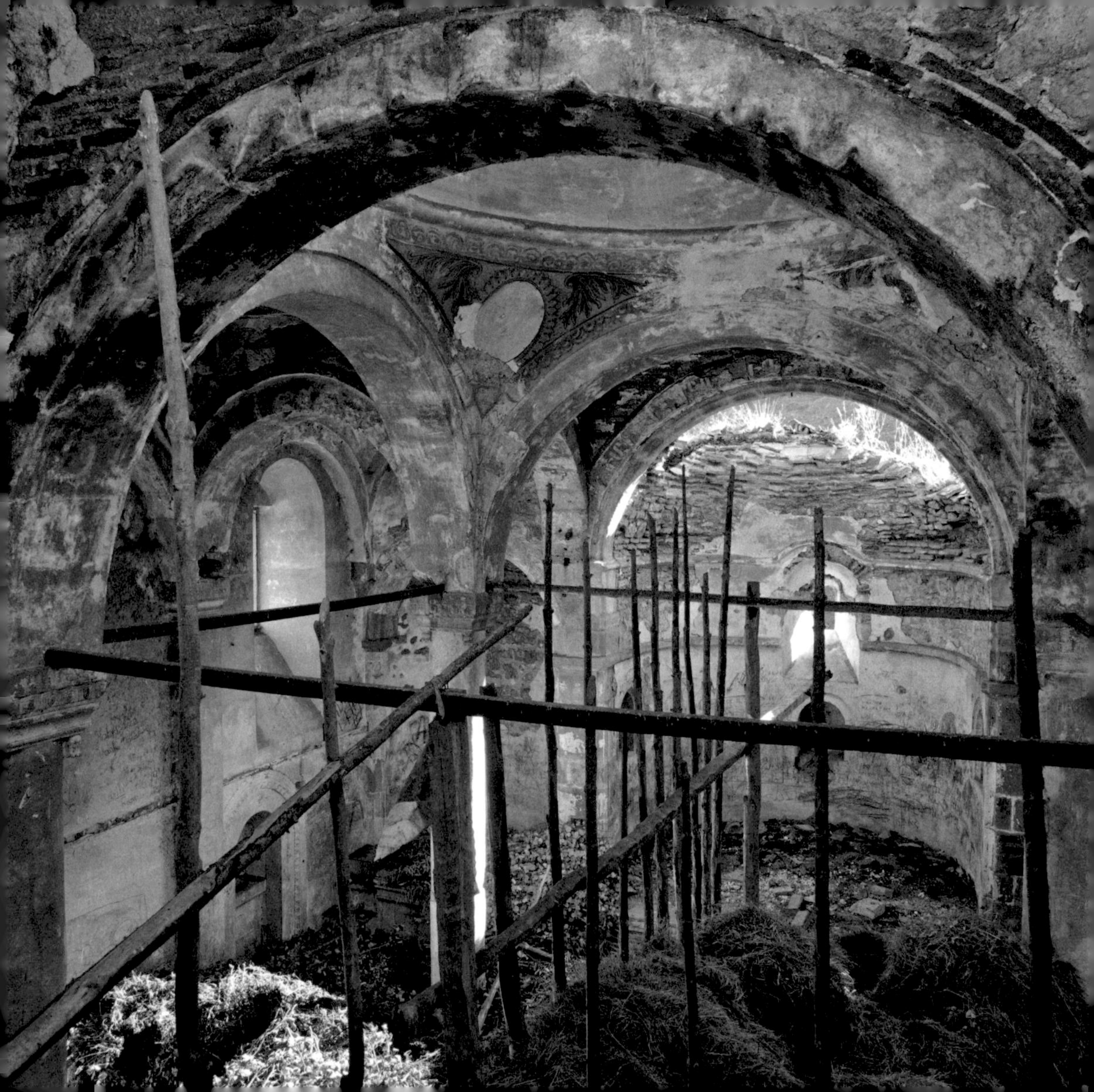

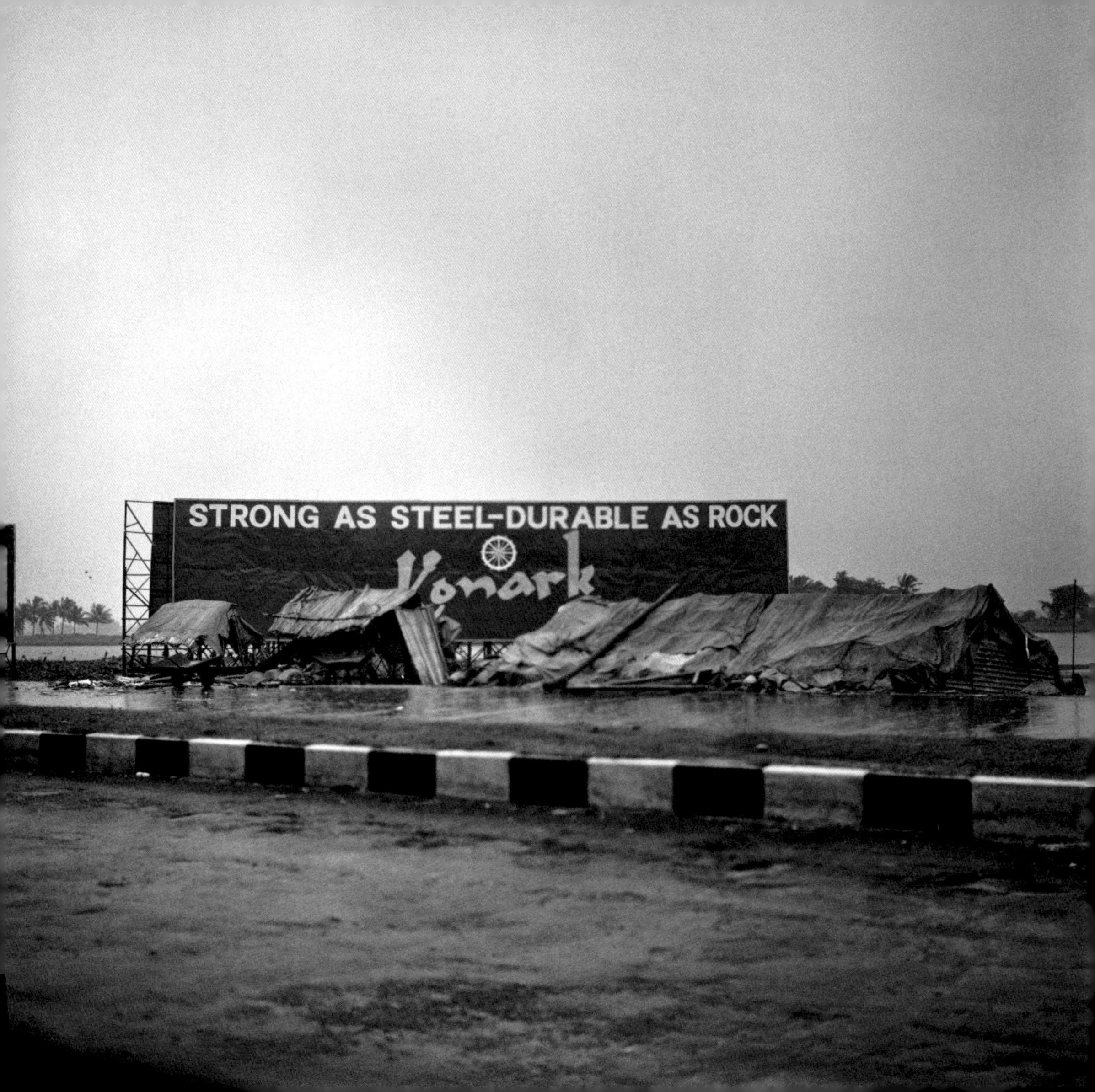
STRONG AS STEEL-DURABLE AS ROCK
Konark

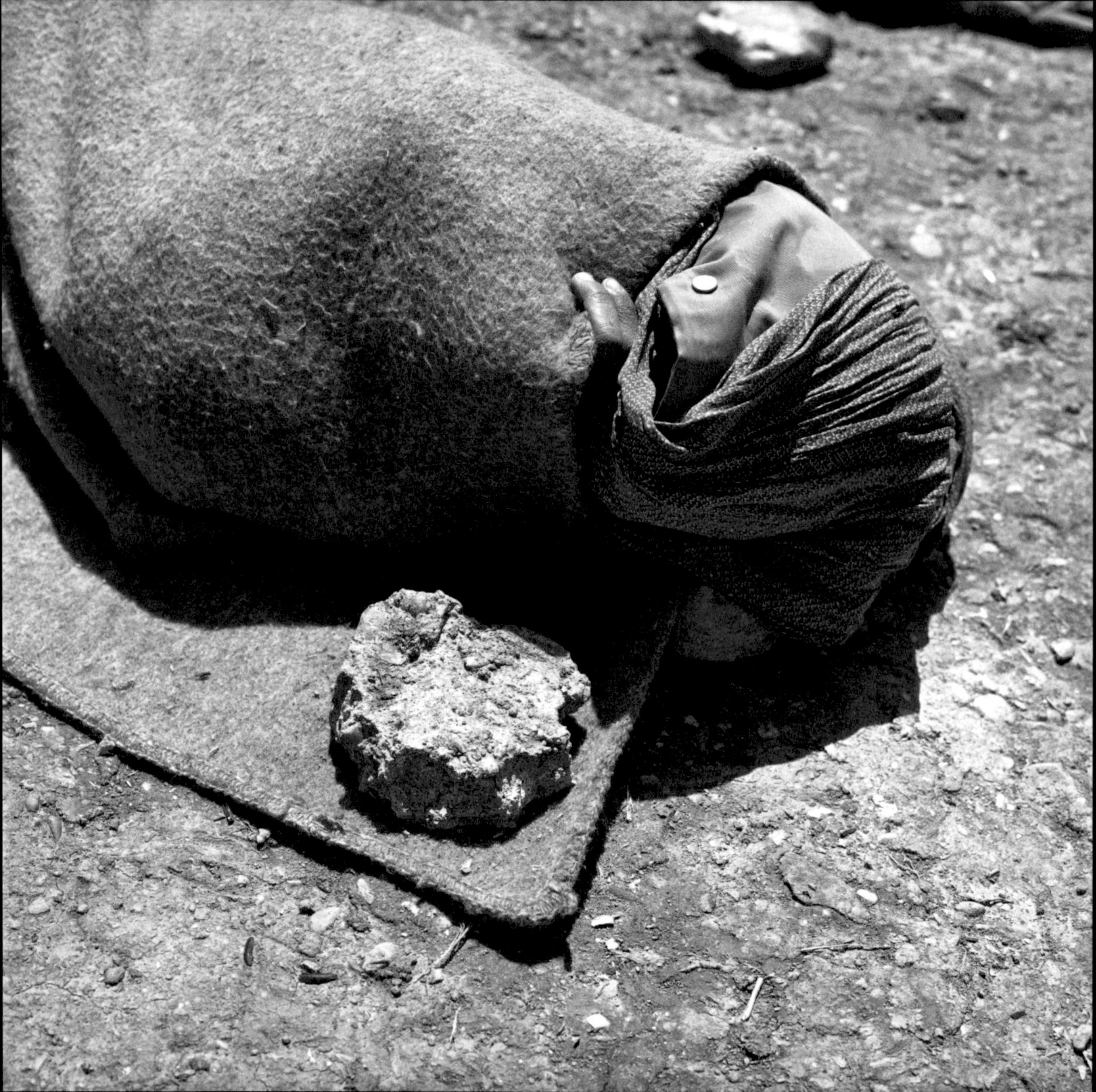

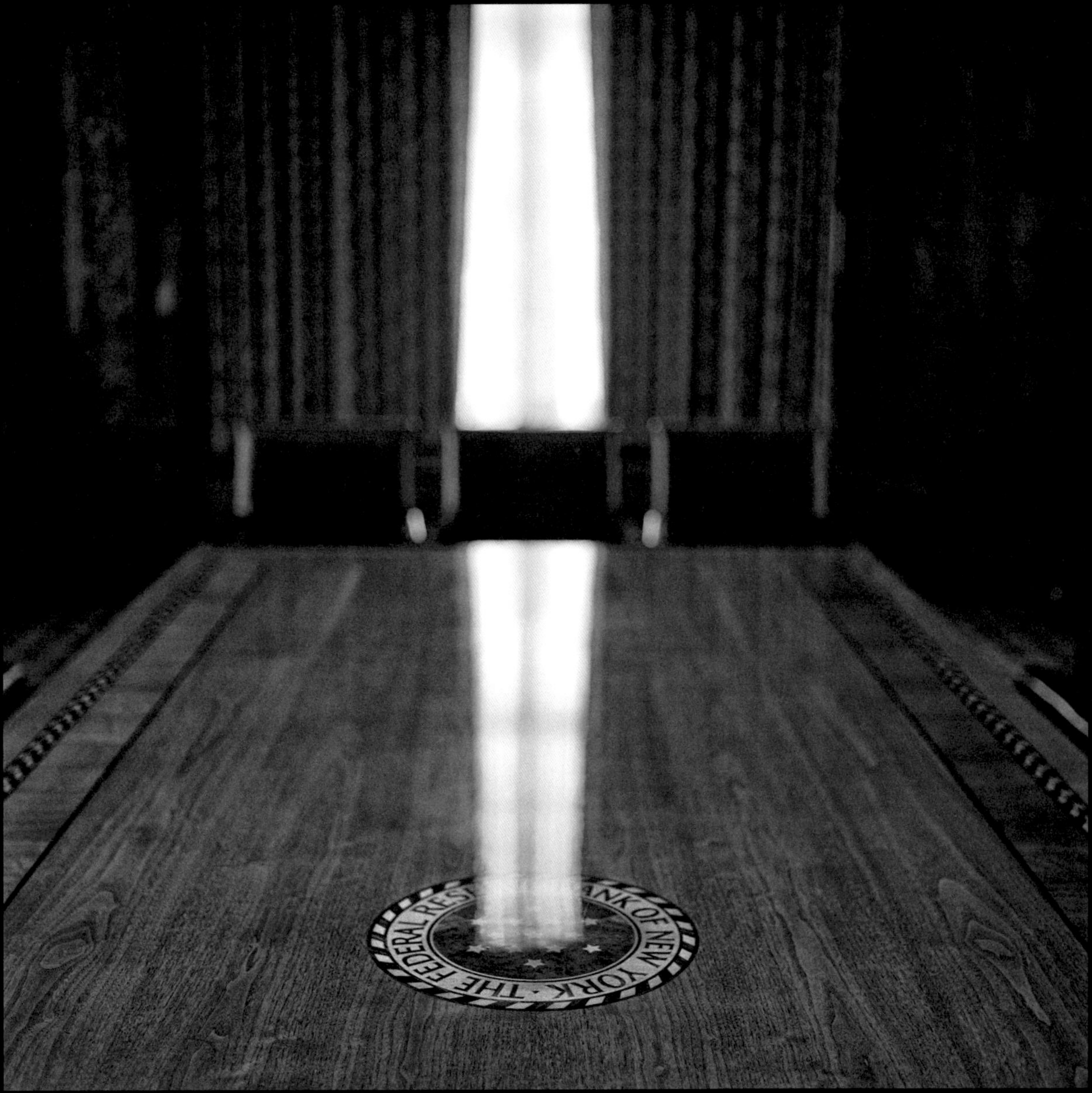
THE FEDERAL RES ANK OF NEW YORK

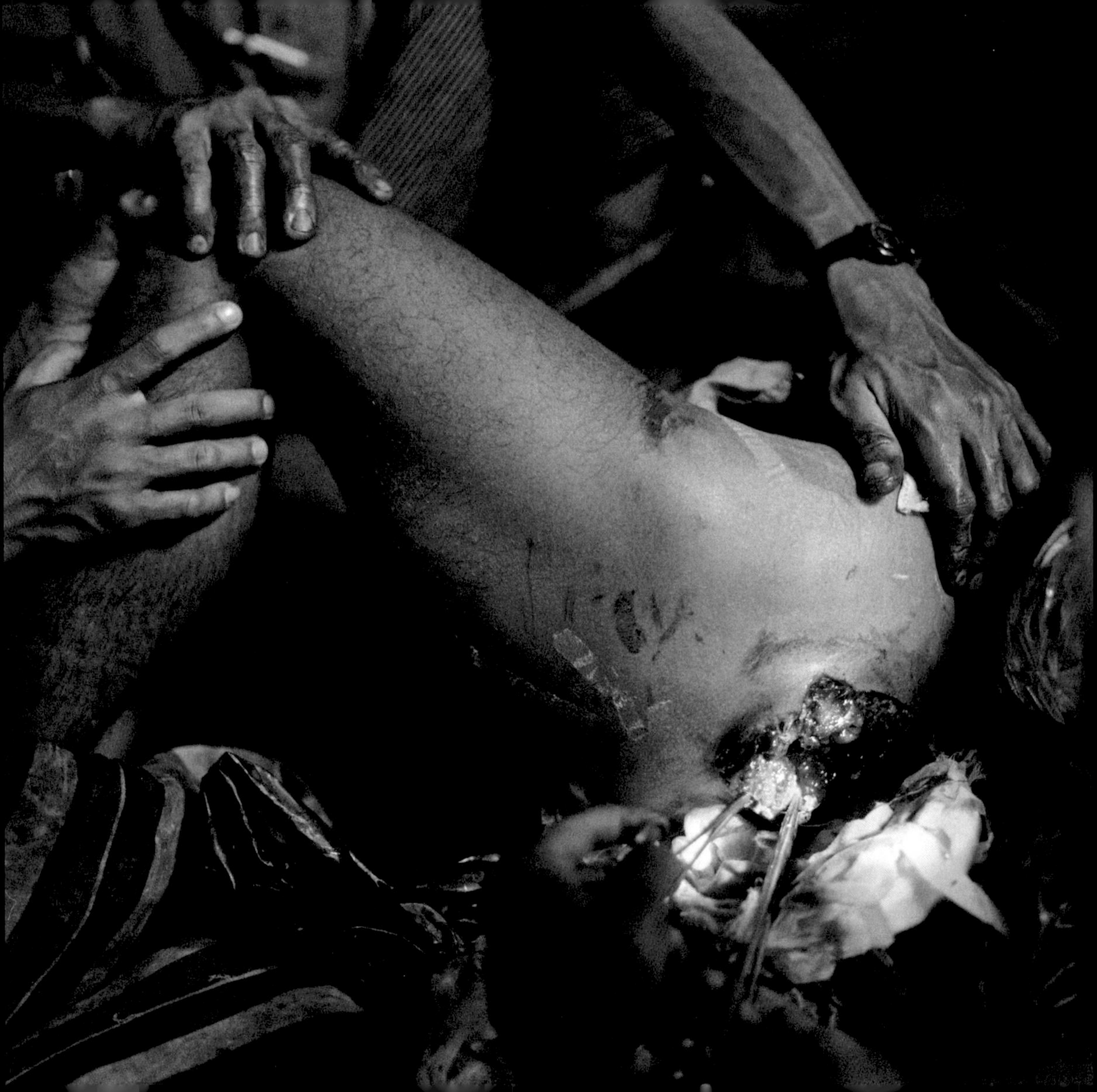

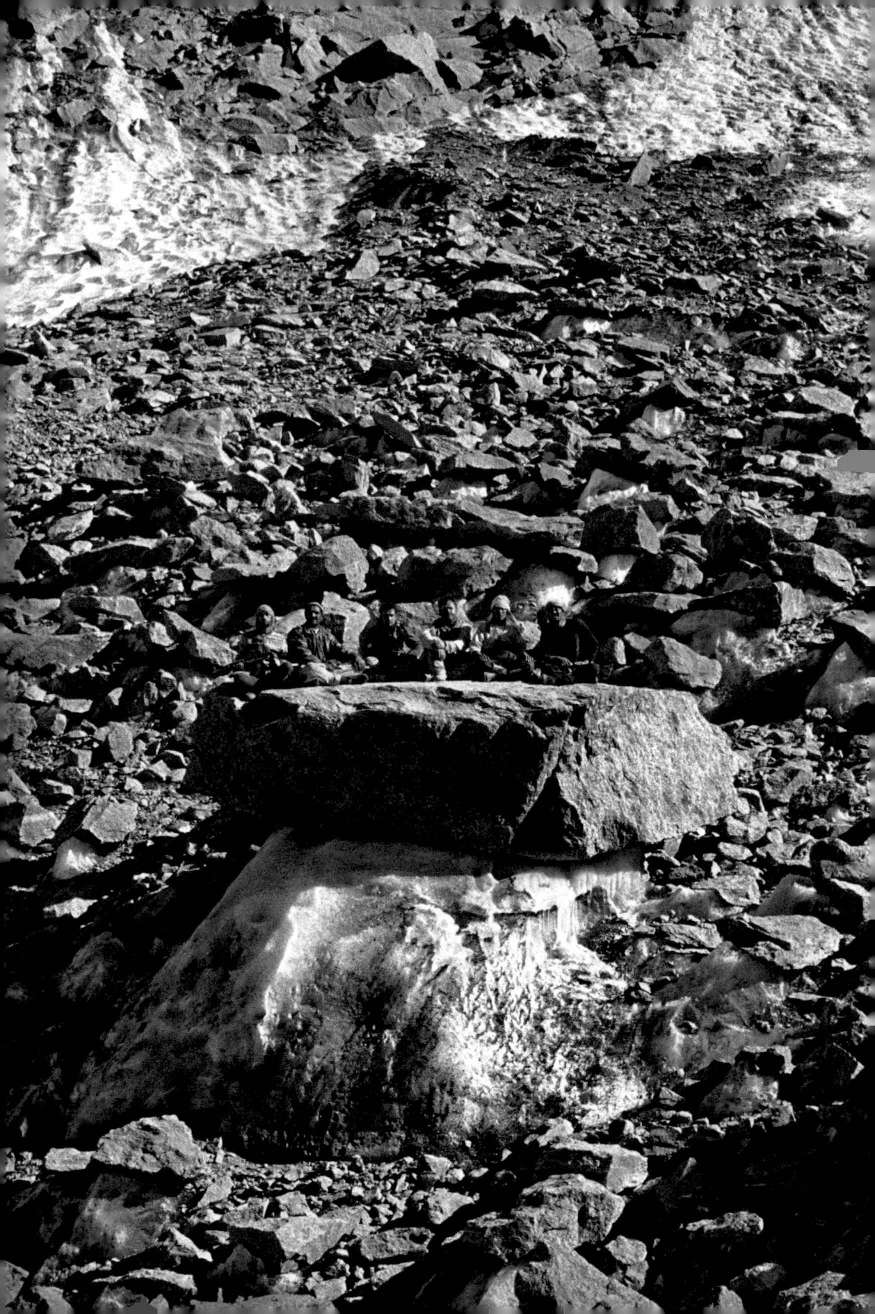

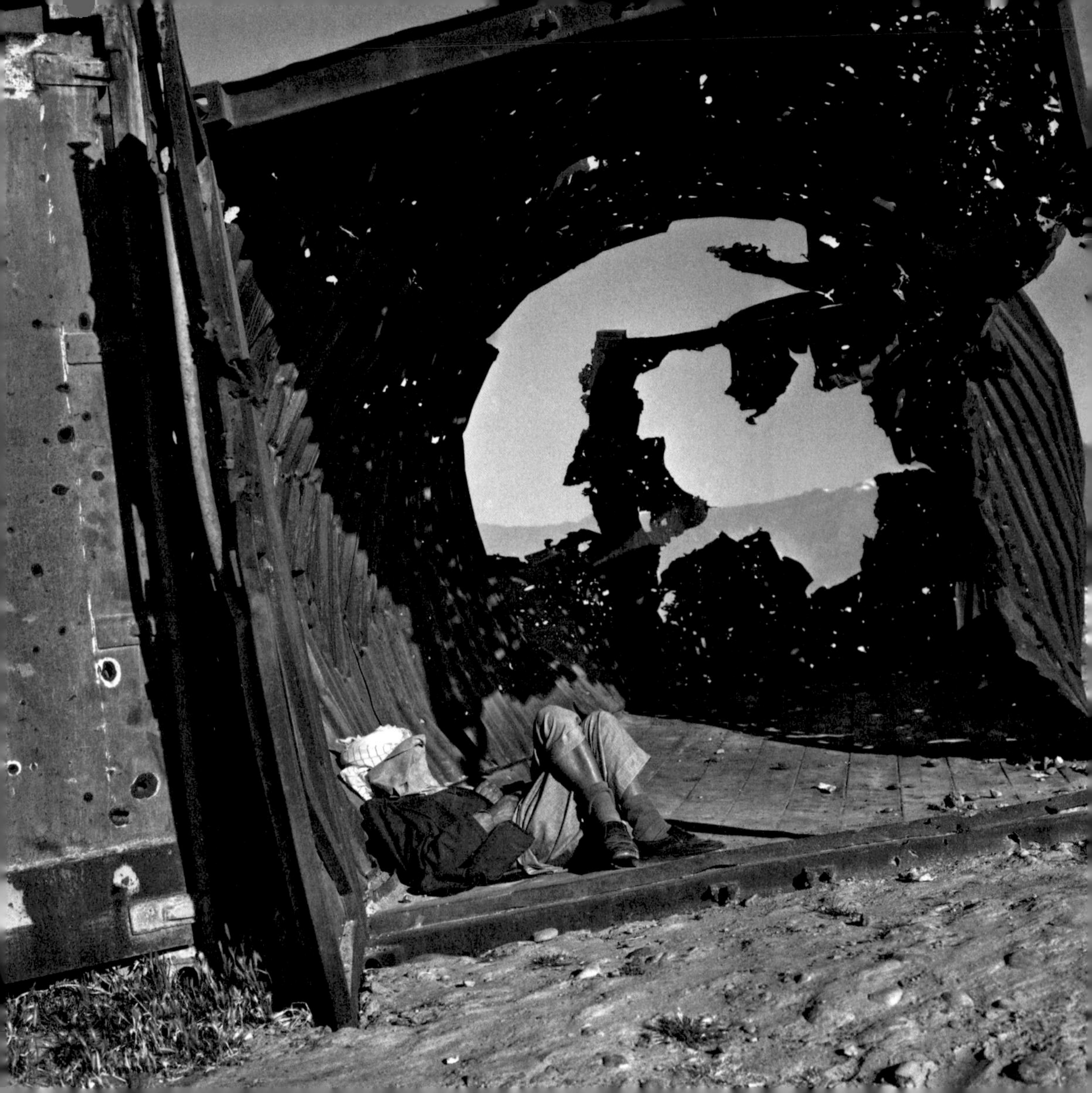

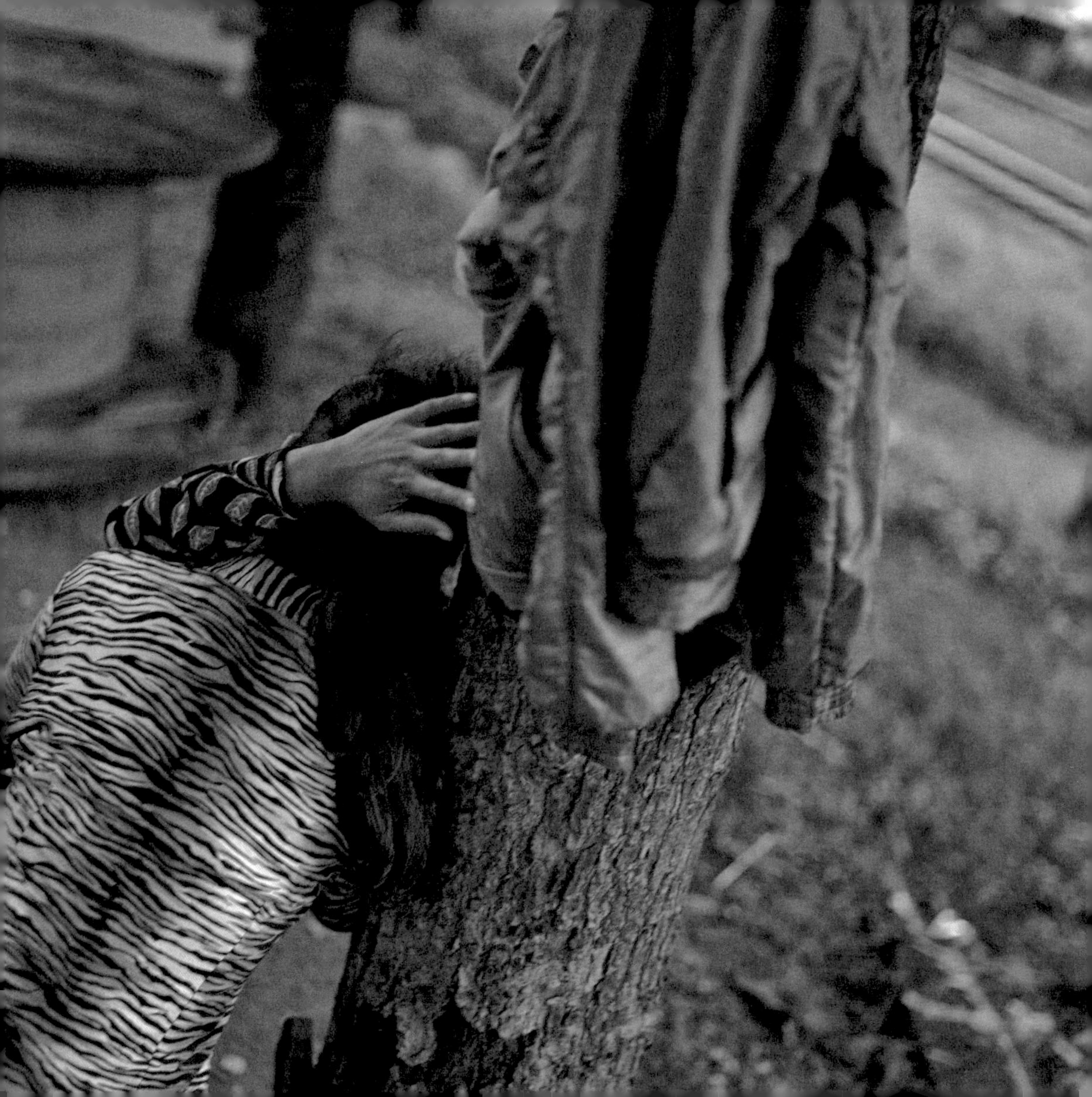

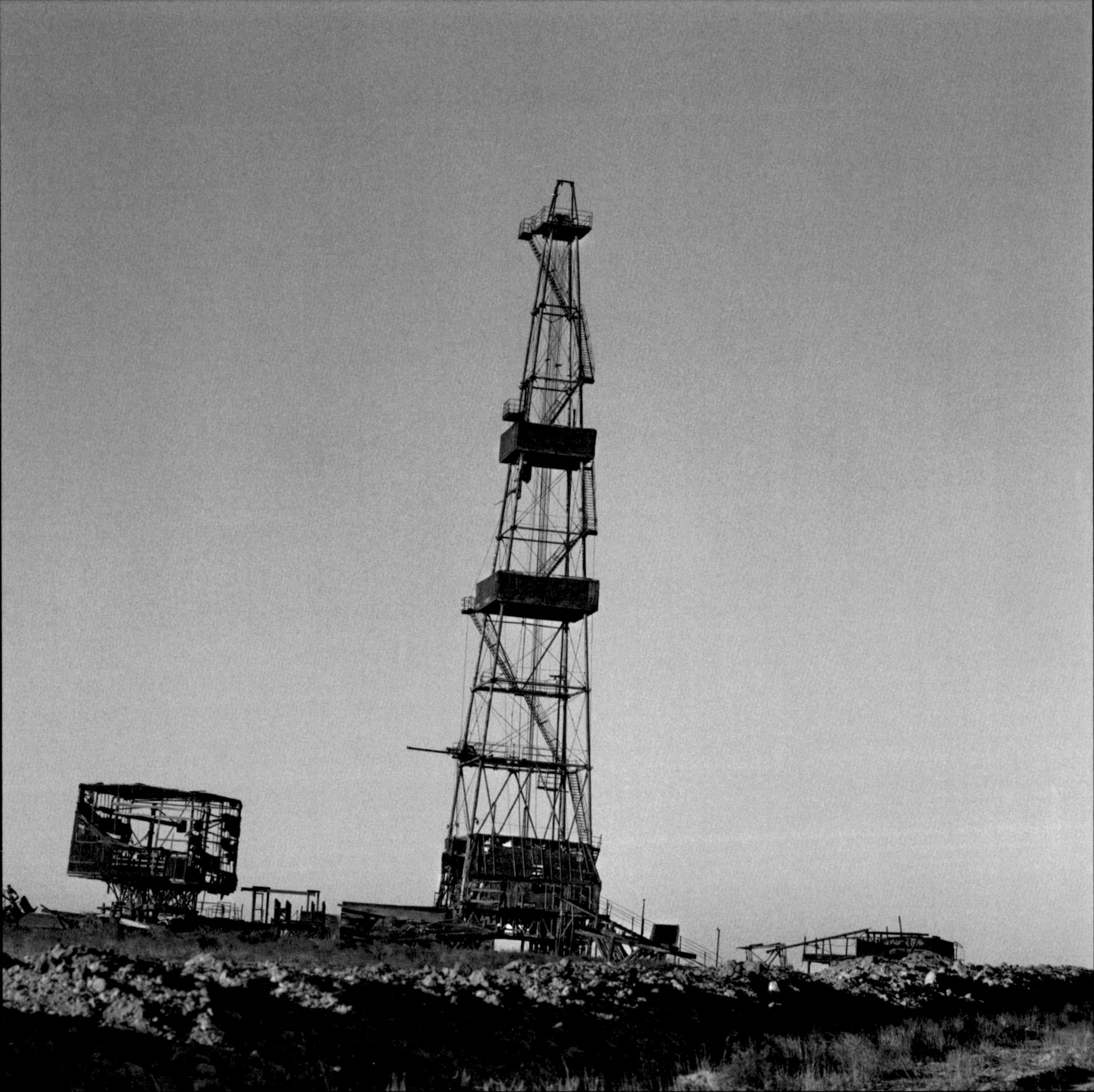

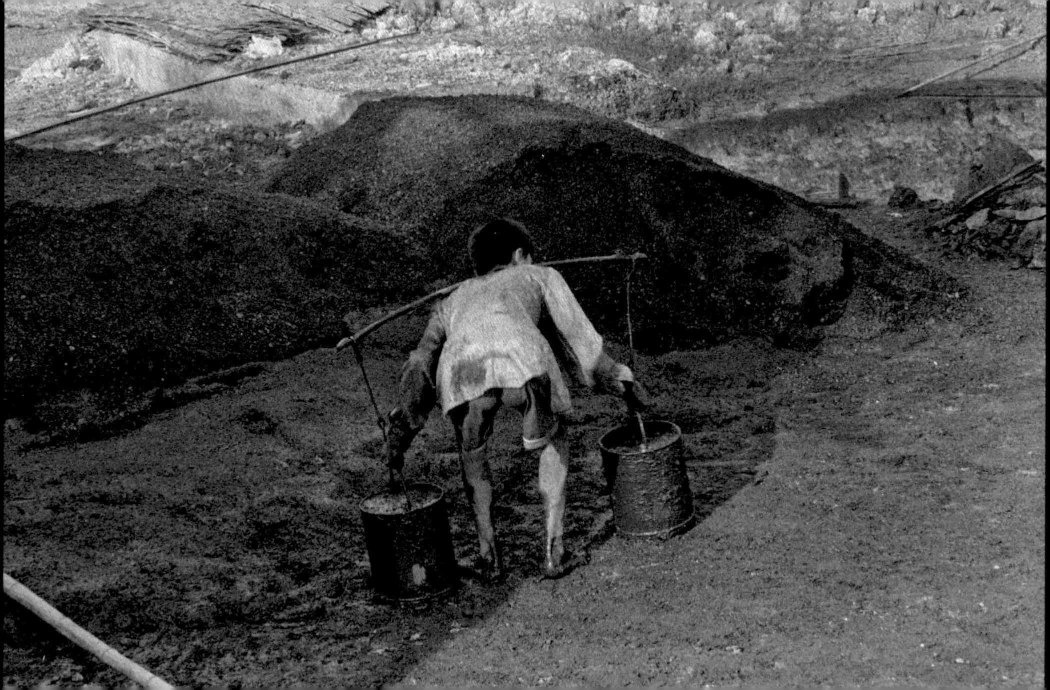

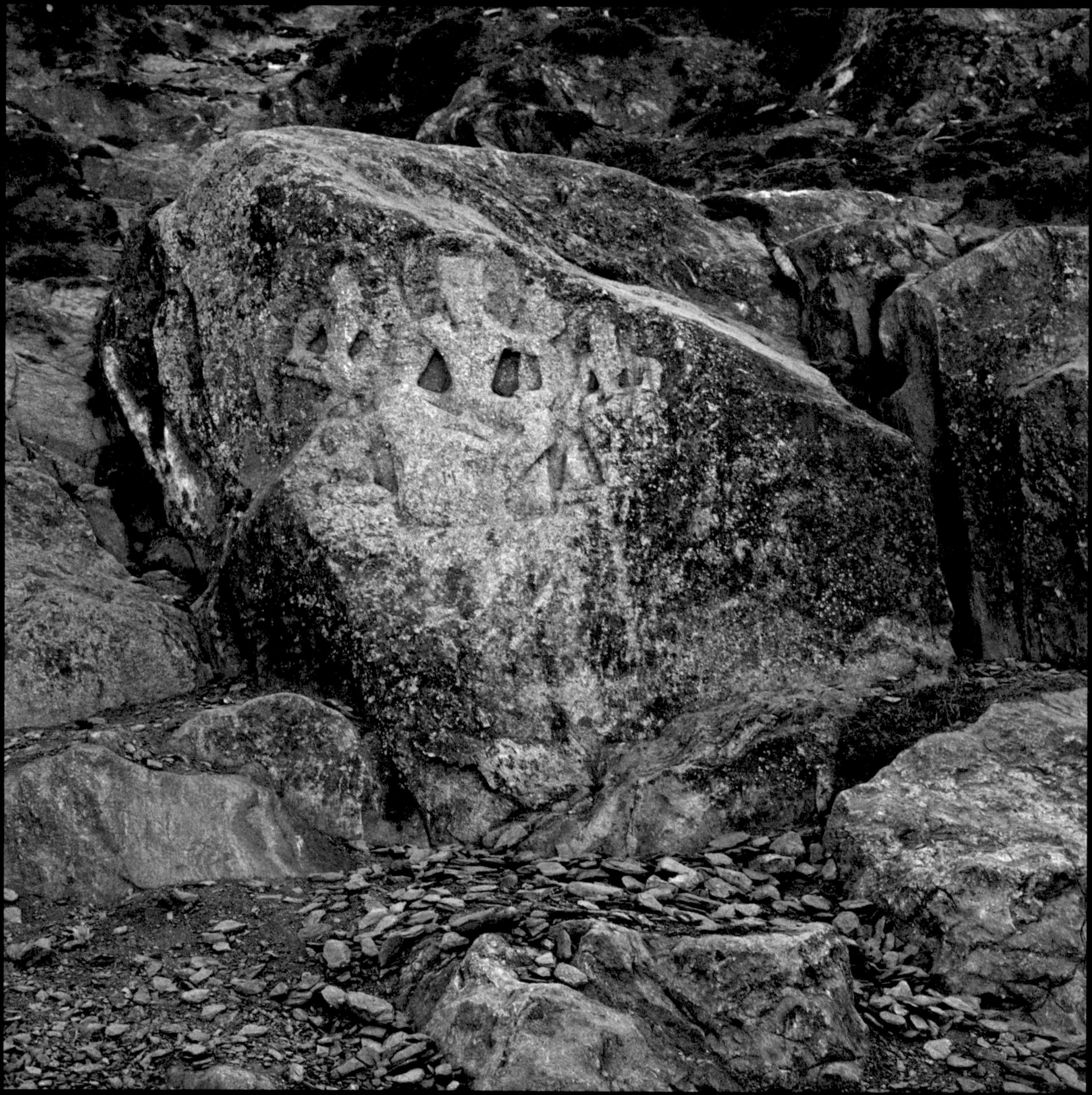

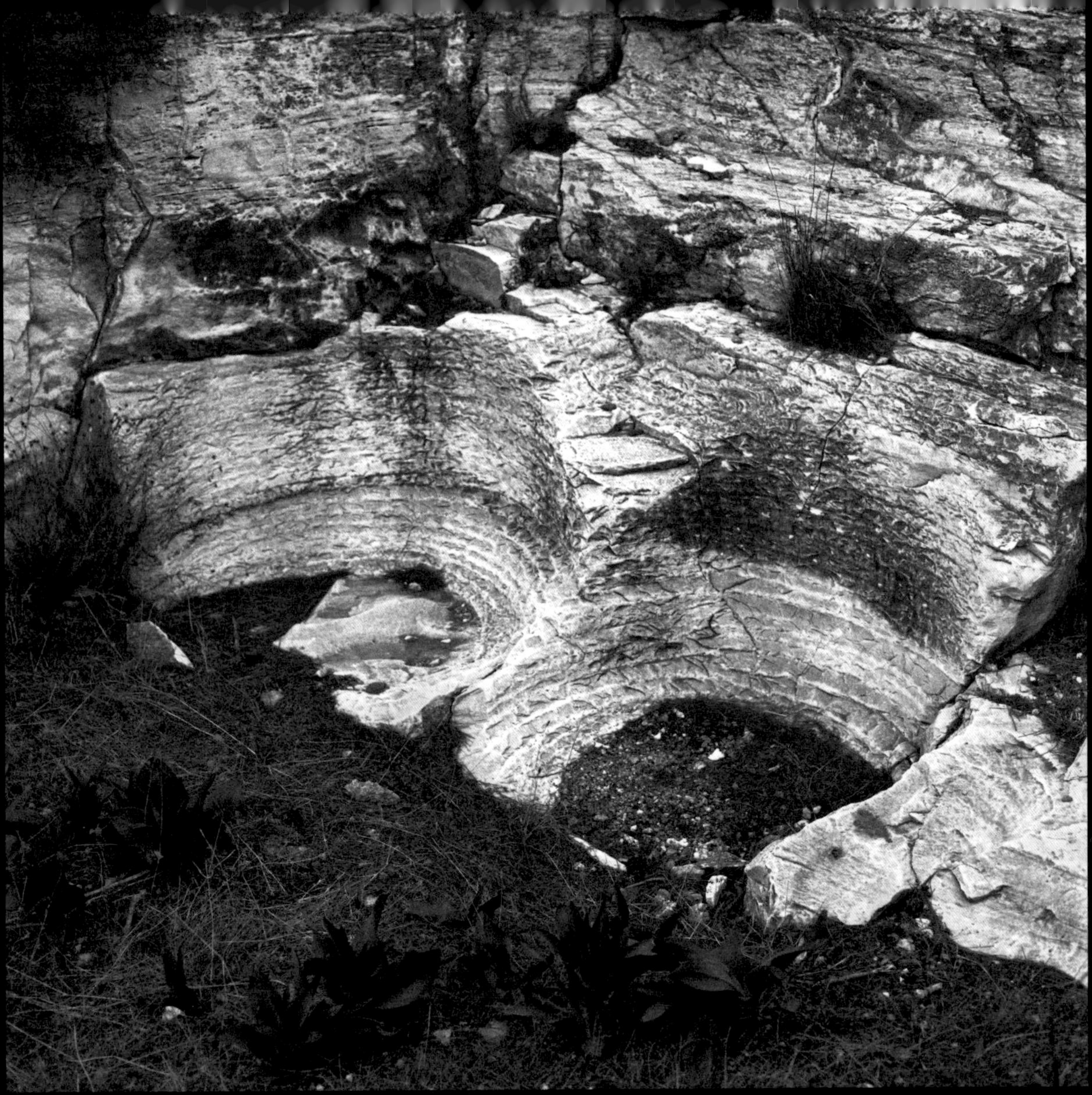

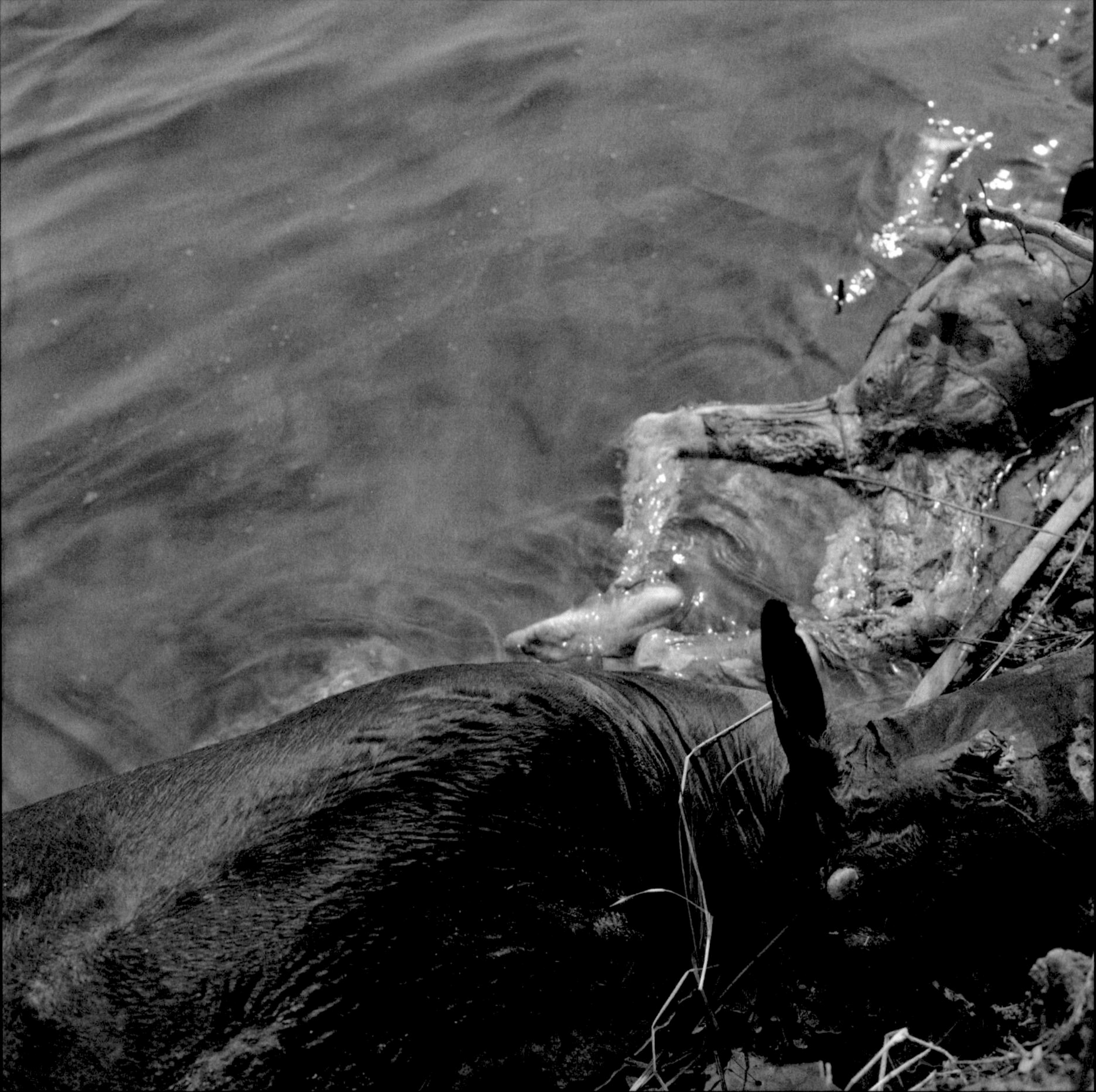

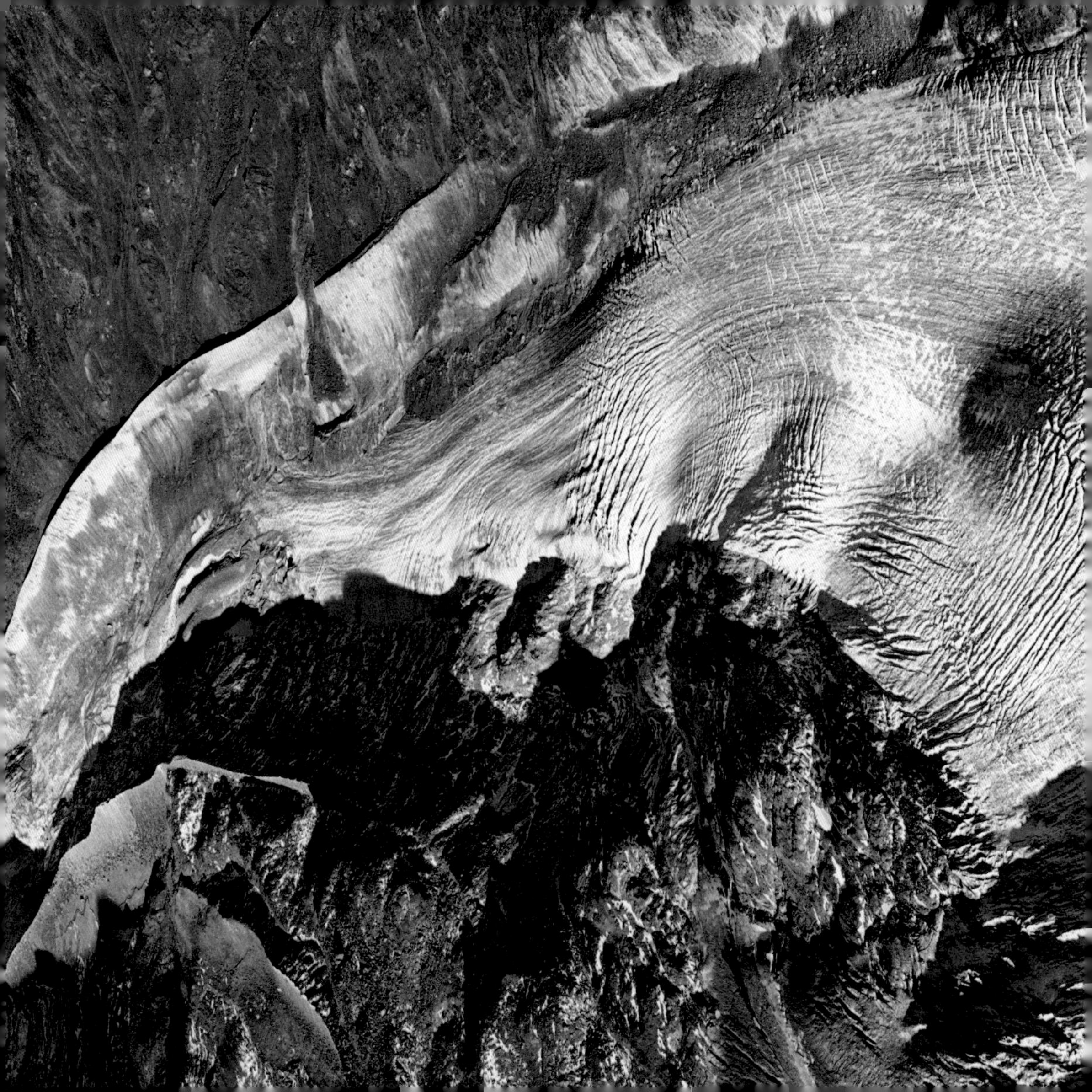

Preceding pages

Plate 43
Transition economy proclaimed
Cholon, Ho Chi Minh City, Vietnam
14 February 2001

Plate 44 – commentary on p. 174
Byzantine-church-turned-barn
Gümüşhane province, Turkey
10 October 1989

Plate 45
Rag picker's shelter on the Eastern Bypass
Kolkata, India
20 October 1993

Plate 46 – commentary on p. 174
After the exodus from Iraq
Piranshar, Iran
18 April 1991

Plate 47 – commentary on p. 174
The boardroom table
The Federal Reserve Bank,
New York City, United States
10 August 1998

Plate 48
Operating on a wounded Karen combatant
Myanmar–Thailand border
30 January 1992

Plate 49 – commentary on p. 174
Armed men on a glacier table
Southwest 2 Glacier, Mir Samir,
Panjshir, Afghanistan
12 September 2018

Plate 50
A container blown up by a rocket
Kabul, Afghanistan
21 June 1998

Plate 51
Sex worker and client
Ciliwung River, Jakarta, Indonesia
22 February 1998

Plate 52
Abandoned oil well
Aktau, Kazakhstan
8 November 2007

Plate 53
The bamboo pole
Quang Ninh province, Vietnam
30 July 2000

Plate 54 – commentary on p. 175
Iconoclasm
Swat Valley, Pakistan
21 December 2009

Plate 55 – commentary on p. 175
Ancient quarry
Agrilesa, Attica, Greece
January 1985

Plate 56 – commentary on p. 175
Child's body and carcass after the cyclone
Banshkhali, Bangladesh
9 May 1991

Plate 57 – commentary on p. 175
Collapse of the cryosphere
Findel Glacier, Valais, Switzerland
2 November 2014

Fig. 3 – commentary on p. 176

Drought in the Murghab canyon
Badghis province, Afghanistan
30 March 2001

Gelatin silver quadruple-exposure print, 2017.
Sheet size 40 × 50 cm (19 3/4 × 15 3/4 in.)

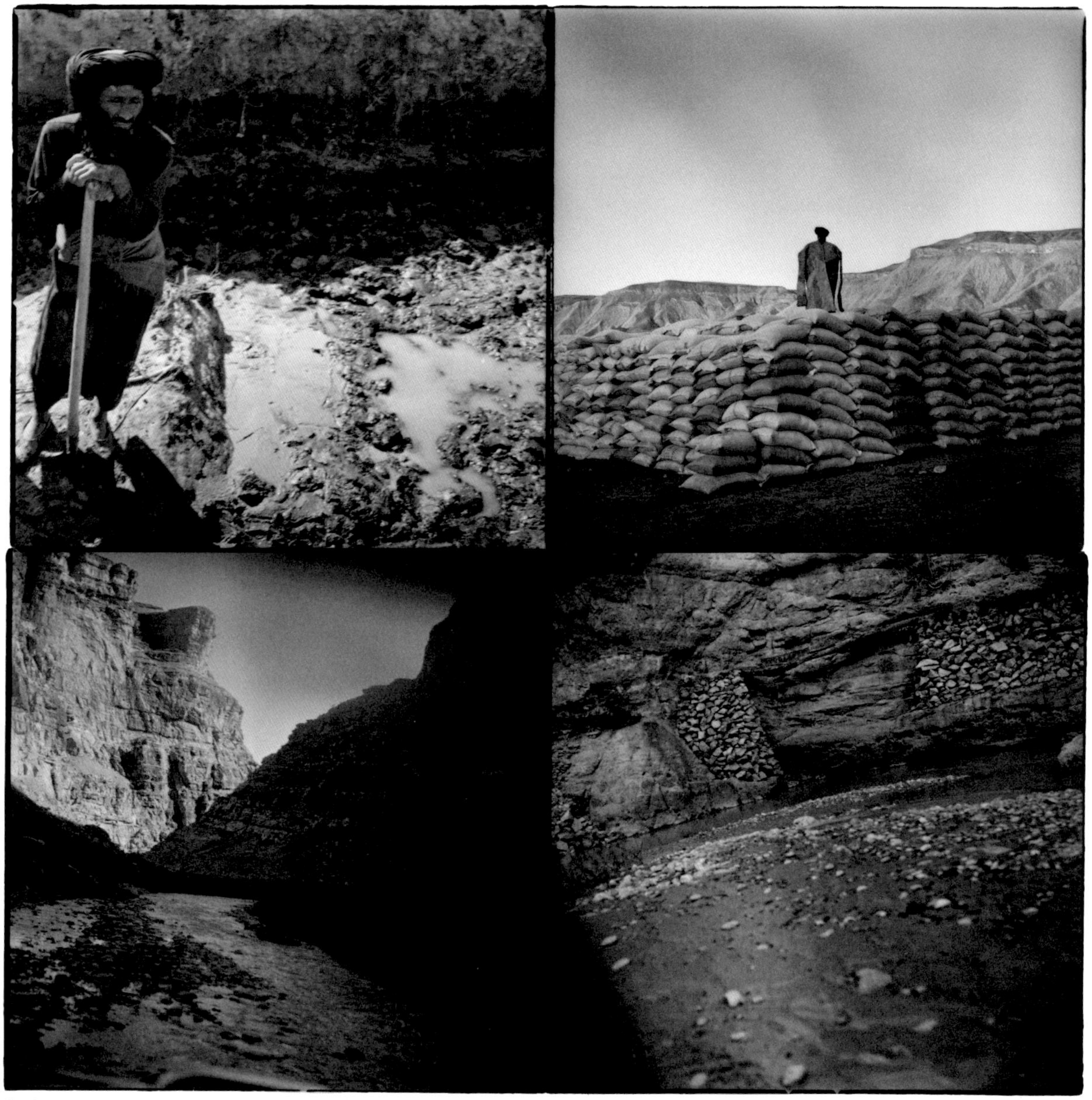

Fig. 3

Beat Wismer: Tracings

It is not as easy as it might initially seem to familiarize oneself with Daniel Schwartz's oeuvre. Firstly: which Schwartz are we thinking of, and which aspects of his work should we consider? After all, as well as the photographer, there is the author of numerous articles and a literary magnum opus, not to mention the diligent collaborator on and editor of socially and politically engaged photography publications, with equal concern for content and form. Then there is the curator of an enviable collection, one of such unbridled diversity it verges on a chamber of curiosities; he is also the keeper of an equally varied, sprawling and even more extensive library, which he cultivates with the same ambition.[1] Of course, first and foremost, Schwartz is an uncompromisingly meticulous photographer who occupies a unique position with his reportage and other unrelated work – a position which is as firmly rooted in the history of photography as it is completely unrivalled in the contemporary photography scene. In the late 1970s, when Daniel Schwartz was a student and capturing his first images on camera, the discipline set about occupying its own category in the fine arts context. Hesitantly at first, but then increasingly, photography was exhibited in institutions and spaces that had until the dawning of this new era been reserved for the fine arts. Photography began to step up – with a self-assured voice – and to make an important and unmistakable contribution to contemporary art discourse. Early in this decade, in the context of minimal and conceptual art, Bernd and Hilla Becher's objectively austere photographs of industrial architecture were exhibited as works of art – first at documenta V in Kassel in 1972, and then in art galleries. Towards the end of the same decade, from 1978 to 1979, the 'WOLS Photograph' exhibition toured Europe. Wols (1913–1951) had been perceived primarily as a Van Gogh-esque *peintre maudit* and an important predecessor or progenitor of the *informel* in painting during the years subsequent to his untimely death. But as the interest of the art world began to extend to photography and Wols gained recognition for his work in this area, his photographs from the 1930s were exhibited in art museums.

Both of these contributions to art history were discussed in depth in the Fotoklasse at Zürich's Kunstgewerbeschule (School of Arts and Crafts), where Schwartz was studying at around this time, and where teachers such as Rudolf Lichtsteiner played an important role in his development. On the one hand, the Bechers' style was seen as being indicative of an emphatic modern-day endorsement of Sachfotografie, the objective photography taught in the Fotoklasse, the course founded in the 1930s by Hans Finsler (1891–1972), which still very much bore the hallmarks of his functionally austere approach. On the other hand, Wols's still lifes, with their depiction of the unapologetically precarious reality of everyday life, his 'view of the bucket and washrag', posed a real challenge for the purist objective photography of which Finsler was an exponent. The contrast between still life arrangements and compositions à la Morandi (fig. 7) and found still lifes was also a point of discussion. Schwartz himself says that his discovery of Wols's images towards the end of his studies had a profound impact on him. At exactly this time, Kunsthaus Zürich was holding the first exhibition of photography by Constantin Brâncuși (1876–1957), whose studio photographs, again, were ultimately found still lifes and provoked a similarly intense response from Schwartz. The discovery of these two photographers, Brâncuși the sculptor and Wols the painter, was instrumental to Daniel Schwartz's still lifes. His images are contaminated by the harsh reality of everyday life – or in his own words, they are 'wild' – and demonstrate an almost dialectical revocation of Finsler's maxim of purity.

The still life study of the two peppers on a tar-bitumen sheet, published for the first time here (fig. 5), is a case in point: Schwartz produced this image when he was nearing the end of his studies in 1979, in a rather cocksure attempt to compete with the series of pepper photographs (fig. 6) by Edward Weston (1886–1958), one of the undisputed icons of still life photography, which was half a century old at the time. It was a daring challenge and a self-assured show of the evolution of his artistry, though executed entirely without emotion: he bought the peppers at the market in the morning, then photographed them with various filters in the natural daylight of the student chamber, developed the film in the laboratory in the photography department and printed the image off. Later, in the evening, he chopped up the peppers in the kitchen and ate them. And with that, the deed was done. This flippant emotional detachment, striking as it may be, diverts the visual memory away from the obvious similarity to Weston's pepper photographs and their virtuoso depiction of surfaces and materiality; instead, we are instinctively reminded of Wols's brutally bare still lifes of rabbits and sardines – photographs that comment in a raw, unsentimental way on basic needs such as hunger and food. Daniel Schwartz did not become a still life photographer in the decades that followed, granted, but it is still interesting and worthwhile to look into this aspect of his reportage photographs and see how, in addition to the somewhat reckless approach to presenting the contents, they have an almost still life quality in places and an intuitively confident, usually very fast composition. His pepper photograph is a virtuoso little *Gesellenstück* – a journeyman's piece, which essentially contains many of the characteristics that became typical of his extensive body of work in the decades that followed.

As a brief aside, it should be noted that from the 1980s, Daniel Schwartz primarily gained recognition for his creative work on the strength of five substantial book publications and numerous reportage features in magazines and newspapers. Each of the book projects Schwartz worked on over the course of several years has a definite thematic framework, though the subjects he deals with are wide-reaching. And the same can be said of the widely varied exhibitions he has produced since the 1980s, which, moreover, were not held exclusively in institutions reserved for fine arts but usually in the respective photography department. Thus far, the reception of Schwartz's photography has been linked to his reportage and therefore tied in with specific themes. *Tracings*, however, both as an exhibition and a book, differs from all his previous projects: for the first time, the focus is not first and foremost on the author of reportage photography; it is on the photographer as an artist and his photographs as thematically independent works of art.

Another image, produced a year earlier than the pepper photograph, in the spring of 1978, offers a perhaps surprising but most certainly revealing glimpse into the mind of Daniel Schwartz the art photographer, providing insights into his sophisticated process of contemplation and recollection. The picture of the peppers was taken in the confines of his student digs, whereas this earlier photograph was a product of his native landscape, which he worked on in the context of a school assignment on the subject of home. The twenty-three-year-old student took his Hasselblad to the forest outside Solothurn to photograph the huge erratic boulder on the Martinsflue (fig. 14), and returned on several occasions until the weather and the light were just right for the shot. With hindsight, this carefully composed picture reveals itself to be a secret predecessor to *A Glacier Odyssey* (systematically compiled between 2009 and 2016, then published as a book in 2017) and serves as an illuminating illustration to Schwartz's most recent themed project, which was seven years in the making. The subject foreshadows the glacier tables Schwartz went on to photograph on the Raikot Glacier on Nanga Parbat, Pakistan in 2015 (fig. 11), and then in Afghanistan in 2018 (plate 49). The erratic boulder framed by slender trees, meanwhile, is just as closely related to the glacial erratic known as *Pierre à Bot* in the forest above Neuchâtel (fig. 12): both were stranded in their current locations after a journey that took place over a period of five thousand years, transported via the Valais ice stream from the neighbouring Mont Blanc region over a total linear distance of around 150 kilometres, at a speed of 30 metres per year. We know that the journey of the Martinsflue erratic occurred in several stages, the last of which was around twenty thousand years ago. Paul Vionnet's photograph of the *Pierre à Bot* dates back to the start of the era of research into glaciers, which in turn coincides with the early days of Swiss photography. The erratic boulders stood in their current locations for thousands of years before the two photographs were taken; Schwartz's images of the erratics in Switzerland, Pakistan and Afghanistan span a period of four decades. Compared to such vast expanses of time, the hundred years or so between Vionnet's photograph and the one taken by the young Daniel Schwartz is a mere blink of the eye for world history. For the history of photography, however, this hundred-year period represents a huge leap: it takes us from the invention of the camera and the first photographs in the mid-nineteenth century, to the heyday of reportage photography, and finally to the incipient but soon inexorable transition from the analogue age to the digital age from the 1990s.

Schwartz published his first two books in the decade after he completed his studies in Zürich: *Metamorphoses. Greek Photographs* (1986), followed by his spectacular, sensational collection of views in *The Great Wall of China* (1990). Looking back, the Swiss photographer now refers to the former as his *Gesellenstück* (his journeyman's piece) and the latter as his *Meisterprüfung* (his master craftsman's examination). This was followed by *Delta. The perils, profits and politics of water in South and Southeast Asia* (1997), a publication illustrated with photographs taken between 1991 and 1995; then he published *Travelling Through the Eye of History* (2009), a series

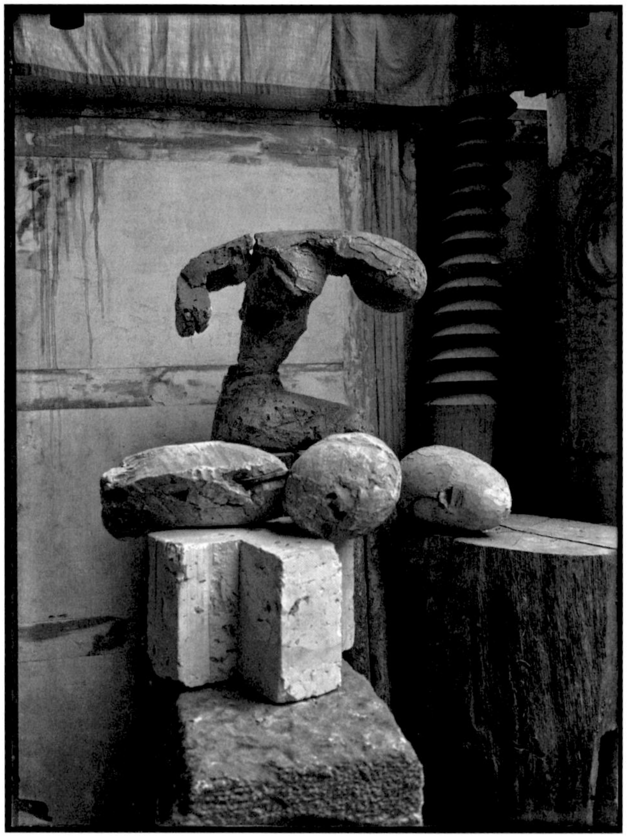

Fig. 4

Constantin Brâncuși (1876–1957)
Narcissus Fountain, 1920–35

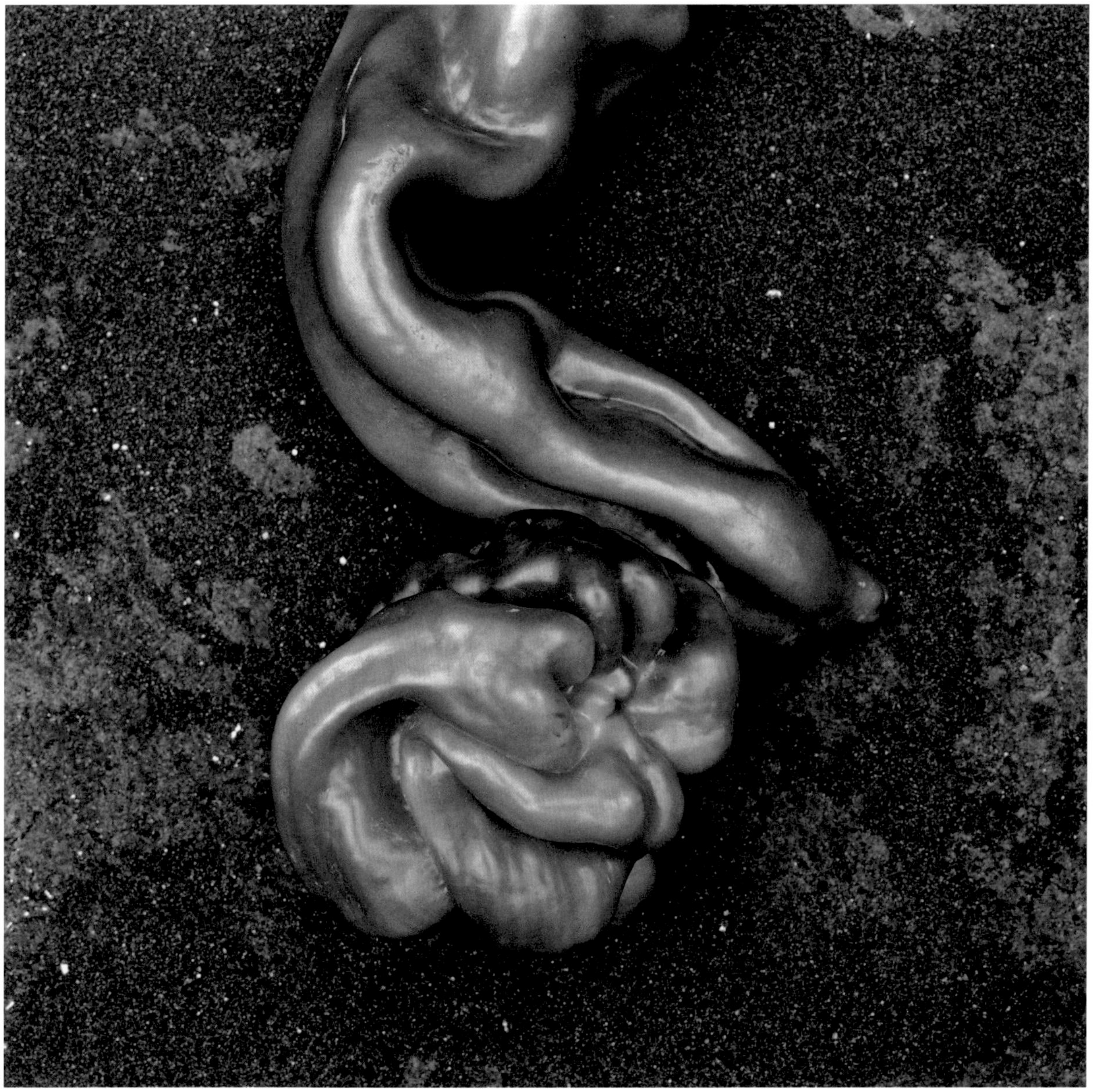

Fig. 5

Two green peppers on a tar bitumen sheet
Still life study, Fotoklasse / Kunstgewerbeschule Zürich
Zürich, Switzerland
1 September 1979

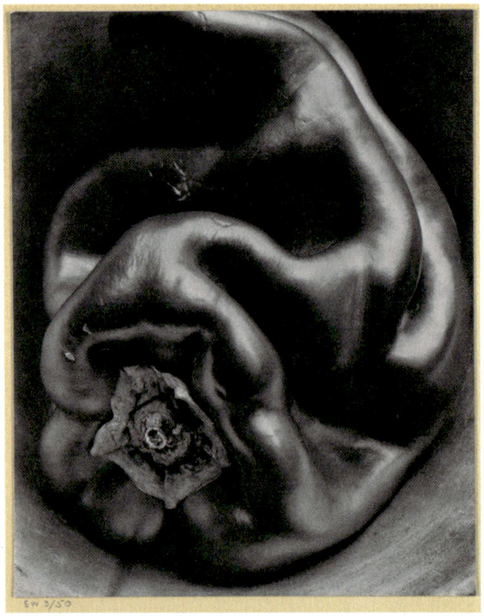

Fig. 6

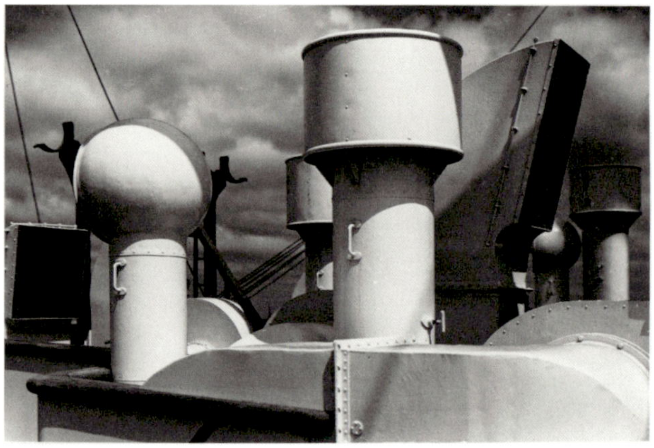

Fig. 8

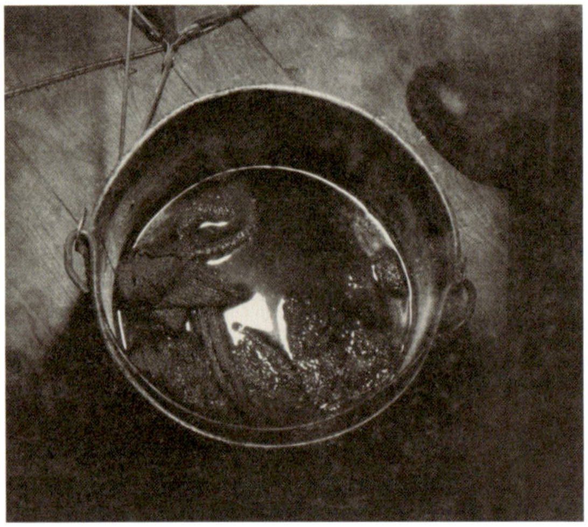

Fig. 7

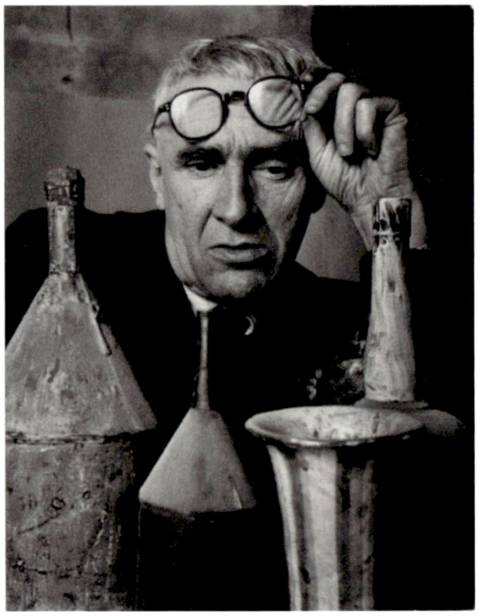

Fig. 9

Edward Weston (1886–1858)
Pepper No. 35, 1930

Wols (Alfred Otto Wolfgang Schulze, 1913–1951)
Without title [Still life – bucket with washcloth],
1938–August 1939

Hans Finsler (1891–1972)
The ventilators of the *Bremen*, 1929
From the series *Norddeutscher Lloyd*

Herbert List (1903–1975)
Giorgio Morandi (1890–1964), Bologna, Italy, 1953

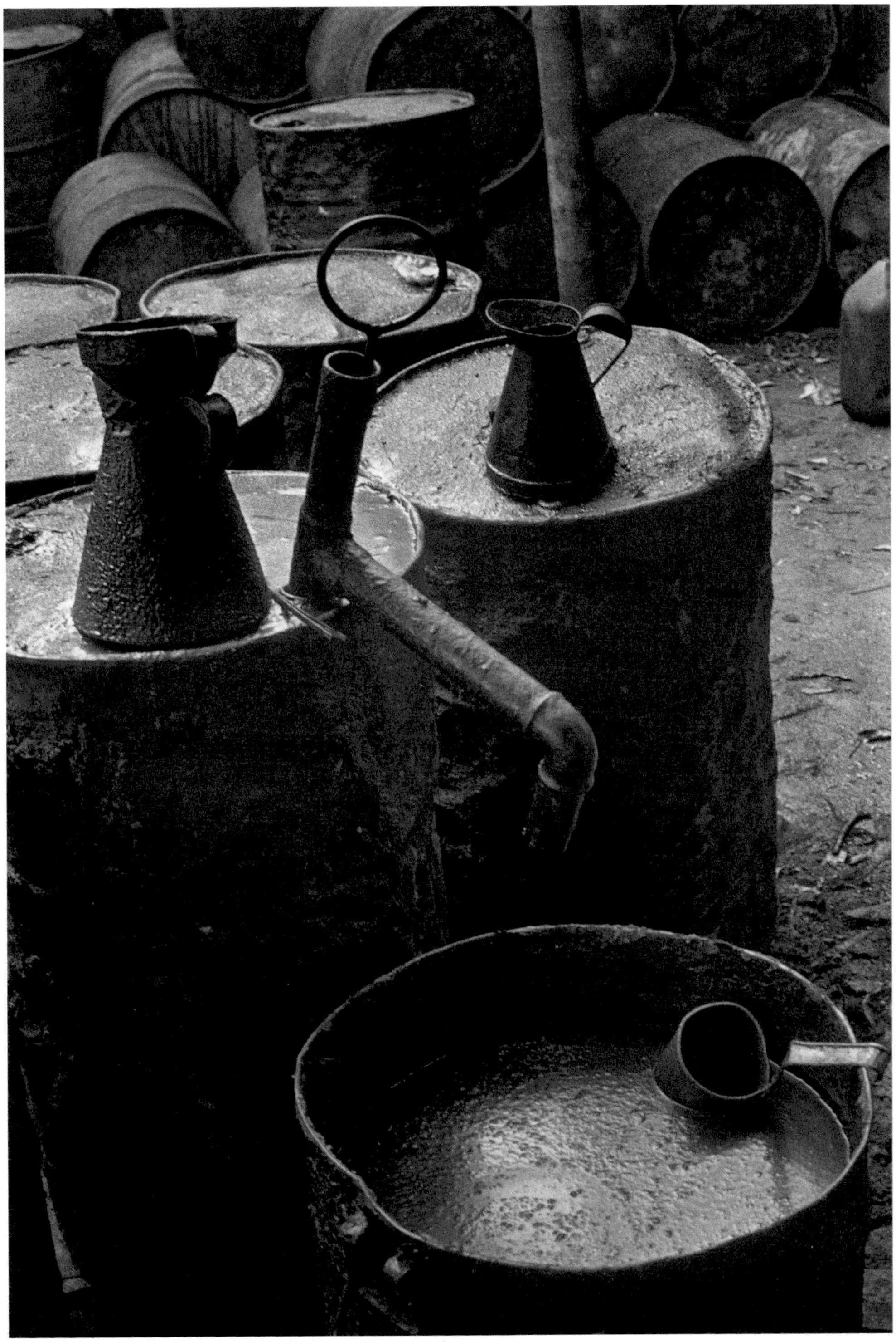

Fig. 10

Lubricating oil
Mawlamyinegyun, Myanmar
6 October 2019

of images he took between 1995 and 2007 while reporting from the 'arc of crisis' stretching from the Caspian Sea to the west of China via Afghanistan. These two books differ from Schwartz's earlier publications not only in terms of the nature of the photographs and their motifs, but above all in their design and the combination of image and text. *Travelling* is his first (and so far his only) book to feature colour photographs; moreover, the number of colour images in the collection far outweighs the black-and-white component. In addition to the inclusion of short, bold lines or blocks of text, *Travelling* also provides a staggeringly long list of incidents of war in Western Asia and Eurasia from the last five thousand years. These two publications bring the author's enlightening sociopolitical consciousness and his environmental conscience and commitment to the fore, while the elements of supplementary text also speak to his awareness of the limitations of the photographic image and what it can express without the help of words. To work his way out of this dilemma, Schwartz uses the contemporary artistic practice of combining photography with text, allowing the image and text to engage in a dialogue that enhances the validity of both media and even injects both forms with more impactful meaning. The solution Schwartz pursues in his book *Travelling Through the Eye of History* bears eloquent witness to his engagement with the 'walking artists' Richard Long (b. 1945), whom he knows personally, and Hamish Fulton (b. 1946). In pioneering fashion, the *Delta* project is an unsparing warning of the devastating consequences of climate change, which human beings have been contributing to ever since the age of industrialization. Indeed, the book was also received as a powerful indictment; immediately after its publication, twenty-five years after the Club of Rome's report on the state of humanity and the limits to growth, a review in the *Financial Times* described *Delta* as a 'visual J'accuse'.[3] Twelve years later, *Travelling Through the Eye of History* became an exhibition with the subheading 'Views from the Hinterland of War' and was shown in Zürich (2009) followed by Berlin (2011). These two publications, combined with the vast portfolio of reportage he produced for newspapers and magazines from the 1990s, played the biggest role in building Schwartz's strong, justified reputation as a reportage photographer whose work focuses primarily on the often forgotten, overlooked and even supplanted hotspots and smouldering fires of history and present times.

In most of his work, Schwartz is concerned with vast stretches of time. Indeed, the subheading of his literary magnum opus, *Schnee in Samarkand. Ein Reisebericht aus dreitausend Jahren* (*Snow in Samarkand. A Travelogue of Three Thousand Years*) sets forth the sheer enormity of his intention.[4] His most recent long-term project, *While the Fires Burn. A Glacier Odyssey* goes even further. These photographs, taken between 2009 and 2016, tell the story of immense periods of time, condensing indefinite spans into the image. Schwartz describes the concept as 'a glaciology in pictures' and his method as 'exploring the relics of Holocene glaciation...leading into the milieu of the Anthropocene to the collapsing glaciers on four continents.'[5] His glaciology, therefore, addresses not only the journey of the erratic boulder over roughly five thousand years, but is also an exploration of the vast glacial and interglacial periods, examining the fluvial and glacial erosion of the Alps in the Quaternary, a process that took place over the space of between 2 and 3 million years. Humans rarely appear in these images; people are merely a fleeting episode in the history of the earth. For a long time, these geomorphological changes, which happened over periods of time we cannot even conceive, were barely visible to the human eye. Only now – and rather cynically, only due to the dramatically accelerated climate crisis – can we directly observe changes of this kind. Schwartz did exactly this, for over seven years. In this new global scenario, which is a source of great interest and even attraction for glaciologists and geologists, though utterly fatal for humankind and the planet, Schwartz realized his glacier project. In terms of its message, this project shares the same objective sense of urgency as the *Delta* book. The visual language, on the other hand, is quite different: to make their statement, the photographs of the disappearing glaciers do not employ a dramatically explicit approach. In this sense, the glacier project bears more similarities with Schwartz's 'documentary reconstruction' of the Great Wall of China from a quarter of a century earlier, albeit with a greater tendency for abstraction. In most of these photographs, Schwartz dispenses with overviews and vista shots; even when he photographs the subject from a great height, he gets closer to it, defines it more narrowly. When looking at photographs of ice, therefore, we may well find ourselves reminded of the thick wrinkled skin of severely endangered mammals (plate 57). These largely abstract photographs, which seldom if ever offer a horizon for us to cling to and so often leave us in the dark as to which way is up and which is down, are perceived as self-contained images. This is both logical and consistent with the photographer's intention. But at the same time, the photographer wants his images, and his art in general, to have the lasting importance and value of valid informative testimonies, including for the scientists of the future. Unsurprisingly but logically, these photographs (some of which are extremely large format) were first shown at art exhibitions and in an art museum.[6] And quite rightly, these images, along with Schwartz's earlier photographs, have come to form part of the discourse around the visual arts.

The photographs from the *Tracings* project, of which this publication is an integral component, will also be exhibited at the Kunstmuseum Luzern. Here, having carefully sifted through his extensive, meticulously maintained archive, Daniel Schwartz takes stock of his creative output from a career spanning more than four decades. As he takes us on a tour of his photographic archive, he also opens the door to the archive inside his mind, his rich *musée imaginaire*, forming complex associative connections between his memories of works from the history of photography and works of fine art. This kind of associative recollection results in pairings such as the photograph of the Khmer repatriation train and a 'Killing Fields' memorial showing the cranial bones of victims of the Khmer Rouge genocide, and, next to it, Paul Cézanne's still life with skulls, with which Schwartz became acquainted in the collection at the art museum in his home town of Solothurn (figs 19–21); it can also lead to such pairings as the images of boulders and the film still of a tank from the First World War, whose savage attack on a tree trunk symbolizes the escalation of industrial warfare (fig. 13). In the introduction

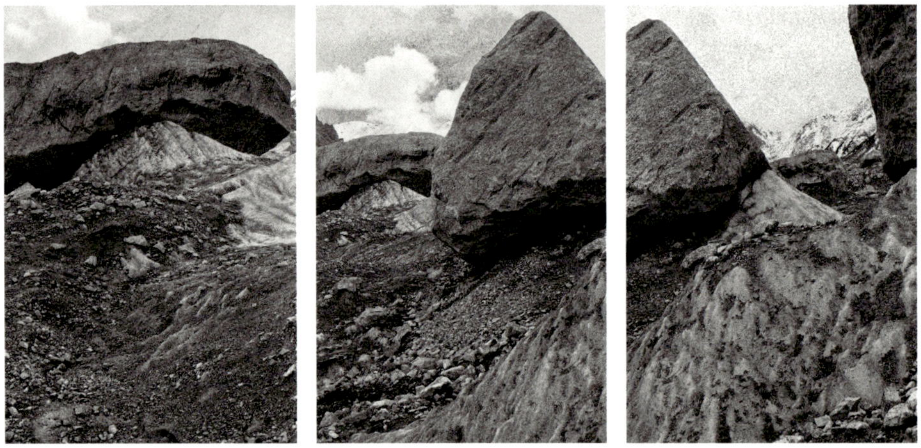

Fig. 11

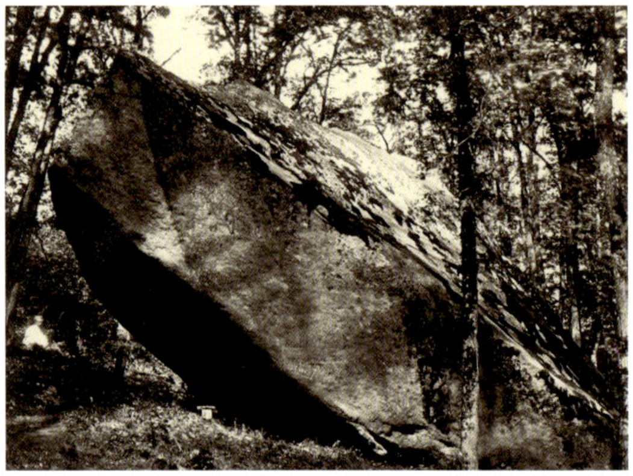

Fig. 12

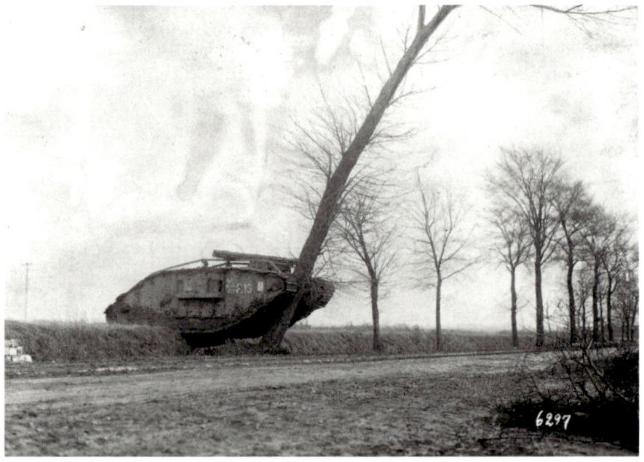

Fig. 13

Glacier tables
Raikot Glacier, Karakorum, Pakistan
27 September 2015

Paul Vionnet (1830–1914)
Pierre à Bot, Neuchâtel, Switzerland, 23 August 1869

Anonymous
First World War. Western Front 1917. Battle of Cambrai, 20 November–5 December. A captured fully functional British Mark IV, driven by a sergeant of a German Motorized Unit. Still taken during the shooting of the NS propaganda film *Nach der Tankschlacht bei Cambrai Dezember 1917.*

– commentary on p. 176

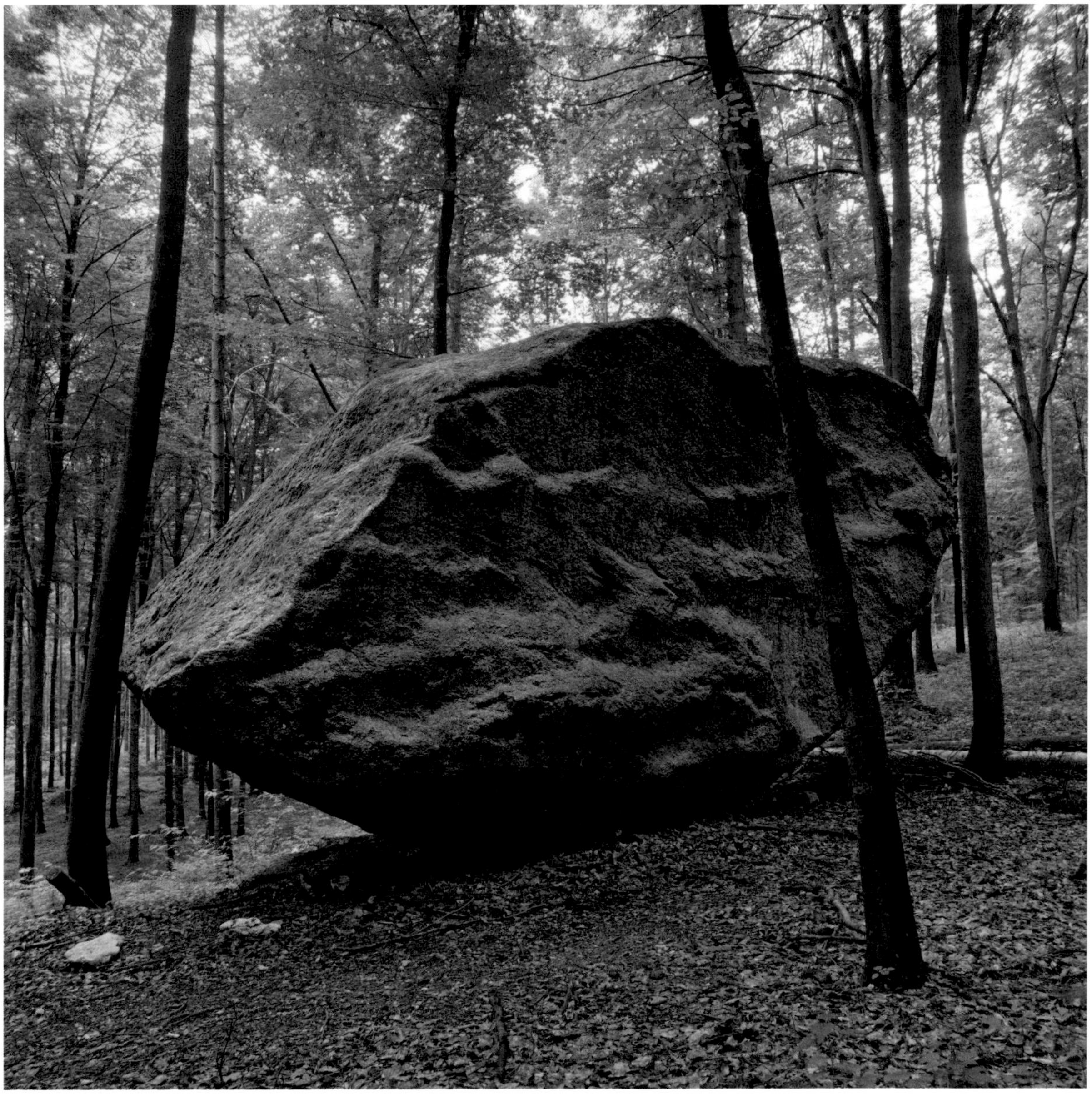

Fig. 14

Erratic boulder
Rüttenen, Switzerland
May 1978

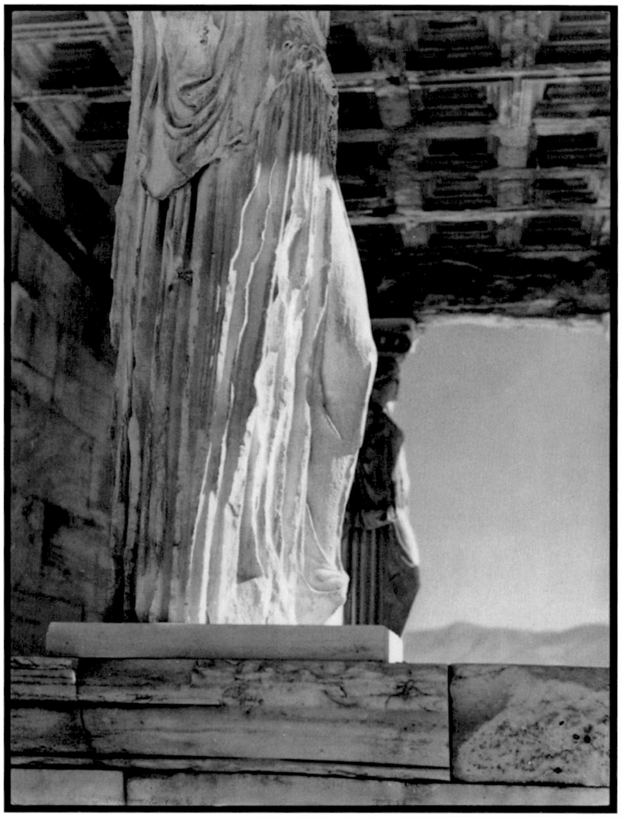

Fig. 15

Werner Bischof (1916–1954)
The knee of the Caryatid, Erechtheion, Acropolis, Athens, 1946

to his first book, his collection of Greek photographs, author and Oxford literature professor Peter Levi compares Schwartz the photographer with a 'short story writer'; this compliment, from over thirty-five years ago, is confirmed by the syntax of the connections of images in *Tracings*.[7] The present collection, which sets off on the trail of the manifest and hidden traces to be found in Daniel Schwartz's body of photographic work, is also a record of such short stories. He served as a photographic contributor at cultural magazine *Du* for fifteen years from 1990; he co-edited *So Many Worlds: A Photographic Record of Our Time*, an important volume on photographic history, with Dieter Bachmann; and in 2003 he edited *Tales from a Globalizing World*, a publication that is still highly relevant today.[8] Since then, titles such as 'When the War Was Over', 'The Creative Moment', 'Work' or 'Cult and Religion' – to name a handful of examples from *So Many Worlds* – are frequently used to break photobooks down into chapters, including publications edited by our photographer himself. 'Dialogues at the Museum', 'Devotion and Surrender' and 'War – as far as we know' are among the subheadings to be found in Schwartz's own publications. Associative in the broadest sense, the terms around which the photographic contents of *Tracings* are structured have a different effect. For anyone who is familiar with the history of Swiss photography, the abstract terms 'Motif', 'Association', 'Absence', 'Form' and 'Observation' that Schwartz has chosen for this book will bring to mind the keywords used by Hans Finsler to structure the sequence of images in the legendary 1964 issue of *Du* devoted to photography.[9] Though Finsler's terms are specific, serving almost as keywords for the photographs selected for the feature, there is a good correlation between the category he refers to as 'Dauer und Moment' (duration and moment) and the concept of 'Fortdauer' (continuance) that is so central to Schwartz's work.

This brings us back full circle to the origins of Daniel Schwartz's oeuvre, which, for all the topical explosiveness of its images, never conceals its firm, solid roots in the tradition and history of classic photography. In his introduction to the *Delta* book – the most explicitly politically opinionated project in his portfolio – the legendary war photographer Tim Page (1944–2022) mentions his predecessor Werner Bischof (1916–1954) and his place in the history of socially conscious photojournalism. A publication on the history of Zürich's Hochschule der Künste (University of the Arts) examines the importance of its famous alumni. Its discussion of the series of high-profile photographers who attended the photography course established in 1932 begins with Werner Bischof, who 'traveled to every conceivable scene of human misery, creating the definitive icons of the human condition in the twentieth century'; it then moves on to René Burri (1933–2014), who 'portrayed the world famous, and yet his lapidary trademark was "photographer of people"'; and it ends with Daniel Schwartz: 'he travels the world, photographing and communicating elementary questions of human existence.'[10] We return once again to Tim Page, the rock-and-roller among Vietnam War photographers, for a pithy summary of the high quality of Schwartz's photography: 'all in the best Swiss tradition.'[11]

Werner Bischof died before his time in 1954. Daniel Schwartz is a whole generation younger: born a year after Bischof's death, he is not much older than his predecessor's sons. In 1946, after reporting from war-ravaged Europe, Bischof travelled through Italy and onward to Greece, where he produced a series of photographs published in *Du* magazine in July 1947. Schwartz first travelled to Greece in 1975. Travelling light, he took with him his copy of *Description of Greece* – the Baedeker for ancient Greece – by Pausanias, the ancient writer from Sparta. But in his memory, as well as Bischof's photographs from 1946–47, he was also carrying the series of Greek photographs that Herbert List (1903–1975) had taken between 1937–38 and 1967, and which were featured in *Du* in July 1973. Along with the images produced by these exponents of modern photography, the historic photographs of Fred Boissonnas (1858–1946) and Walter Hege (1893–1955) also played a particularly important role in the pictorial memory of this young photographer. While Boissonnas's pictures depict an idealized image of ancient Greece, untainted by the modern world, Hege's interpretations of architecture from the 1920s demonstrate his interest in spatial structures. These contrasting visual stimuli flowed into Daniel Schwartz's conception of Greece, a study of the complex relationship between contemporary Greece and the weight of its legacy as told through the tradition of ancient Hellas. It was on this visit, and others in the decade that followed (1975–85), that Schwartz took the photographs which formed the basis of his book *Metamorphoses. Greek Photographs*, images of landscapes and temples, including temple construction sites; studies of ancient ruins, exhibitions and the contemporary, sometimes problematic handling of these artefacts; classical architectural photographs in the aforementioned tradition; and even two images of Lesbos and Attica, which are reminiscent of Herbert List's work but are explicitly declared an *Homage to Pausanias.* But in addition to these studies of Greece, it also contains a series of photographs which take a surprising, almost surreal turn. This first book is our only encounter with photographic experiments such as solarization or attempts at staged photographs. A result of the time Schwartz spent training under lecturer Rudolf Lichtsteiner (1938–2022) and studying his experimental photography, this photographic art is perhaps also reminiscent of Duane Michals' (b. 1932) innovative photo sequences. It may be tempting to interpret such images, which are surprising to us today, as a secret homage to Lichtsteiner; held in high regard by Schwartz, his teacher was an important photographer who has been wrongfully neglected and perhaps even deliberately overlooked in the historiography of Swiss photography. Perhaps in the cocksureness of youth, but certainly with plenty of ambition and self-confidence, Schwartz gave one of these experimental images the title *ON PHOTOGRAPHY, Zürich 1985.* It is the last picture in his first book, and, as we learned earlier, Schwartz thought of it as his journeyman's piece.

Schwartz first travelled to Greece thirty years after Bischof. Forty years before Schwartz, Bischof travelled to Indochina. From 1991 to 1995, Schwartz was in South and Southeast Asia working on his photographs of the devastation of war and environmental disasters for his *Delta* project. In 1952, Bischof reported back from the

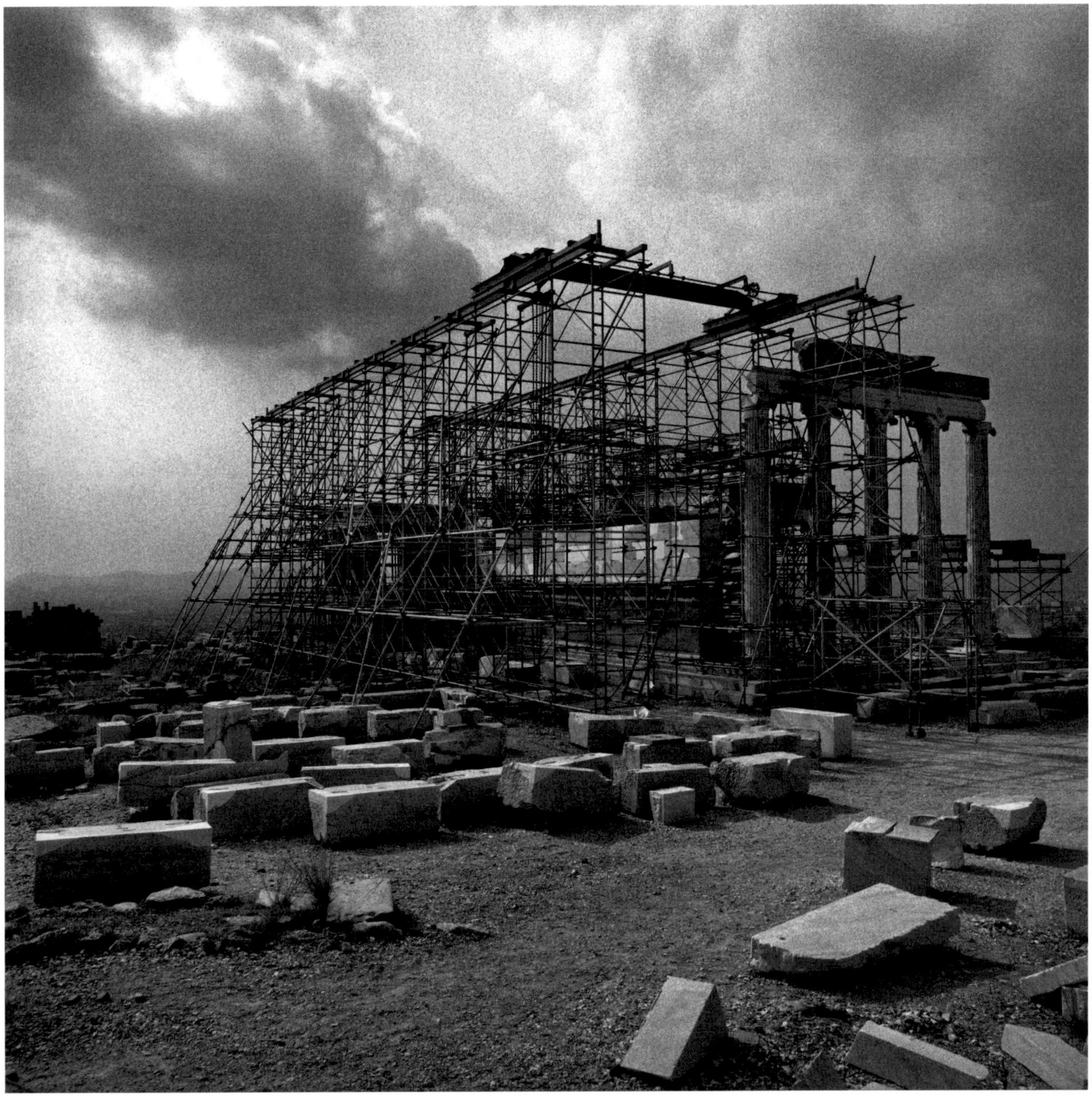

Fig. 16

The Erechtheion
Acropolis, Athens, Greece
September 1983

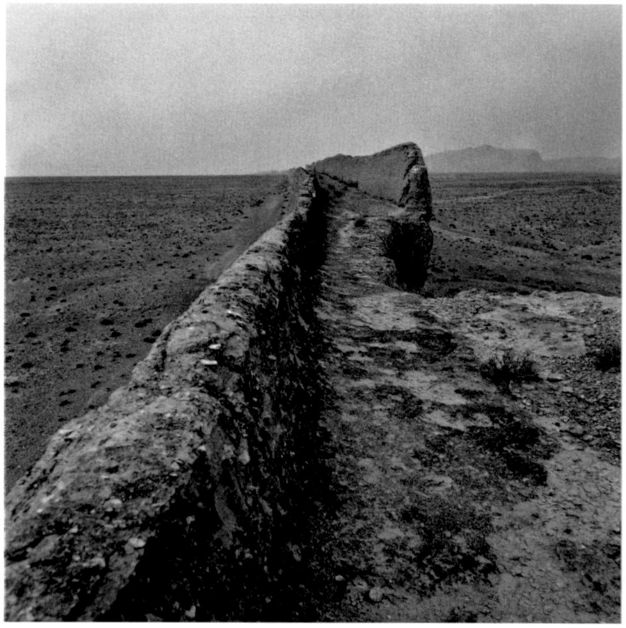

Fig. 17

Qingtongxia section of the Great Wall
Helan Mountains, Hui Autonomous Region of Ningxia, China
20 May 1987

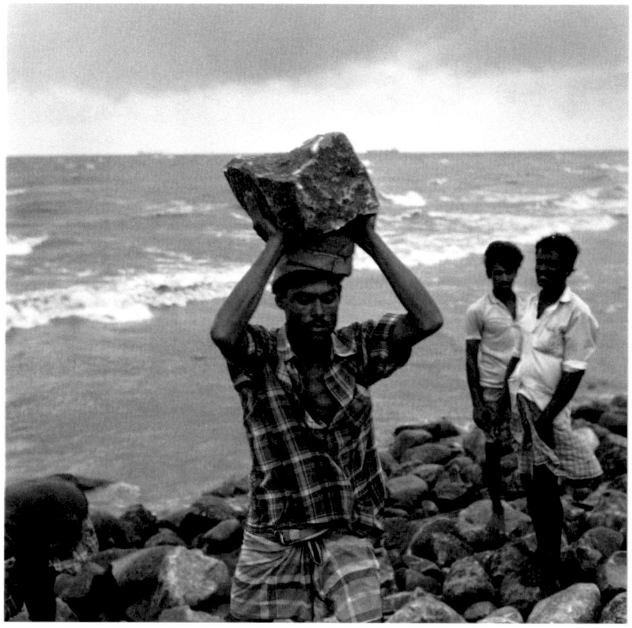

Fig. 18

Coastal embankment construction
Patenga, Chittagong, Bangladesh
6 July 1994

First Indochina War, where he had been posted as a war correspondent for *Paris Match.* It was on this assignment that Bischof took his famous photographs of his legendary journey on the armoured train 'La Rafale', which was repeatedly bombed and under fire from the troops of the Vietminh while heading northwards from Saigon. These images were used by the editors in Paris to illustrate a major tabloid feature. How similar they are to the photograph Daniel Schwartz took four decades later on the roof of the Khmer repatriation train in Cambodia (fig. 21)! Bischof's haunting photograph of jobseekers at the railway station in Rouen was taken shortly after the war ended in 1945; more than half a century later, in the spring of 2001, Schwartz produced his wonderful colour photograph of a group of people displaced by drought at a refugee camp in Afghanistan, with the minarets in the background (figs 24, 25). Again: how similar these images are! Maybe not at first glance – though it would certainly be worth examining Bischof and Schwartz's photographs in greater detail to see specifically how they deal with the theme of looking back. The similarities go beyond the photographs themselves; it is more a matter of the respect shown towards the subjects, the way that the face looking into the camera reveals the eye contact of the man behind the camera. Though the Indochina job was not the only gruelling task in Bischof's career, this last assignment in a war zone only served to reinforce his intense scepticism of photojournalism. 'Can there be another photographer who has been so acutely conscious of the conflicting demands of aesthetics and journalism, and who, as a result of this dilemma, has left us such an exemplary body of work?' writes Hugo Loetscher in his introduction to the major Bischof monograph.[12] Loetscher, with whom Schwartz worked several times from 1981 onwards, is here referring to the dilemma of modern photography, which has since intensified and grown almost exponentially, on multiple levels. In a brief statement on the occasion of Bischof's hundredth birthday, Schwartz himself spoke of this dilemma: 'Werner Bischof's reservations about journalism go to the heart of this matter, today more than ever, as the profession struggles with new roles.'[13] Digital photography first appeared over thirty years ago, but when Schwartz was still just a student, no one had a clue that the world would eventually be flooded with selfies and smartphone photographs. The field of photography has changed categorically over the recent decades. This is also evident from the work of Daniel Schwartz, who works strictly with analogue cameras, and mostly in black and white. His images – all in the best tradition – attest to what photography once was and what it still could and can be. By following the ramified trails to be found in Daniel Schwartz's oeuvre, this is exactly what this book aims to demonstrate. In this sense, the ambitious intention set out by the young photographer at the end of his first book has proven to be justified: along with the untiring humanitarian dedication of the man behind the camera, the form is central to this vast body of work. Everything he does is 'on photography'.

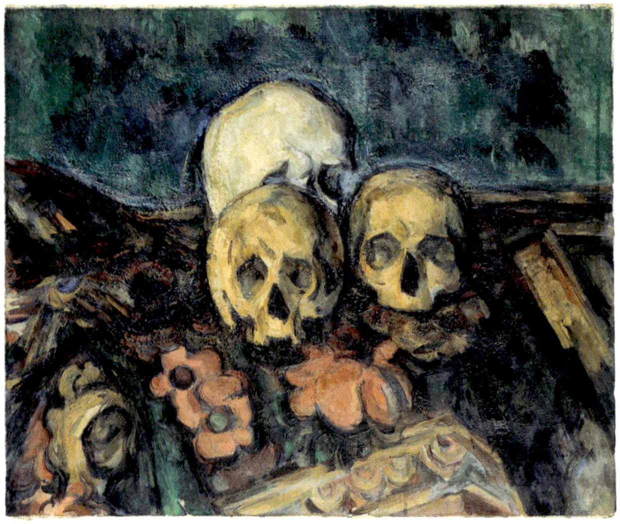

Fig. 19

Paul Cézanne (1839–1906)
Three Skulls on an Oriental Rug, 1904

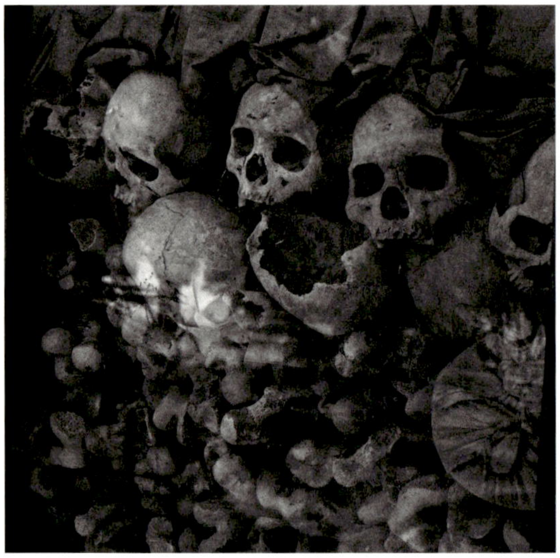

Fig. 20

Killing Fields memorial
to victims of the Khmer Rouge genocide
Siem Reap, Cambodia
12 January 2002

– commentary on p. 176

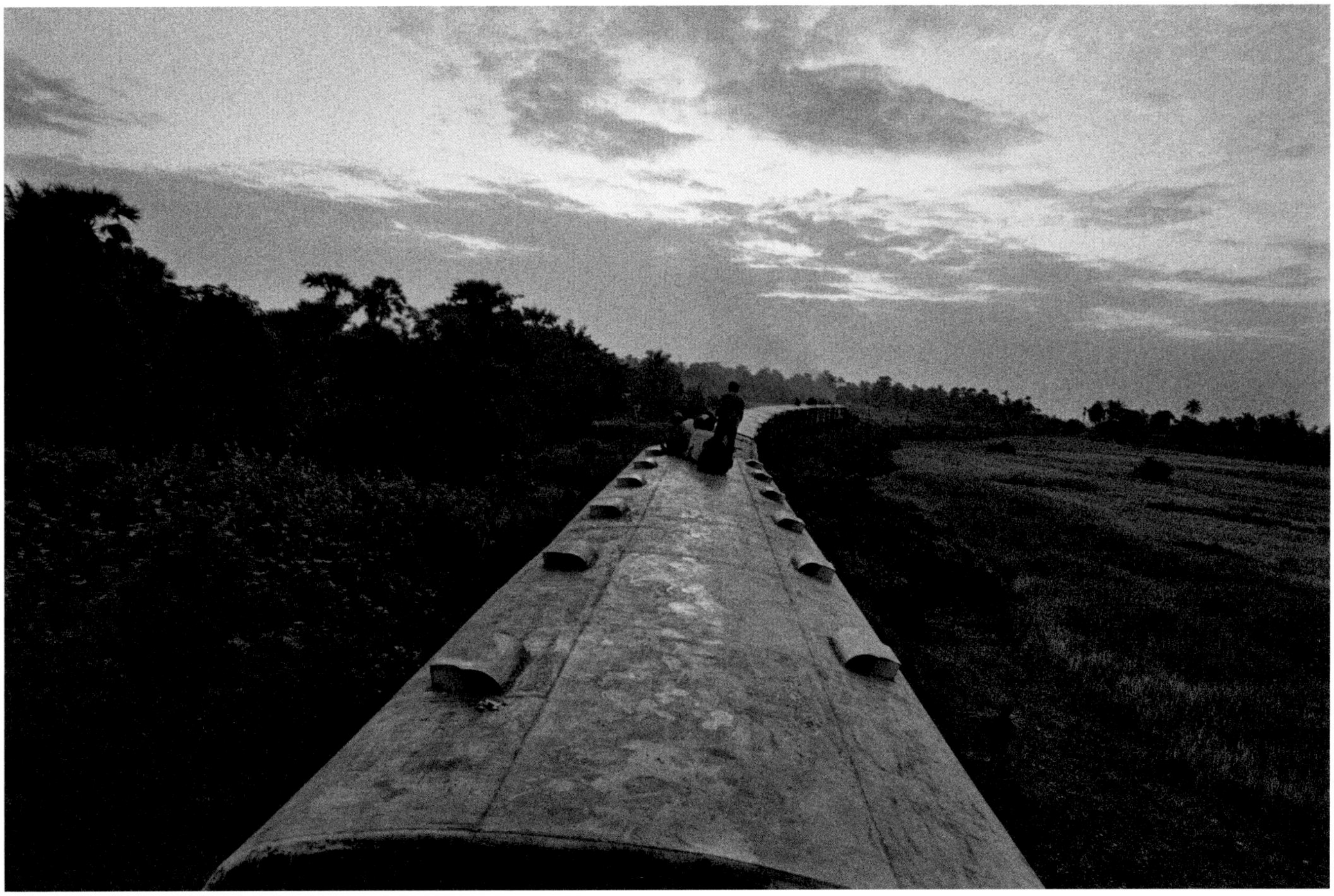

Fig. 21

Repatriation train for Khmer refugees, a.k.a. *Sisophon Express*, destined for Phnom Penh
Pursat province, Cambodia
6 November 1992

– commentary on p. 176

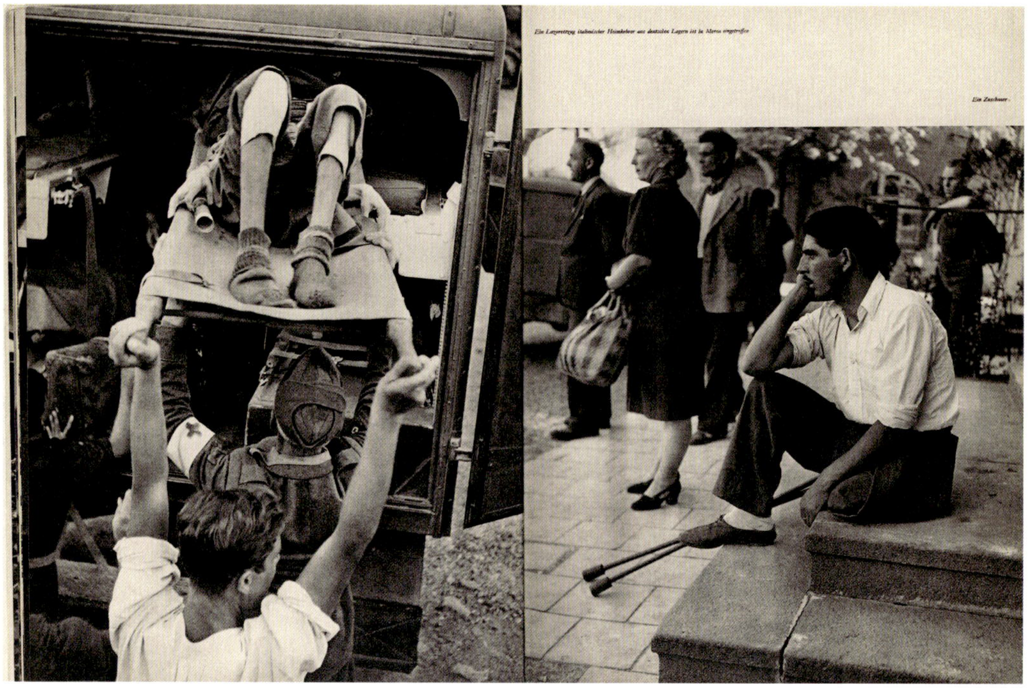

Fig. 22

Werner Bischof (1916–1954)
Return of Italian prisoners of war, Meran, Italy, 1946
Double spread in *Du*, Zürich, Heft 63, *Europäische Aufnahmen*,
May 1946

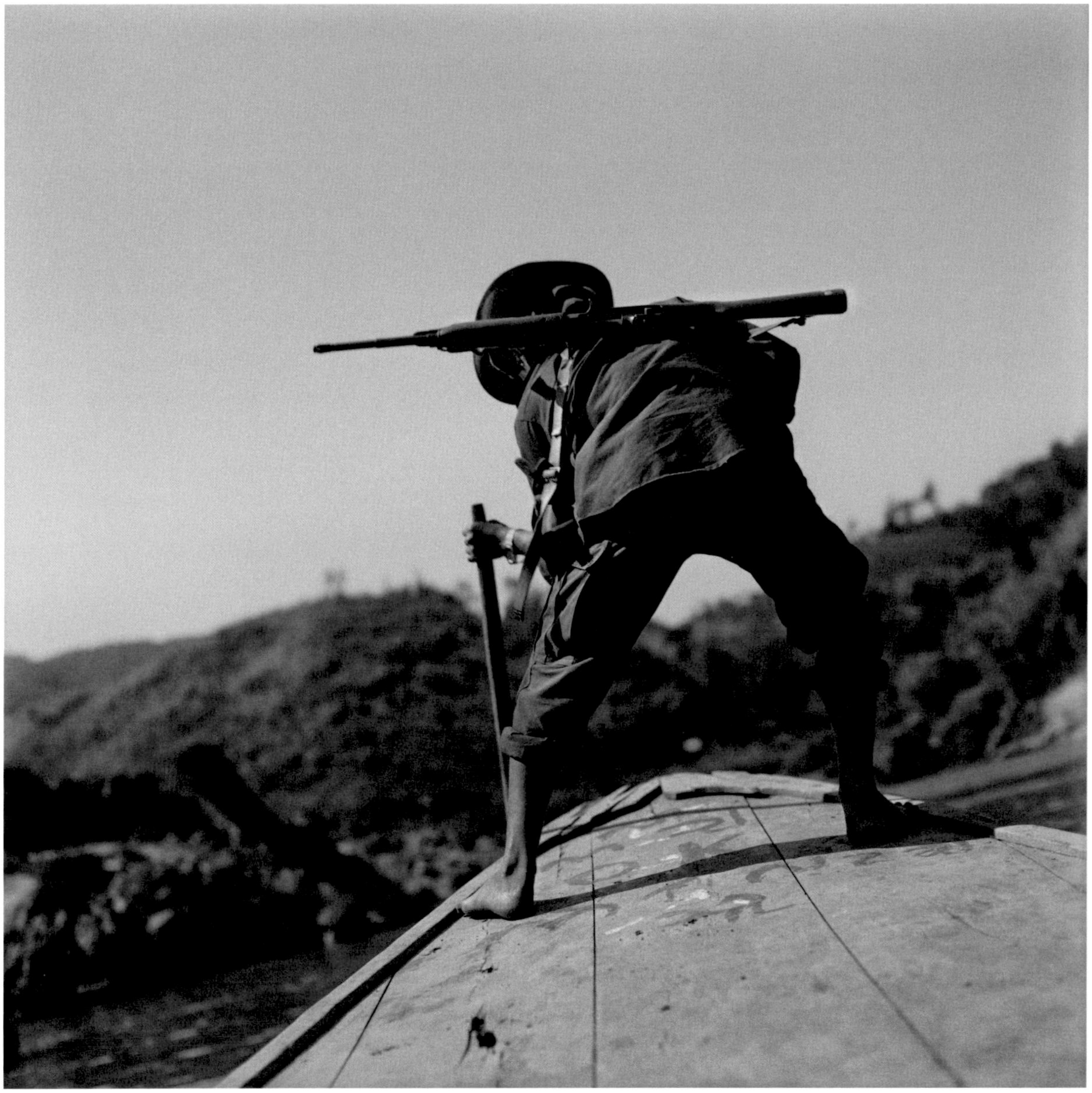

Fig. 23

Karen National Liberation Army combatant en route to the front line
Salween River, Myanmar–Thailand border
29 January 1992

– commentary on p. 176

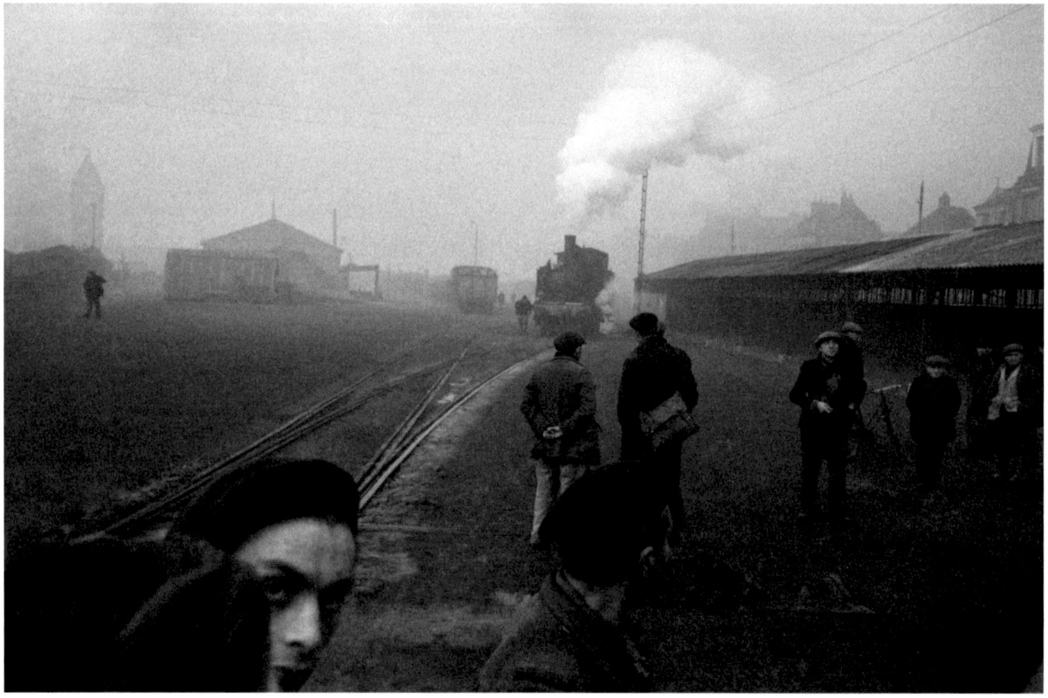

Fig. 24

Werner Bischof (1916–1954)
Looking for work. Port of Rouen, France, 1945

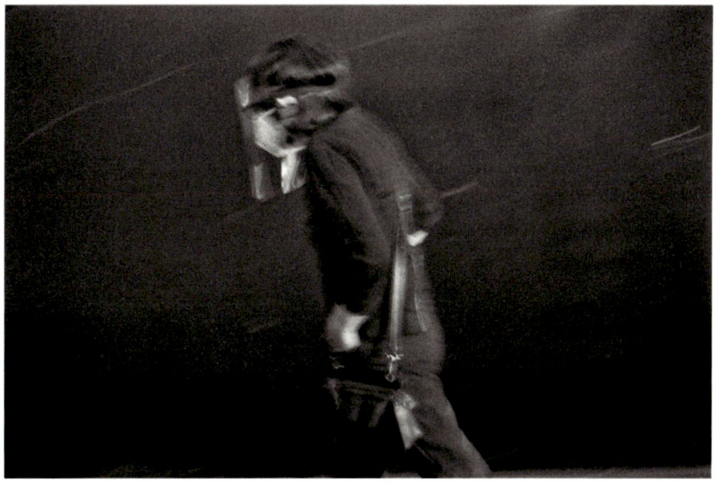

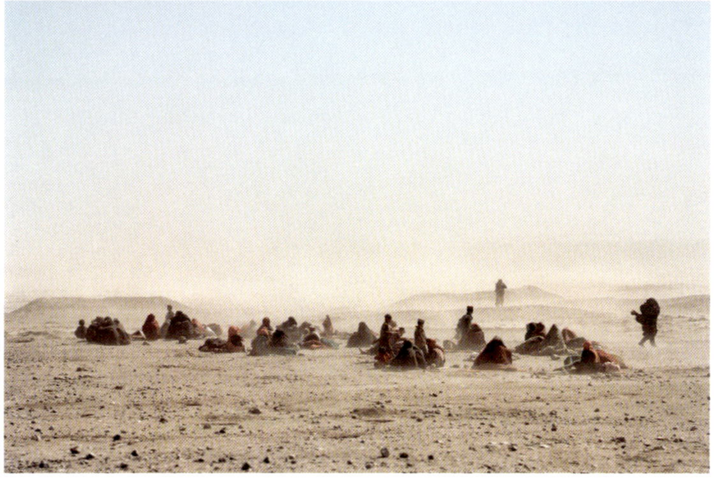

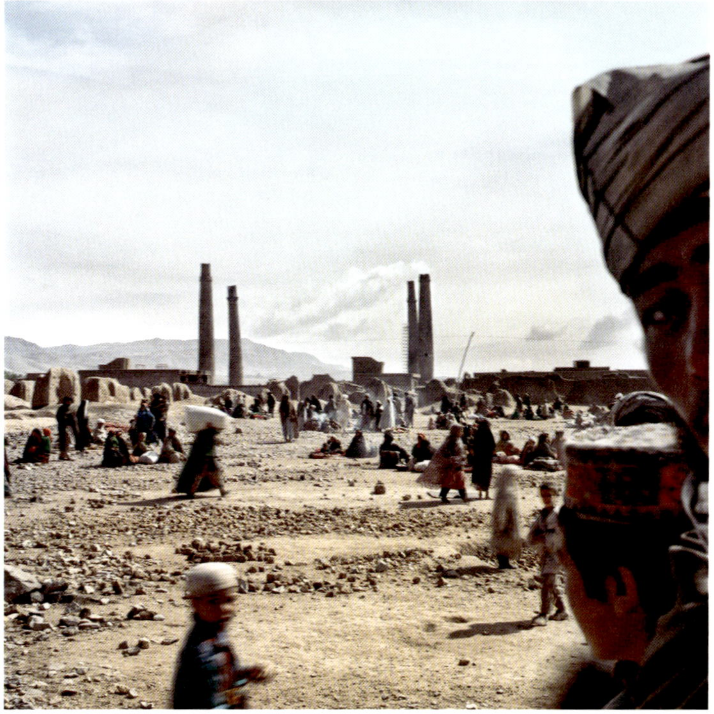

Fig. 25

The face of the Covid-19 pandemic
Zürich, Switzerland
4 July 2020

Fig. 26

Displaced by the drought in Badghis province
Herat, Afghanistan
2 April 2001

– commentary on p. 176

Fig. 27

People displaced by the drought in Badghis province in a transit camp near the last minarets of the Timurid musullah, built in the early fifteenth century under Queen Gawhar Shad, wife of Shah Ruk, son of Tamerlane
Herat, Afghanistan
28 March 2001

– commentary on p. 176

Fanni Fetzer: Persistence
Contemplating the image – or, why lingering is worthwhile

'One must imagine Sisyphus happy'
Albert Camus, *The Myth of Sisyphus* (1942)[1]

Where does the photographer actually stand? Literally and metaphorically: is he standing on the opposite side of the valley? Why is he even taking a photograph of this incline?

In the low plains, a couple of barely distinguishable lines: walls made of loosely gathered stones; the kind typical of all rocky landscapes. These makeshift heaps of stone pave the way for agriculture, keeping livestock and cultivating the earth. Between them, a river carrying water and debris, whose levels vary depending on the season but which, presently, is flowing harmlessly through the valley. Was the striking horizontal line perhaps carved out by this stretch of water? No: it does not mark the peak water level; it is a channel that runs along the slope and slices through the image (fig. 28). The land below the channel is green, and above it, stony grey. The slope is obviously made not of rock but of loose material. Hence, too, the fine lines – paths for people and animals – which zig-zig their way up the slope and eventually trail off into the scree. Alongside them, clear lines that lead steeply down the hill: landslides.[2] Together, these assorted lines make the image a landscape photograph; they indicate the scale and provide the context for the textures we see before us. They tell us we are looking not at a close-up of a mossy rock but a place where people live.

So much converges in this landscape: trails created by humans to access inhospitable areas; age-old knowledge of mountain survival; erosion and accumulation caused by the weather. Formally striking, this barely coloured photograph contains variations of grey, green combined with varying degrees of brightness; bold horizontal lines and a few other, fainter, diagonal, jagged or unstable lines; textures and moiré effects in the rock and the scant strip of green.

•

Daniel Schwartz is always on the move, but never in a hurry. As he travels the world, he is not pulled by the tide of current events; he does not actively seek the turbulent present, but he does not evade it either. Being on the move is the good fortune of the curious. Schwartz is not pursuing a mission in his work. Nevertheless, his curiosity for Central Asia and neighbouring countries is unmistakable. Sometimes his enduring interest aligns with the general awareness of a specific conflict, historical event, or simply the present

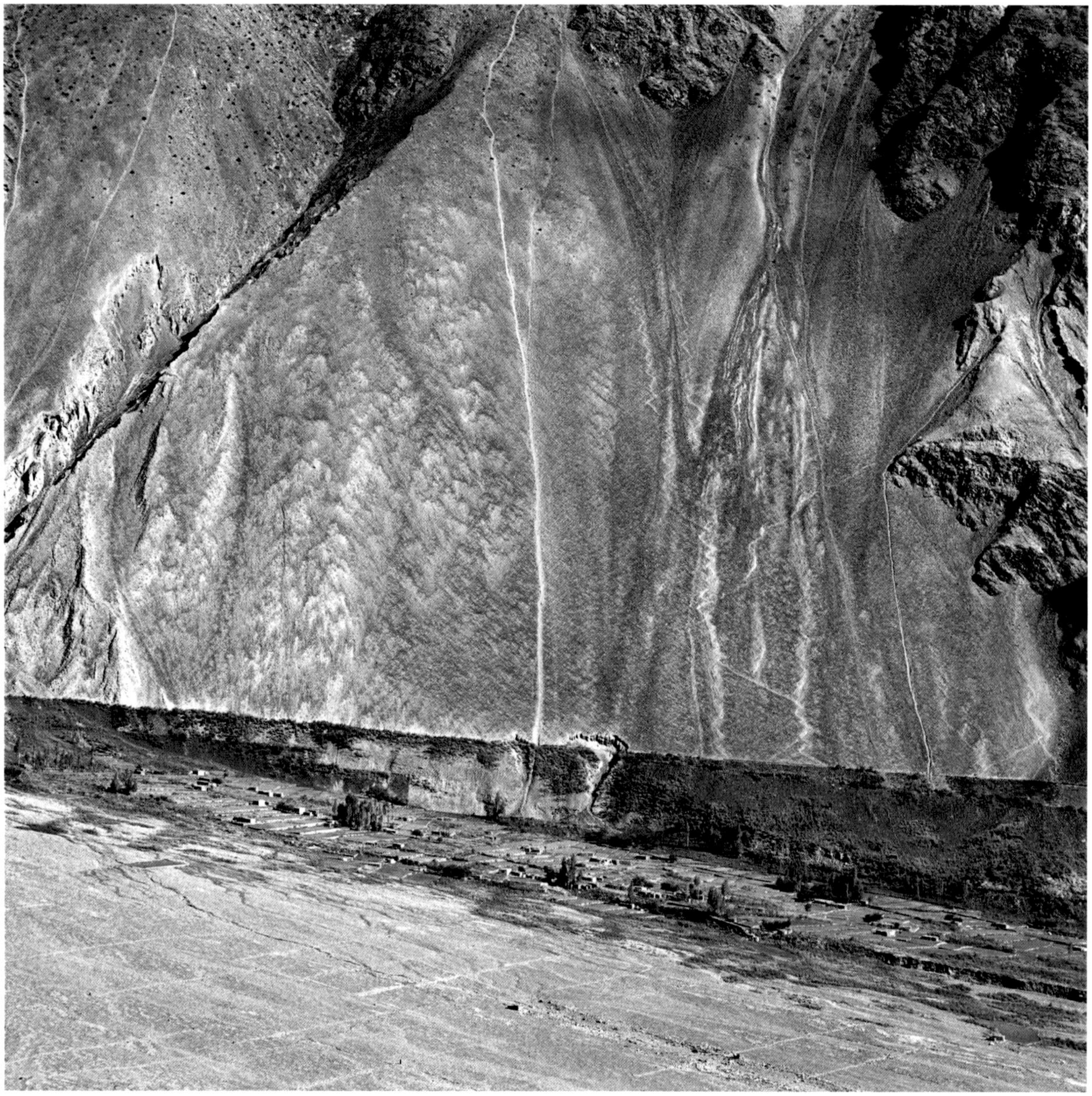

Fig. 28

Upper Indus Valley
Gilgit-Baltistan, Pakistan
24 May 2001

international situation. But when public attention turns to other regions, Daniel Schwartz stays behind. He stays because he knows that Central Asia has everything that is of interest to him: the landscape between mountains and deserts; elevation and vast expanses; the melting pot of cultures; trade, big and small money; the trail of conflicts and wars; consequences of the climate disaster; water; confidence; resignation.

Schwartz is tireless in his pursuit of these subjects. If he fails to capture a scene on camera the first time, or if the image he has taken does not meet his standards, he travels back to the same spot. He addresses these voids as part of the wider conversation. He does not simply drift and let the surprises come his way – which, of course, they do; his activities on his journeys always have a clear purpose. If a picture is missing, or another important aspect comes to light when he is reading, then Daniel Schwartz sets off on the trail again.

Of course, the physical exertion, long ascents or light sleep at high altitude are all part of the appeal. But at heart, Schwartz persists because he knows what he does best: he wants to tell of the absurd beauty of this world – not by ignoring conflicts, but by moving them to centre stage, even when that means transcending the current political discourse. The tenacity and patience of his endeavours suggest that this persistence is precisely where this photographer finds his satisfaction. Not because he knows better than the rest of us, not because he wonders what his images might at best achieve, and not because he was there before us. In any case, his motivation has almost nothing to do with us, the potential audience for his images. He does what he does because it interests him, and because he believes that his role as a photographer is to get close to human chaos, clashes and interventions.

•

The problem with photography is that authorship often overshadows the actwual subject. Photographers, with all the bags, tripods and photography equipment they carry, like to act important. The vest where photographers used to put their exposed films in generations gone by – and still today, in Daniel Schwartz's case – has somehow survived as a work uniform. The khaki-coloured trousers rich in pockets, all the zips and eyelets to ventilate the ego – these things turn the protagonists of photography into adventurers from a different era, nineteenth-century figures who are completely out of place in the postcolonial discourse of the present day. Daniel Schwartz's work gear is much the same; perhaps it is suitable for Central Asia. But this kind of armour, which the rest of us, who stay at home, would never wear in our everyday life, is bold. It demands our attention and it promises action. This performance element therefore always inferences the reception of photography, because it shifts the focus from the photograph itself; because the heroic photographers who travel here and there in particularly precarious circumstances thrust their way between the image and the audience. This is not the case for many photographs, and certainly not for this particular image. The image[3] does not tell a tale of hustle and bustle or political upheaval, and there is no sense of urgency. The circumstances in which the photograph was taken are irrelevant. It is almost an anti-reportage image, which does not report on the outside world but instead calls upon us to stop and take a closer look. With this photograph, Daniel Schwartz invites us to really look and trust in our own ability to read the image. Soon we will see what there is to be seen here. In fact, we find ourselves lingering as we contemplate the lines, the shades varying from light to dark on the slope. But none of this is bold; nothing tells us where we are or what it is all about. In this sense, this photograph sets an example by calling upon us to see for ourselves. It does not provide us with content as such, but it does offer us the possibility of bewilderment (where do those narrow paths lead, who walks along them?). What is interesting is how we contemplate the image. How our eye skims the subject, makes its own connections, lingers on a particular pattern; how the brain steps in, tries to understand what the eye has seen. From this photograph, we learn the slowness of seeing as a process of perception.

Images are not always easy to access. Sometimes, we have to read them. They can be deciphered, like texts composed of letters, though not usually from left to right or from top to bottom. Often we have to spend a little longer looking at them: Why is a photograph out of focus? Aha, because it was taken through the window of a moving car. Why does something fail to make sense to us right away? Because a black-and-white photograph withholds important information that a metallic object, a piece of fruit or some clothing would make immediately clear. Because we are accustomed to receiving clues about proportions; because we have to draw on our own internal images for comparison; because seeing is not limited to how clearly we can see close up and faraway, but is also based on experience. The art of looking is something we need to practise, like other activities such as music, sport and crafts. It is not about knowing the context or the canon. It is about trusting our gaze and taking the time to really look.

•

At a later point, once we have looked at Daniel Schwartz's photograph and are perhaps hurtling through the winter landscape on the train, the faint colours of the detached houses, cars and industrial buildings – in short, the human infrastructure – harmonize due to the frost and a touch of snow, becoming almost beautiful. As we look closer, perhaps we find ourselves thinking of Daniel Schwartz's steep slope, the settlement with the terraced gardens in the valley below. The pale landscape outside the window may not remind us of this barely coloured photograph[4], but the process is the same. In our immediate environment, we are recognizing the things we practised deciphering in Daniel Schwartz's photograph: the trails of human activities, the interplay of nature and culture, political decisions and economic events. 'All Sisyphus' silent joy is contained therein. His fate belongs to him. His rock is his thing.... The absurd man says yes and his effort will henceforth be unceasing. If there is a personal fate, there is no higher destiny, or at least there is but one which he concludes is inevitable and despicable.'[5] Everything is there, inscribed in our immediate environment; we just have to read it. We are standing at the beginning, and it is our world. Our life and persistence are worthwhile.

Giovanna Calvenzi: The Anatomy of Books

Generally speaking, photographers are familiar with one another's work before they meet, and more than anything, it is the subject matter that creates a connection. Gabriele Basilico and Daniel Schwartz were brought together by a shared interest in architecture. Basilico photographed François Mitterrand's Grands Projets for an issue of the Swiss art and culture magazine *Du*, entitled 'Paris – Modern Times' (574) in 1988. Towards the end of the same year, Schwartz was busy collecting material for his book project on the Great Wall of China, some of which was initially published as a preview in *Du* (580) in 1989. Not long afterwards, the two photographers met at the office of Dieter Bachmann, the editor-in-chief of *Du* at the time. Their mutual admiration deepened into a friendship at the 45th Venice Biennale (13 July to 10 October 1993), where Schwartz was participating in the 'Muri di carta' exhibition at the Italian Pavilion on the invitation of Arturo Carlo Quintavalle.

Around this time, Basilico had been working on his Roman vedutas for *Du* (584, October 1989), a subject he revisited twenty years later when he exhibited a series of his photographs alongside copperplate etchings of the same architectural scenes by Giovanni Battista Piranesi (1720–1778).[1] Comparing these works side by side immediately brought home the passage of time and all its different faces. The observer was confronted by two forms of artistic expression that conveyed contrasting perceptions of the same scenes with diverging intentions. On the one hand was Piranesi's study of Rome, incorporating the architectural structures and people that shaped the appearance of the city in the mid-eighteenth century. On the other was Basilico's reinterpretation of the same theme based on changes to the urban landscape – an homage by a contemporary explorer of places to a great architect of the past. The dialogue was based on carefully chosen analogies, and the only obstacle to a completely harmonious conversation was History itself, along with the changes that had happened to the cityscape over the years. Basilico's intention was clear: besides aiming to spark a dialogue between past and present, he wanted above all to highlight the extraordinary ability of this Venetian artist to respect and reinterpret the laws of perspective.

Basilico explicitly seeks to initiate a conversation between his own photography and Piranesi's copperplate etchings, and the practice of engaging images in a wider dialogue also forms an integral component of Daniel Schwartz's work – but with different objectives that are far more complex to decipher. In the five book projects the Swiss photographer has worked on between 1986 and 2017, the relationship between the images shown across a double page was always the more or less direct result of a clearly identifiable quest. There are surely

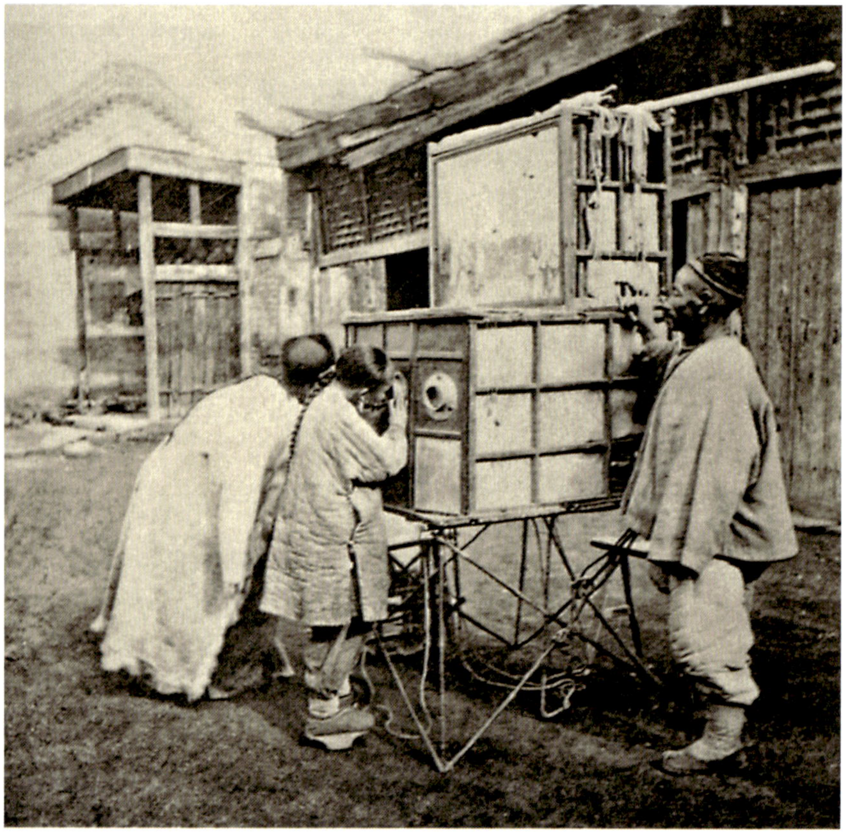

Fig. 29

John Thomson (1837–1921)
The peep-show, China, 1871–72

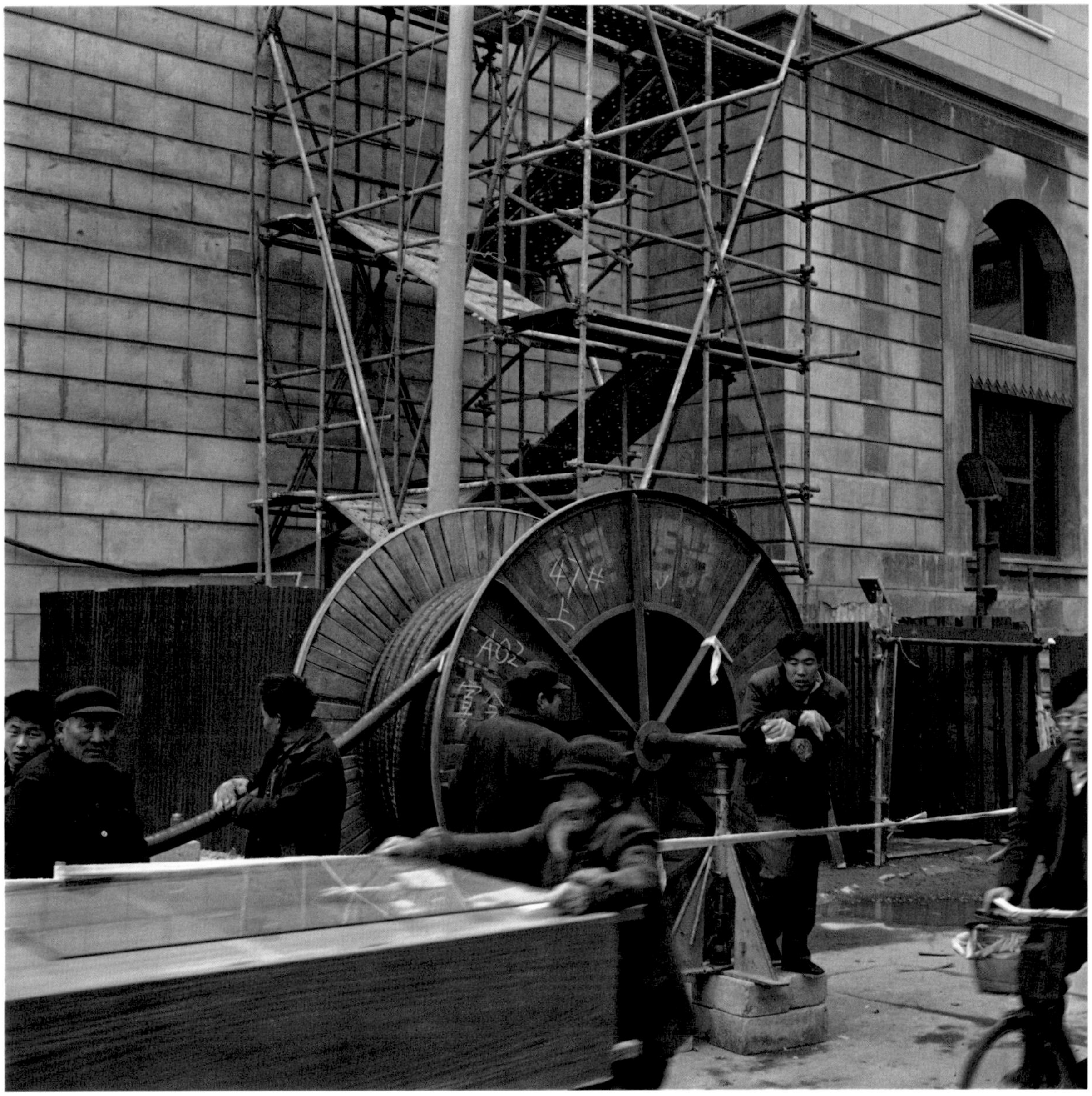

Fig. 30

Construction of the Beijing Hotel's E-block, behind the 1917 wing
Beijing, China
1 March 2000

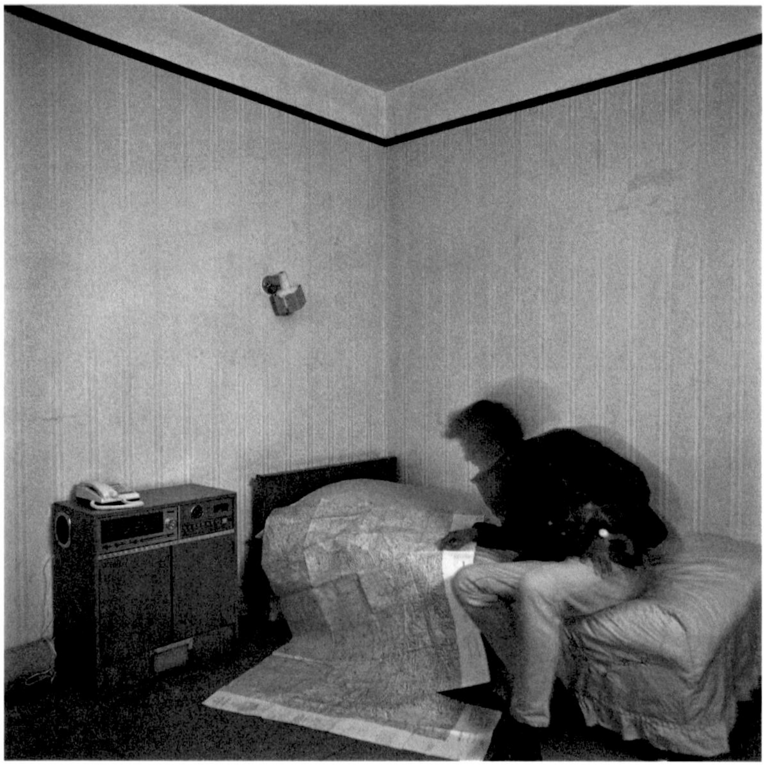

Fig. 31

Self-portrait in confinement
Yulin, Shaanxi province, China
26 November 1987

– commentary on p. 177

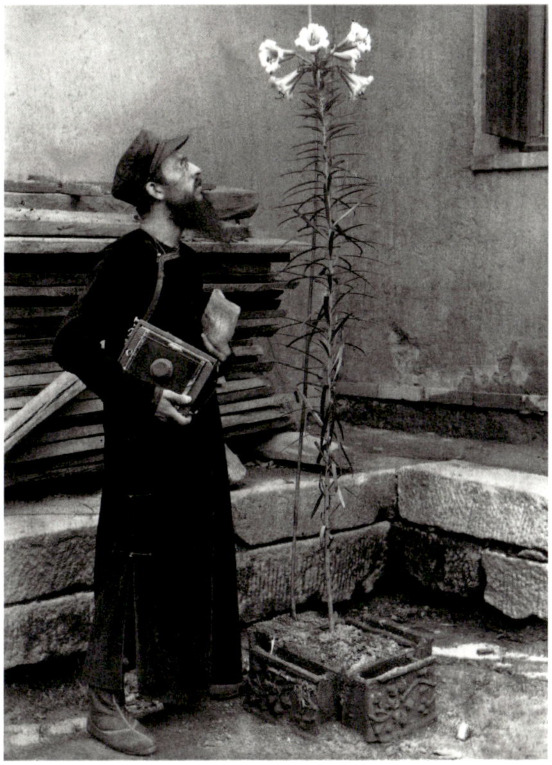

Fig. 32

Leone Nani (1880–1935)
Self-portrait, dressed in a *changshan*, the Qing dynasty long gown and his inseparable camera, Shaanxi province, China, 1904–14

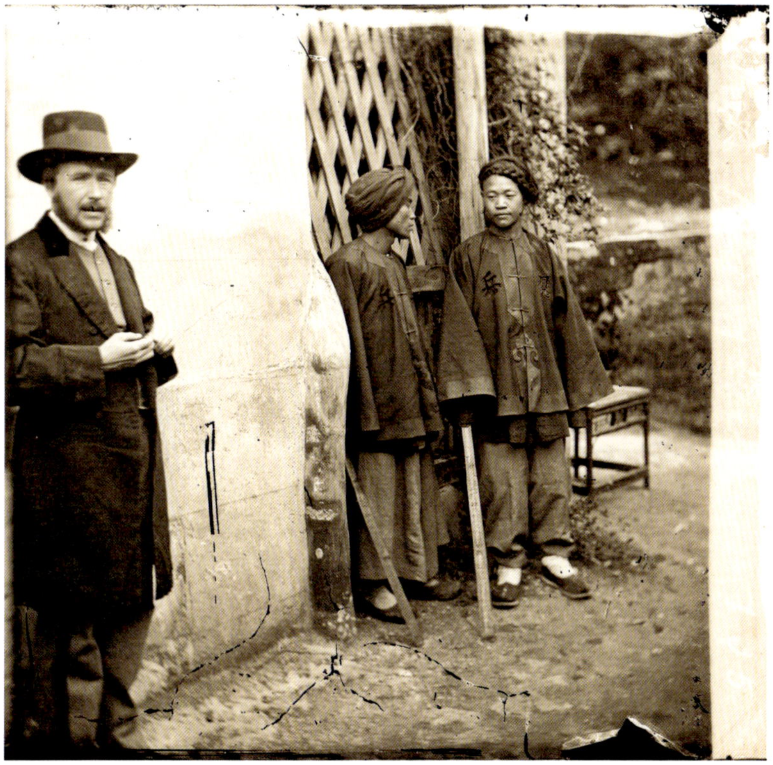

Fig. 33

John Thomson (1837–1921)
Self-portrait with Manchu soldiers. Fujian, China, 1871

similar motivations underpinning the pairs of photographs in this book, too. These images speak to the artist's desire to use his material and his intellectual archive to engage with the sources of his vision. Schwartz has opted for the term *Tracings* as the title for this publication. The trace these photographs contain, however, is not necessarily an obvious one; it is merely a clue we are invited to track down, dig up, discover. Perhaps there is a premise to be found here, an assumption supported by the musings of Umberto Eco (1932–2016), who once described photography as a 'trace' of reality and related it to memory. In 2010, the great Italian thinker held a lecture in Rome entitled 'Ero troppo occupato a fotografare e non ho guardato' (I was too busy taking photographs and I did not look).[2] This statement could perhaps explain why Daniel Schwartz has always probed the past when developing ideas for his long-term projects. In his new book, the photographer sets his mind to 'looking' in a particularly methodical, systematic way.

The path to *Tracings* was deliberately demanding. While searching for images to be published in the collection, Schwartz set himself various guidelines, which in turn formed the basis of his memories and the analysis of his archive. This allowed him to sift through a body of work amassed over a period of more than four decades, and to place the mostly unpublished photographs in a rigorous narrative – without necessarily having to follow any transparent, let alone predictable, selection criteria in the process. Each of the chapters is named after one of six thematic terms chosen by Schwartz himself: Motif, Association, Absence, Form, Observation, Duration. The reader is left to decide whether to agree with Schwartz, or whether to question or even reject the analogies and distinctions he makes, and, most importantly, to deduce the cross-references contained in these photographs, both in terms of form and content. Though these visual encounters are ultimately a challenging experience, they also open up new ways of penetrating the visual mode of thought that structures Schwartz's work.

Tracings came about as a process and in response to a need to retrospectively identify connections that have arisen since the mid-1970s. According to Schwartz, each of his books represents a particular stage in the development of his way of seeing, and each book reflects his altered experience as an observer.

In his first book, *Metamorphoses. Greek Photographs* (1986), rather than being concerned with making stunning images of the ancient artefacts to be found in modern-day Greece, Schwartz is interested in establishing a dialogue between myth and reality. It is a book with a symmetrical structure, incorporating diptychs, triptychs and sequences. The title of each group of photographs reveals the criteria for each category. The process is deliberately laid bare, and we are invited to draw our own conclusions from the images grouped together by the photographer.

In the subsequent two publications, the emphasis is on Schwartz's historical and sociopolitical engagement. While he remains faithful to his characteristically evocative visual idiom, the information aspect is also paramount here. In *The Great Wall of China* (1990) Schwartz follows the entire course of China's famous frontier wall in a series of photographs that depict the landmark as an epoch-making monument that shapes the vast surrounding landscape. *Delta. The perils, profits and politics of water in South and Southeast Asia* (1997) is a book of photo-reportage from densely populated regions of South and Southeast Asia exposed to the threat of rising sea levels and other fatal consequences of the climate crisis. In his suggestive introduction, Tim Page writes: 'It is rare that the art photographer, that outsider to the craft, turns his eye to journalism and takes to the field, to the coal-face. Werner Bischof did so, and the effect is here in these angled images surrealistically addressing the fundamental issues confronting twenty per cent of the planet's populace. [...] Schwartz collages the micro together with a broader brush: global minimalism, superbly printed, finest grain – all in the best Swiss tradition'.[3]

In the two subsequent projects, we see the journalistic obligation to inform combined with expressly artistic ambitions. In *Travelling Through the Eye of History* (2009), Schwartz reports back from his travels through the elusive cultural space of Central Asia, dividing his journey into thematic chapters. The black-and-white photographs are displayed alongside colour images for the first time, interspersed with textworks inspired by world history and topical political events. The origins of these commentaries can be traced back to *Metamorphoses. Greek Photographs*, a project structured around a series of journal entries.

In Schwartz's most recent collection, *While the Fires Burn. A Glacier Odyssey* (2017), the visual narrative system becomes even more complex. Here, the photographer exposes the disappearance of glaciers and writes what he calls a 'glaciology in pictures across four continents'. The material displayed across these double pages reaffirms the author's sociopolitical engagement. Further intensifying these statements, Schwartz interposes his own black-and-white photographs with historic visual documents from art, photography and cartography, with additional blocks of text to supply the scientific context.

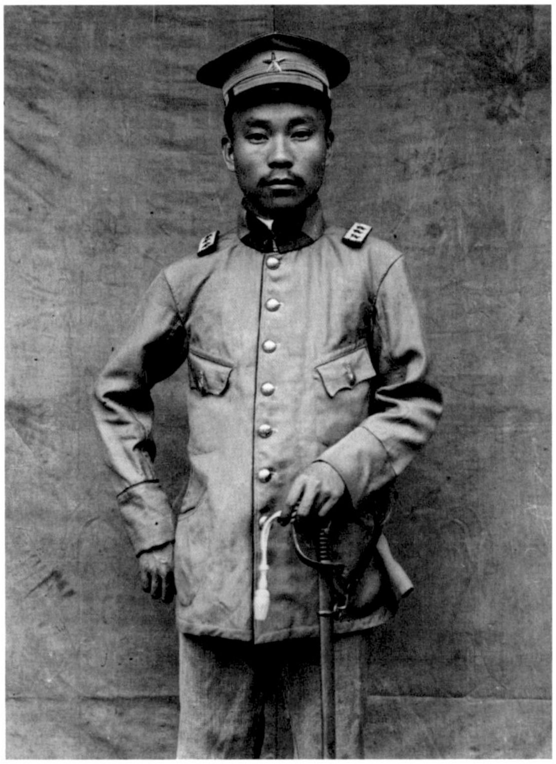

Fig. 34

Leone Nani (1880–1935)
Officer of the new Republican Army, a safety pin closing his collar, China, 1912–14

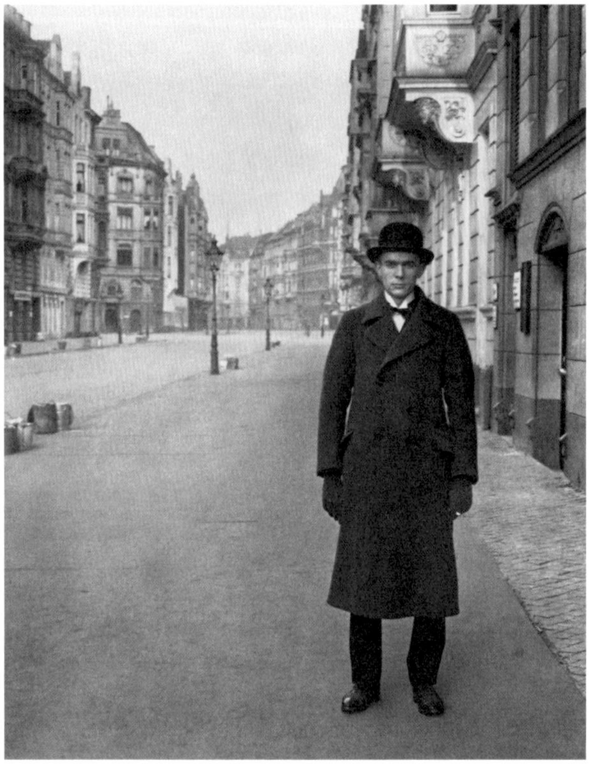

Fig. 35

August Sander (1876–1964)
Painter [Anton Räderscheidt], 1926

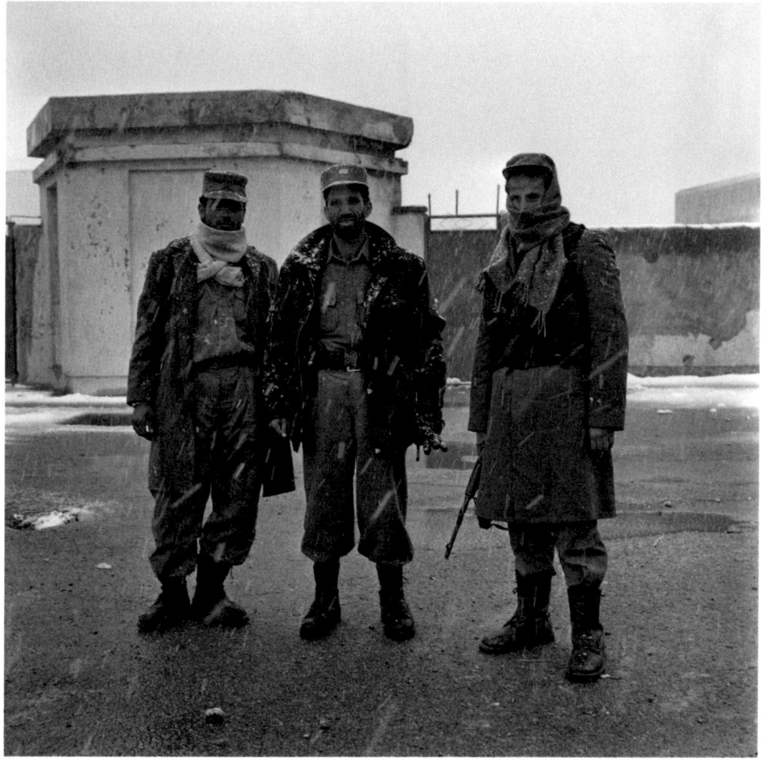

Fig. 36

Security forces on Darulaman Avenue
Kabul, Afghanistan
2 December 2006

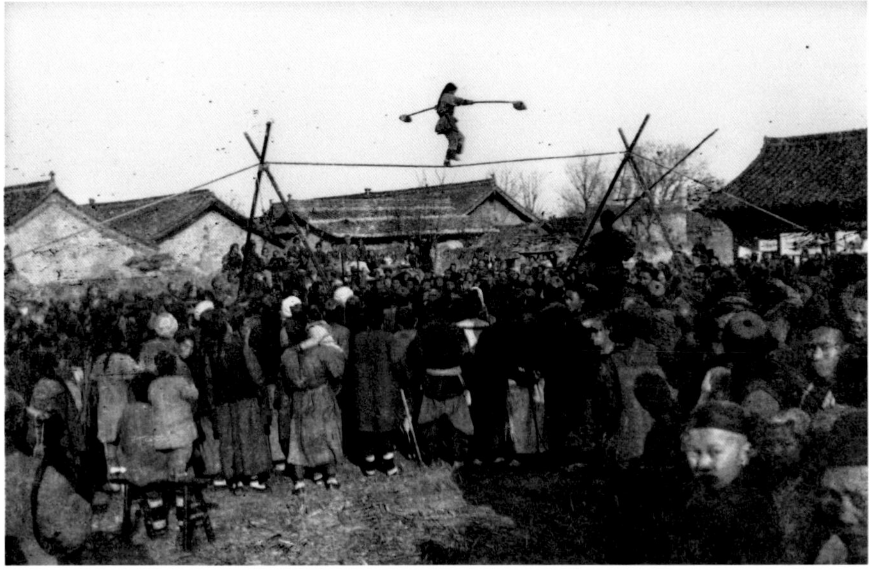

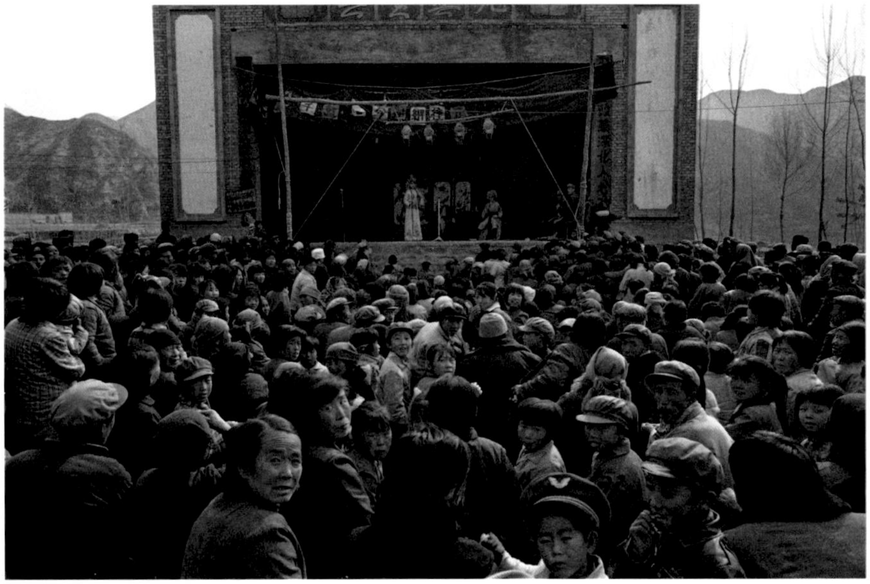

Fig. 37

Leone Nani (1880–1935)
A woman tightrope-walker performing before a crowd of spectators, Shaanxi province, China, 1904–14

Fig. 38

Once the photographer's arrival was noted,
the performance of the Hebei local opera was interrupted
Shuipu, Laiyuan county, Hebei province, China
14 November 1987

We follow the author on his travels from the Delta to the Glacier, from the disasters there to the dramatic environmental changes taking place here.

Though *Tracings* emerges as a culmination of his past experiences, Daniel Schwartz does not limit himself to his own recollection. He also studies the work of other photographers who have potentially fed into his own visual memory, either unconsciously or deliberately. The vision of the great Scottish travel photographer John Thomson, a fellow witness to the reality of the various regions of Asia, accompanies him in China (figs 29, 33).[4] Schwartz also acknowledges a kind of aesthetic, emotional kinship with Leone Nani, an Italian missionary in China whose photographs from between 1904 and 1914 he discovered only recently (figs 32, 34, 37).[5] A sense of anthropological curiosity and attention to everyday life and cultural traditions are qualities he shares with these two predecessors.

Over the years spent working on this collection, Schwartz's use of cross-references has grown increasingly complex. As well as obvious formal or typological congruities between the photographs, the focus of *Tracings* is also on invisible traces. Schwartz finds himself wondering whether, as Tim Page suspected, Werner Bischof was a formative influence, with his exemplary craftmanship and empathetic eye. Or whether the documentary approach of August Sander, with his indefatigable determination to be an 'objective' witness to the faces of the German people, fed into his own depictions of people from other cultures. When Daniel Schwartz suggests Sander's austere portrait of a painter from 1926 (fig. 35) alongside his own image of a group of Afghan security guards (fig. 36), are we to take this as a sly hint from the Swiss photographer? Or is he simply trying to tell the reader that his vision really does come from far away?

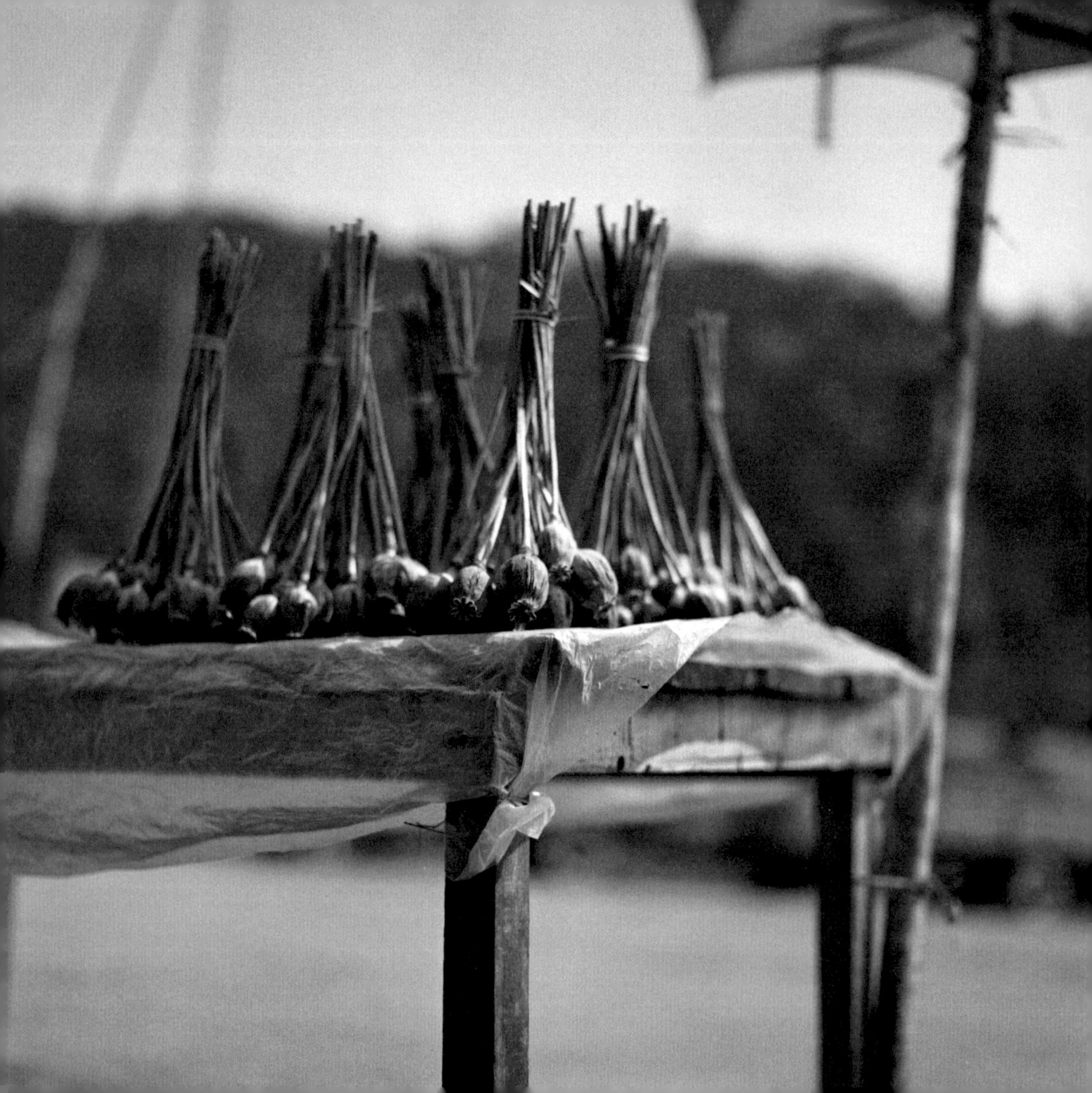

IV Form

Looking at photographs taken by someone whose reputation is primarily based on sociopolitically engaged reports, the question of form may come as a surprise. It helps to know that Daniel Schwartz explicitly dealt with still lifes in photography and painting during his education. We are reminded of this by the early picture of the *omphalos* (plate 60), the cult stone from the Temple of Apollo at Delphi, which was worshipped by the ancient Greeks as the navel and centre of their world. A found, radically reduced still life. Schwartz's formally purist shot corresponds to the found sculpture and its simultaneous timelessness and puristic modernity, which radiates in the manner of Brâncuși: a pure image.

The photographer's sure eye produces images that explicitly testify to his admiration for works from the history of still life painting and photography. But these are never constellations of objects that he has put together; they are always found still lifes that catch the photographer's eye. Trained in this way, however, the gaze is implicitly directed across the entire body of work, including all the images that may initially attract our curiosity for their content. It is informative and worthwhile to think about the question of form, especially in the case of incendiary testimonies: it is this rigorous attitude towards formal precision, or high formal ambition, that raises the content and the message of many photographs from urgent to unrelenting.

An image of the battered feet of a man breaking stones in Bangladesh (plate 69) seems to stand in counterpoint to the purist art image of the cult stone. The active person, the person working under precarious circumstances, is the focus of the photographer's observation, who hardly shows what the person is creating with their work, but rather what the work and the conditions under which it is carried out do to the person, the marks it leaves on people. Contemplating this impressive, albeit on the surface unassumingly modest memorial to an unknown worker, one may perhaps recall Gustave Courbet's *Stone Breakers* – and think not only about the still life but also about engaged realism in Daniel Schwartz's photographs.

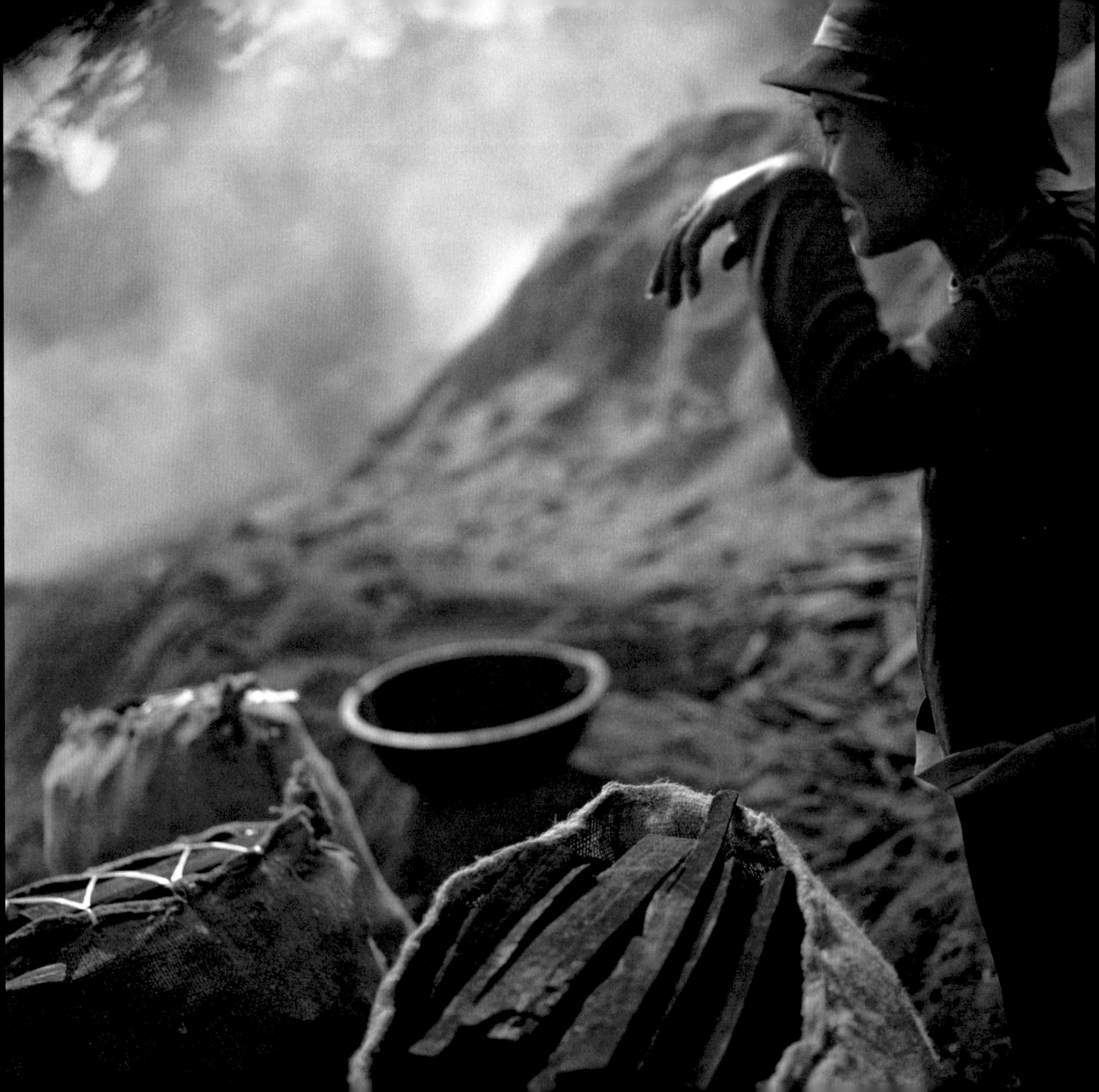

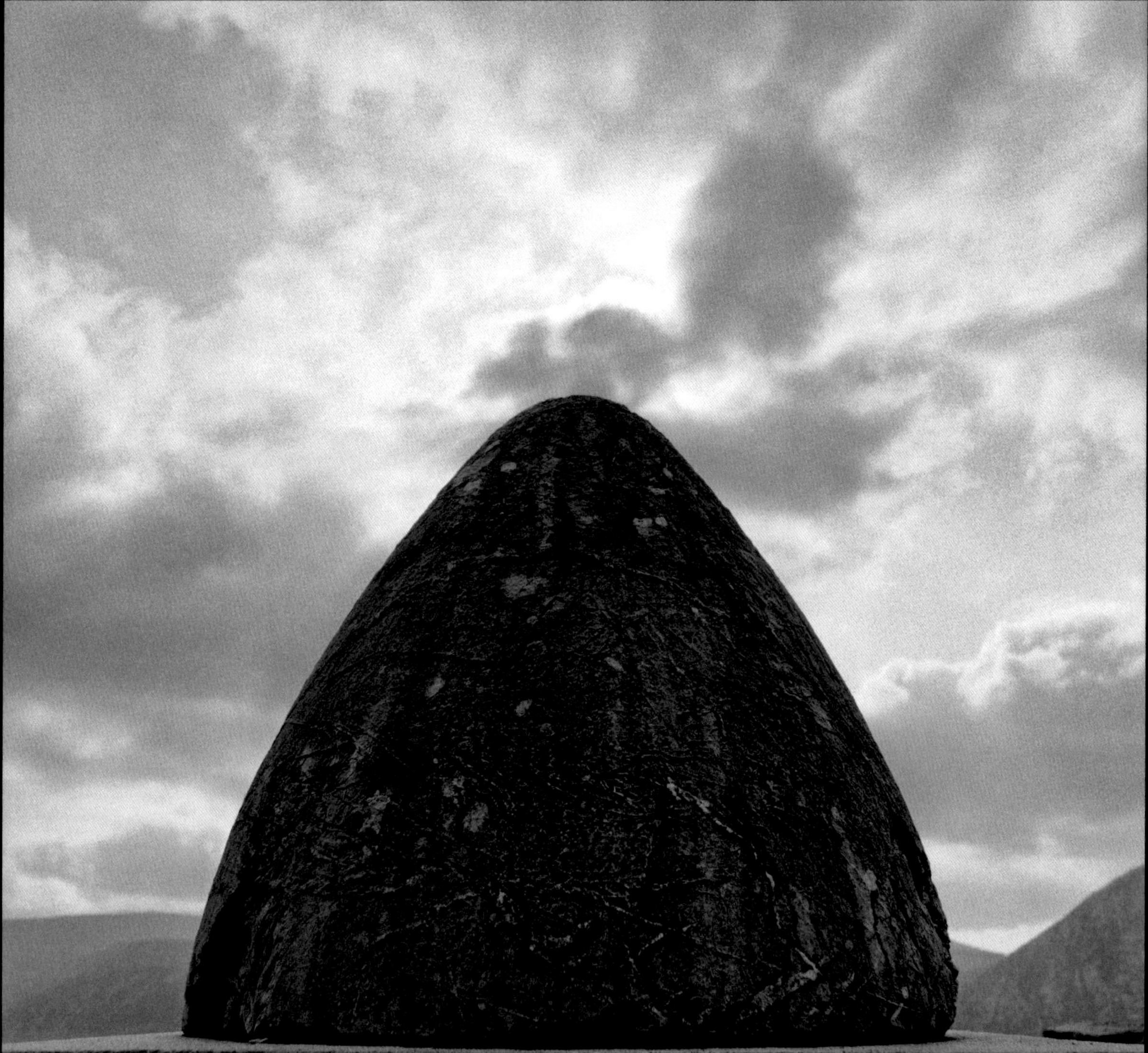

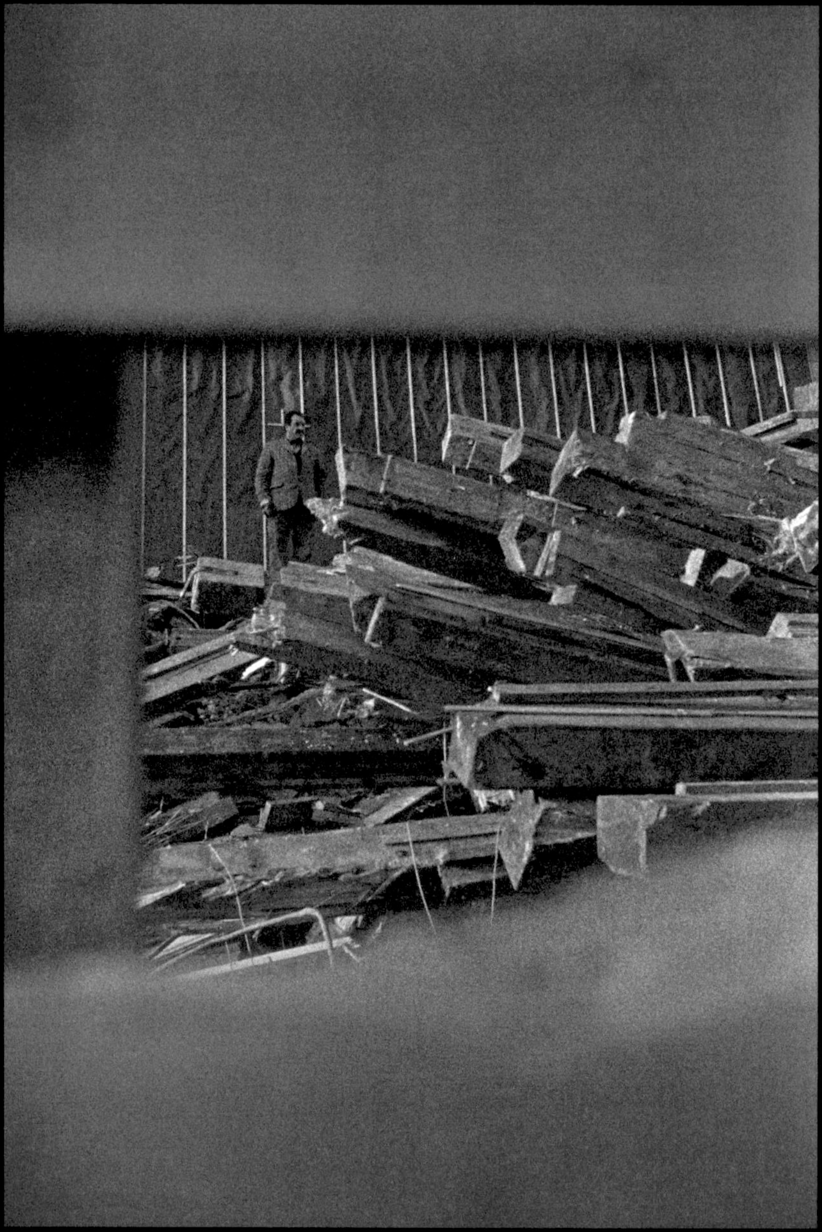

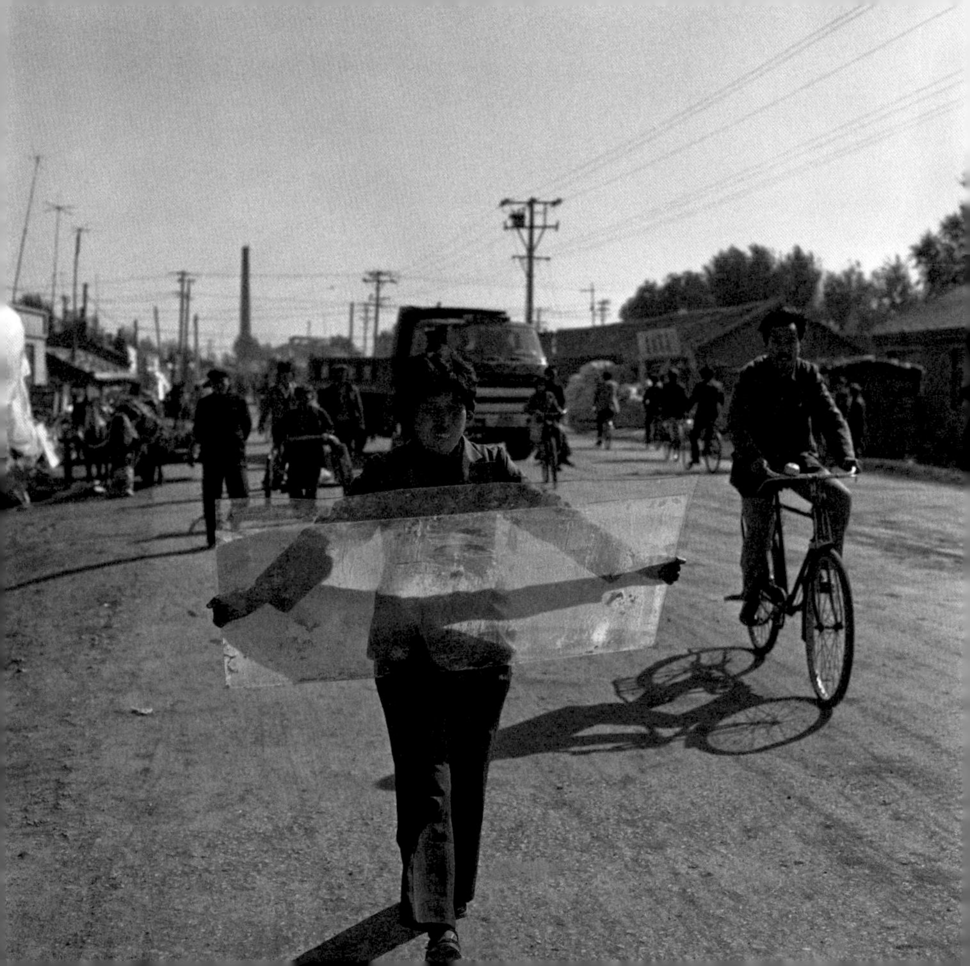

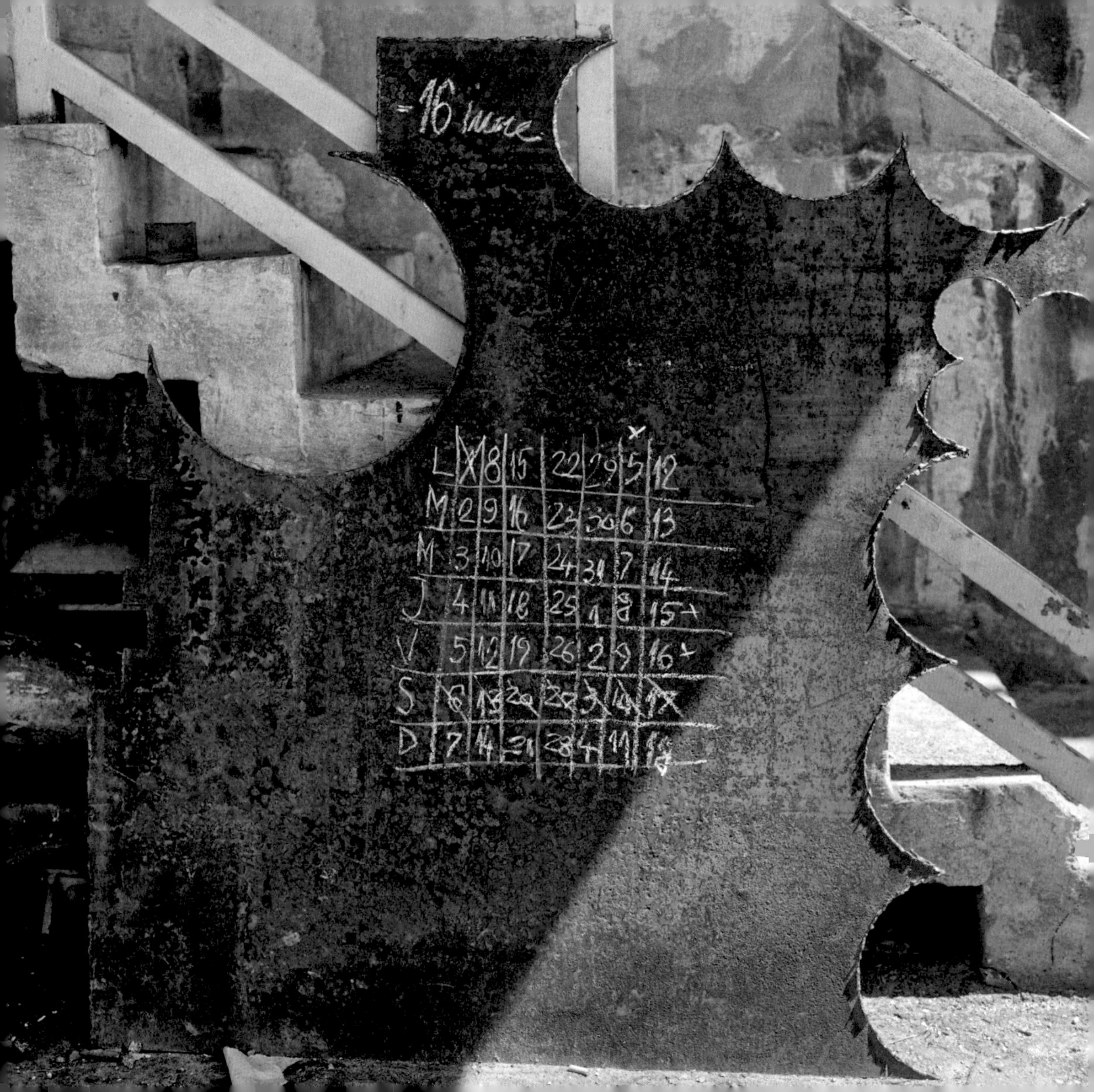

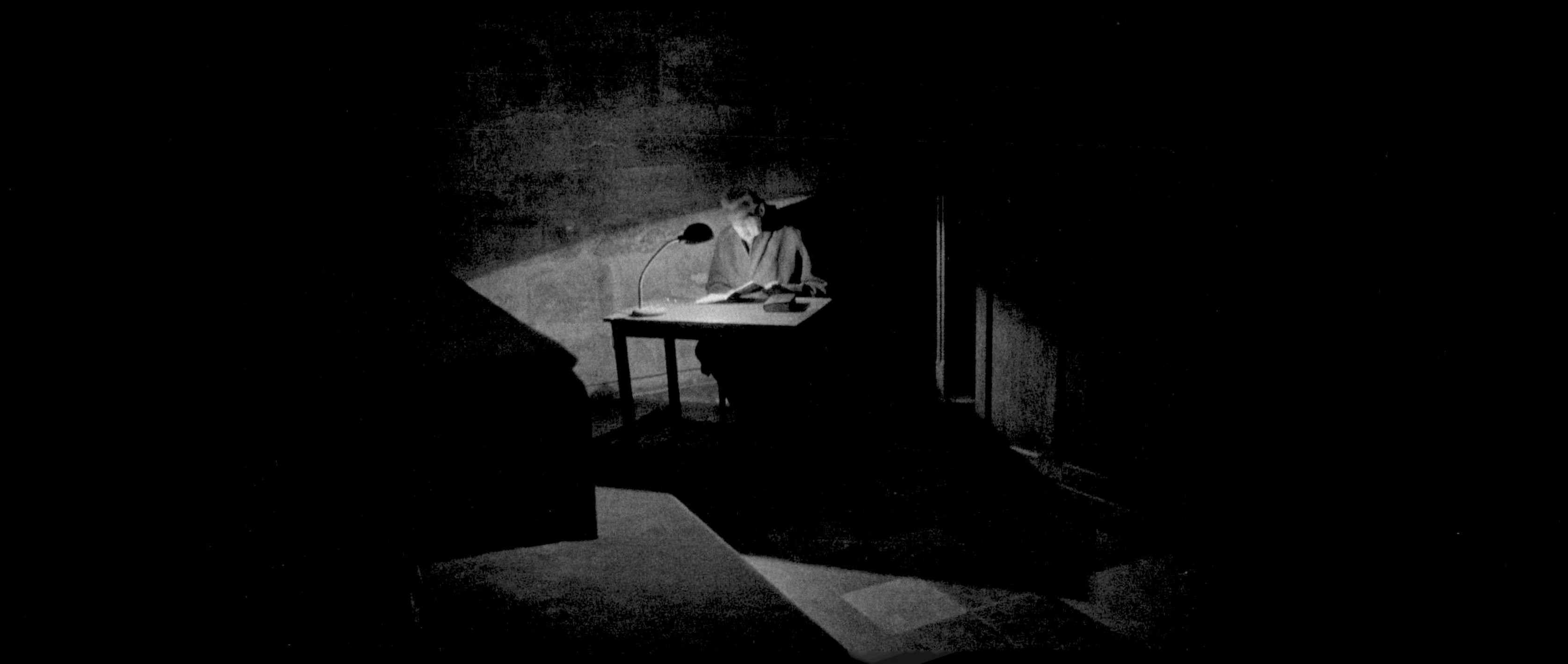

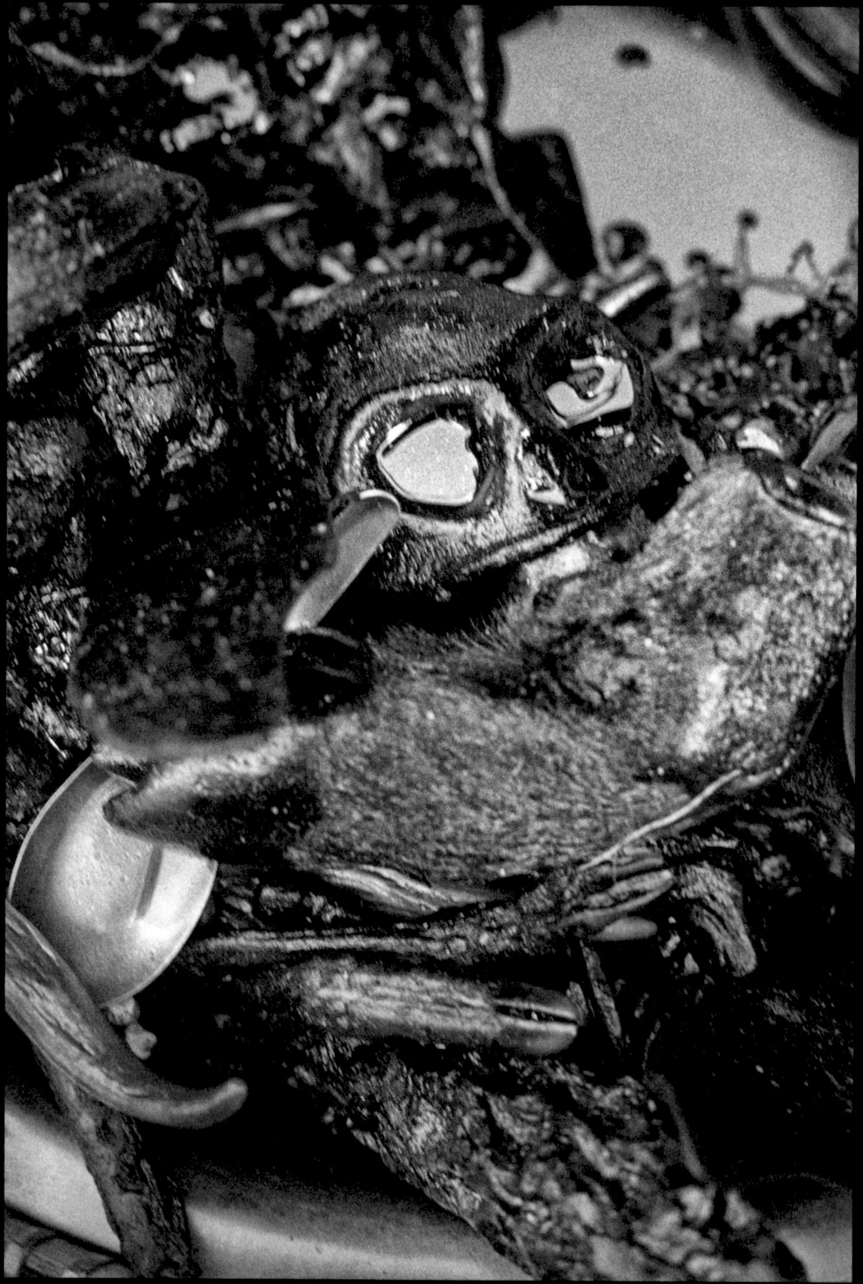

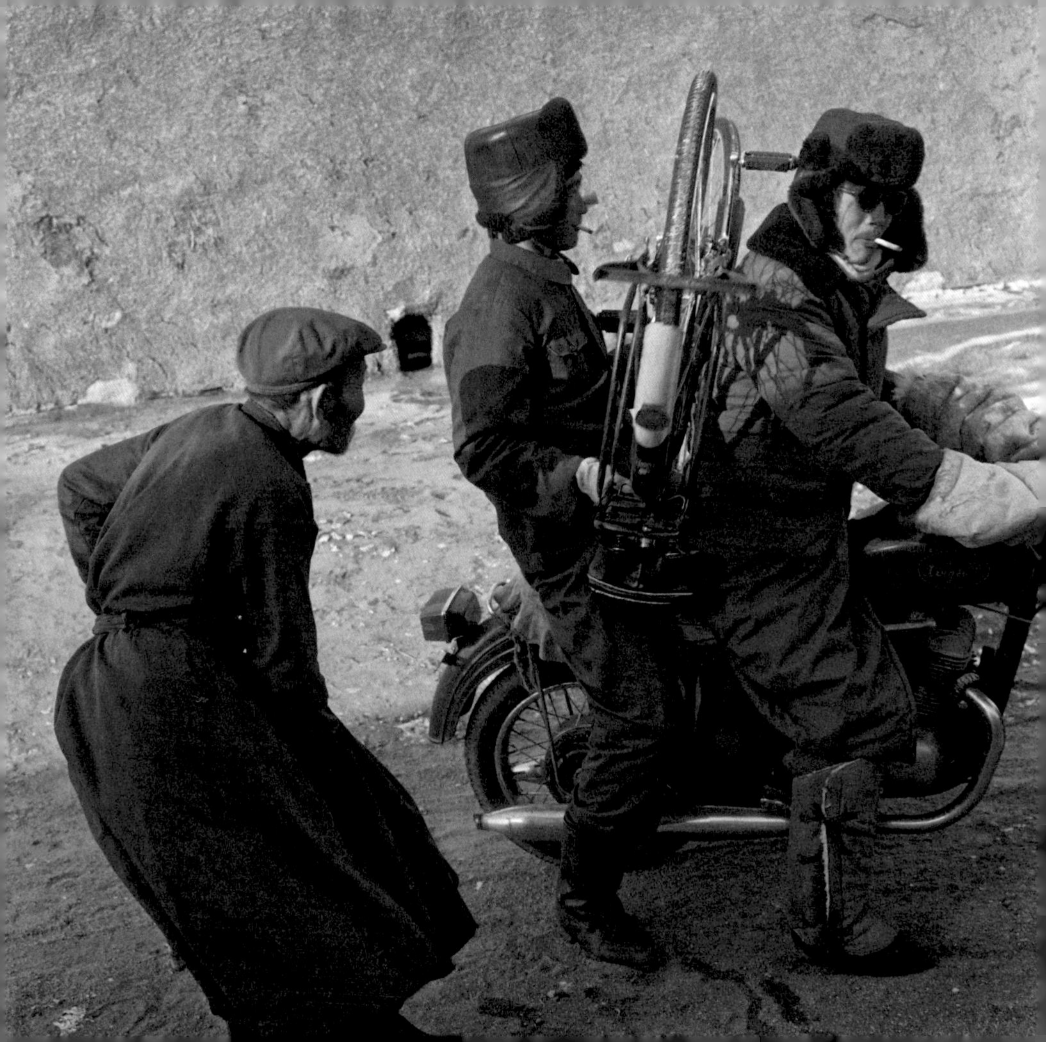

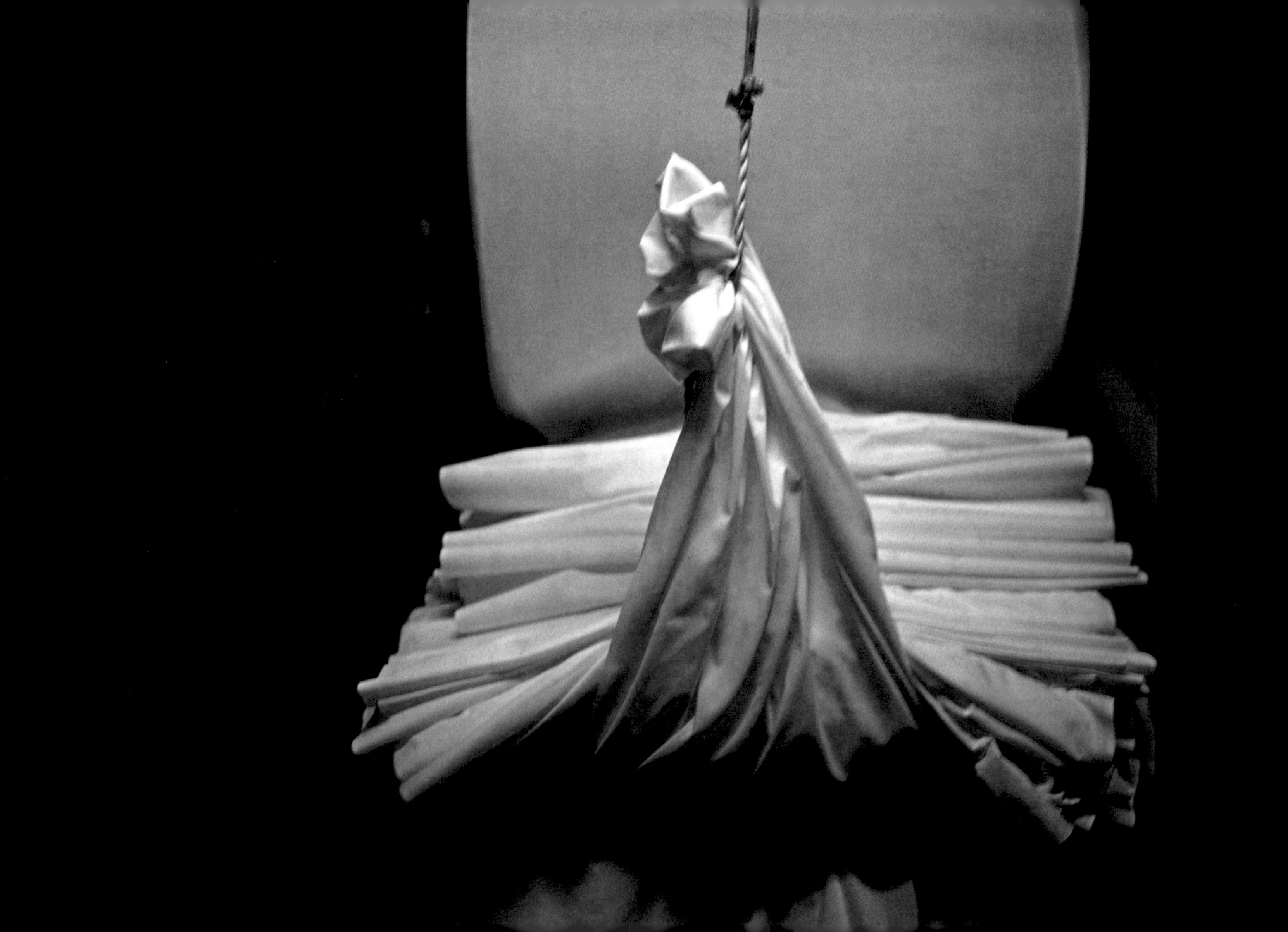

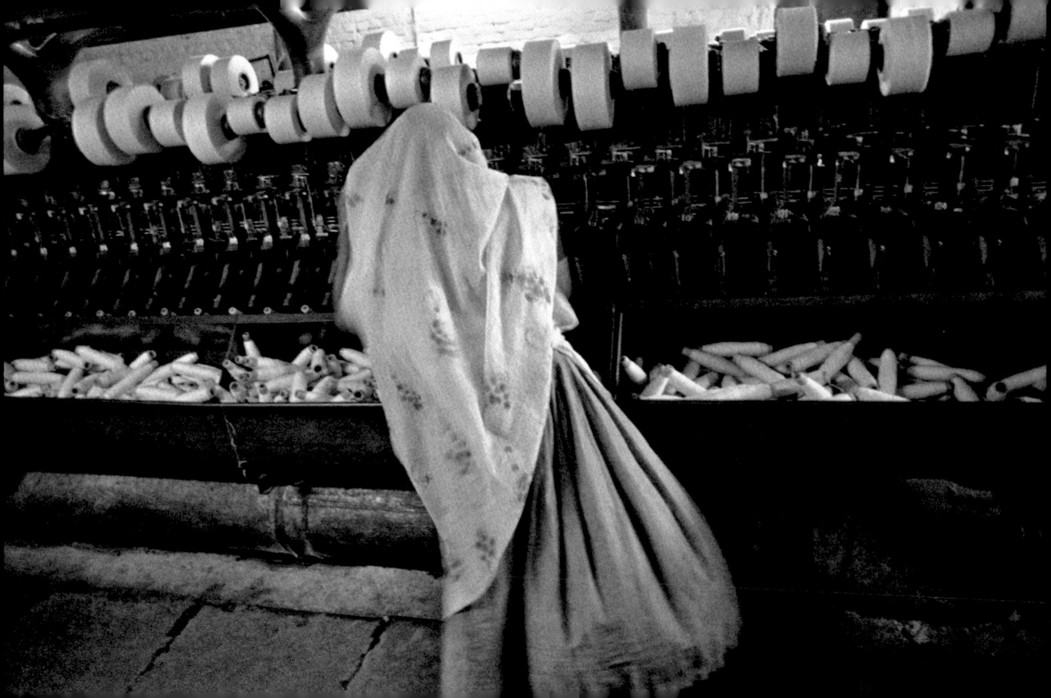

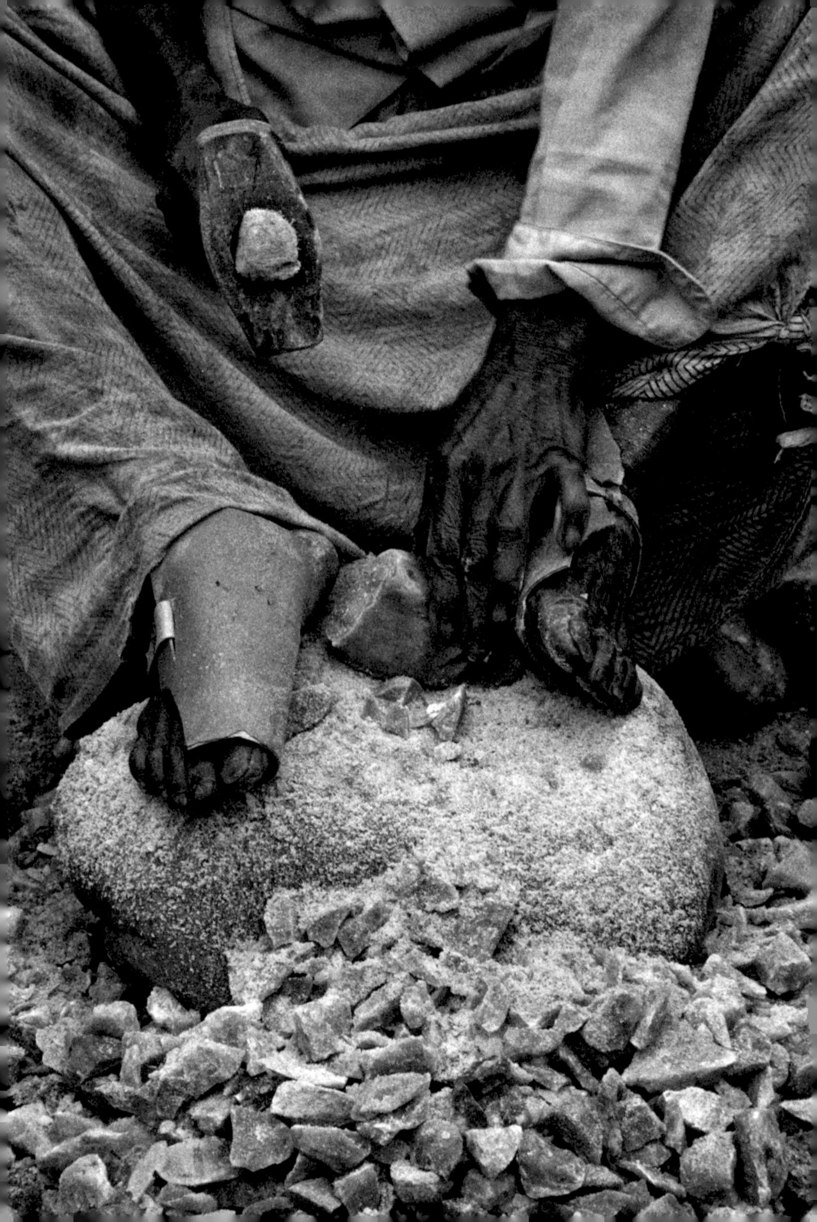

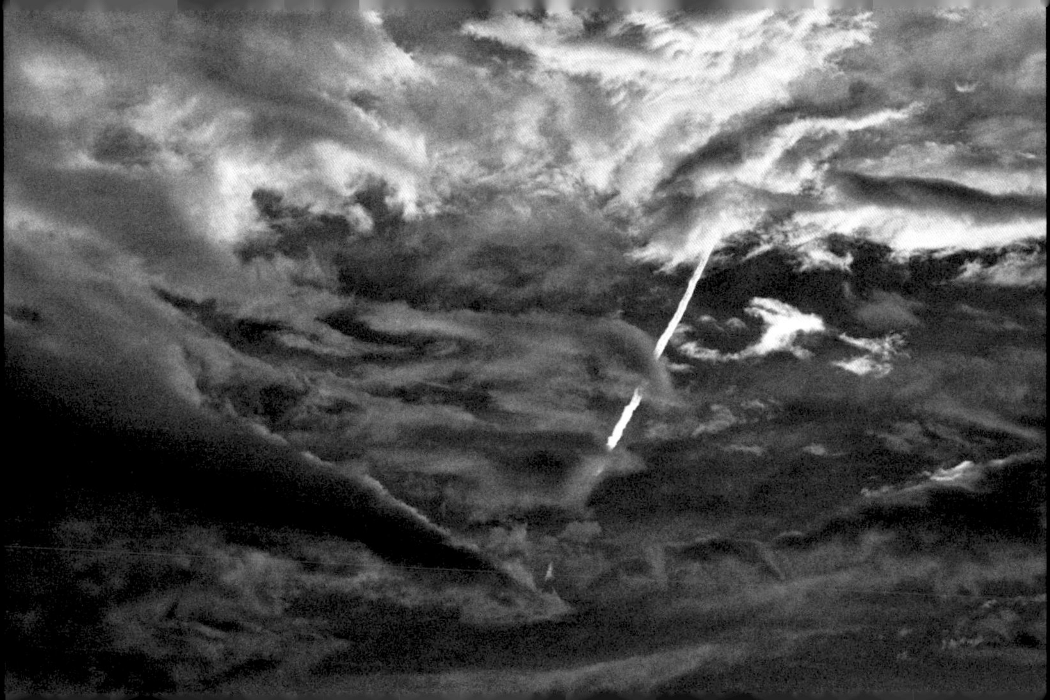

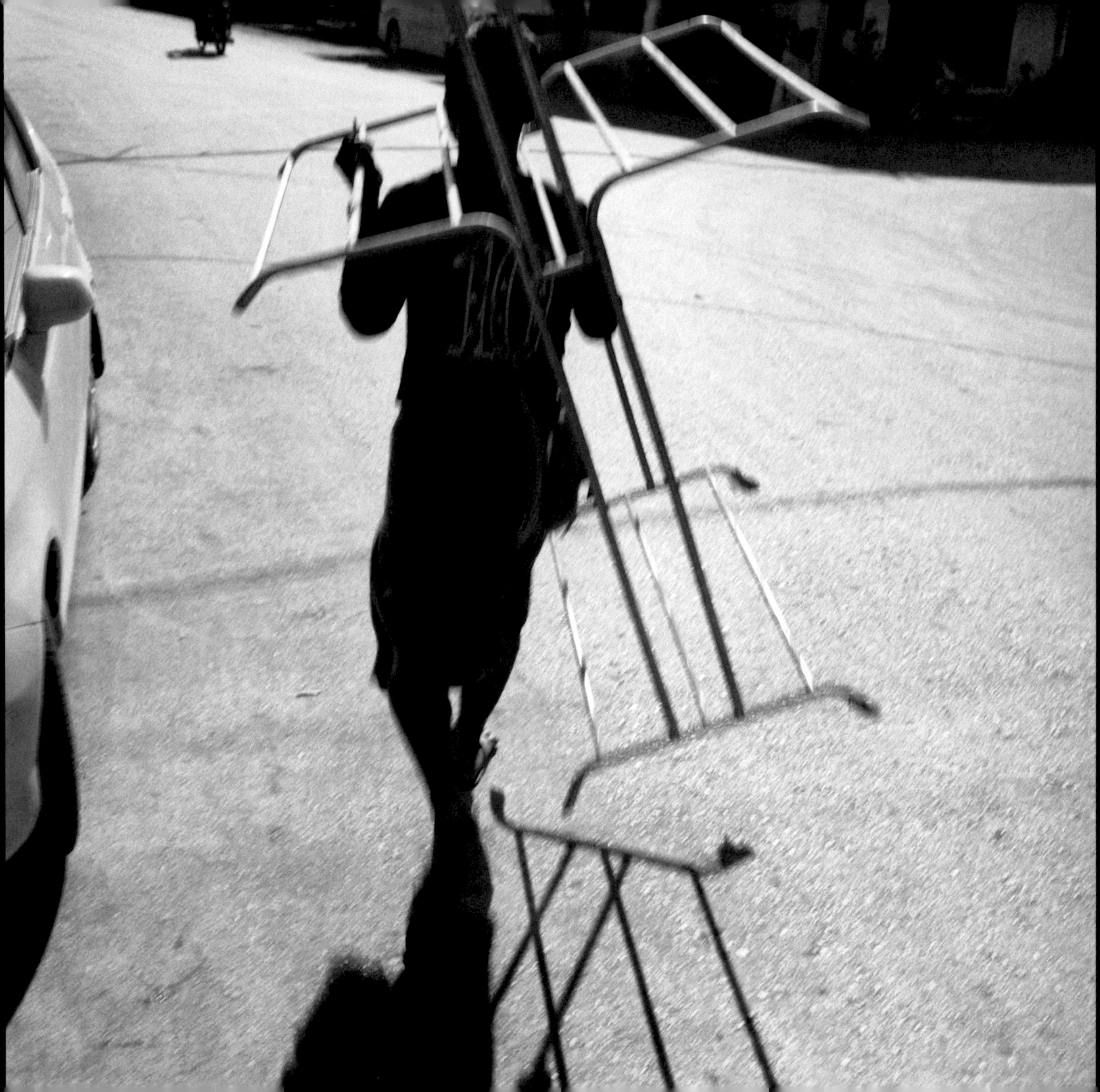

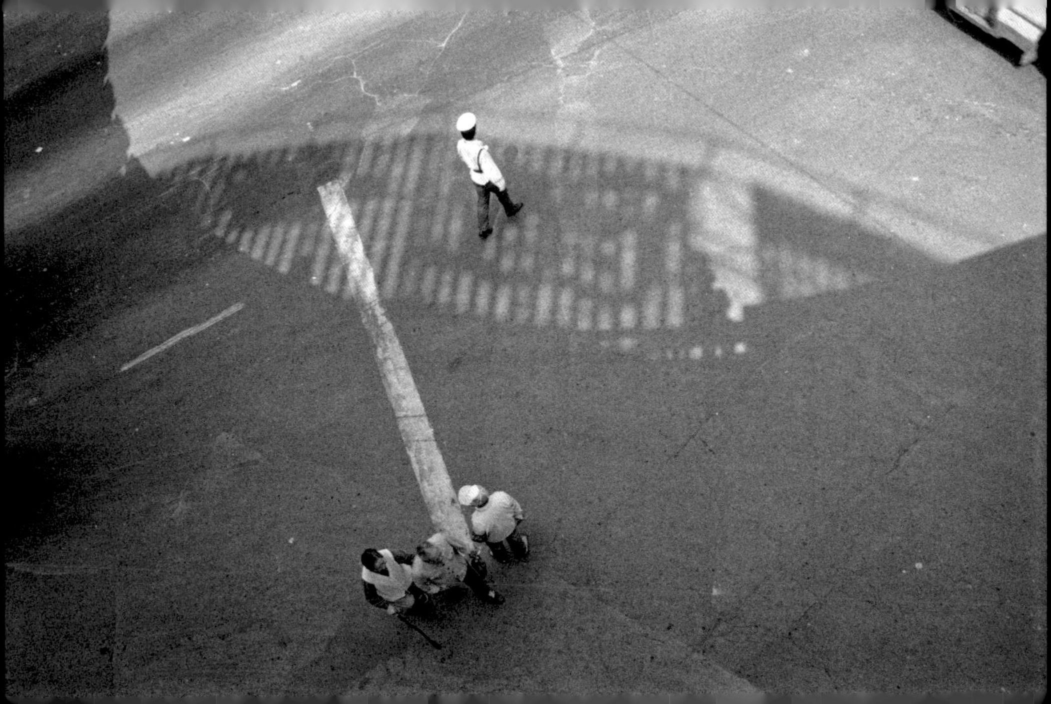

Preceding pages

Plate 58
Opium Poppy (*Papaver somniferum*)
Luang Namtha, Laos
14 March 1996

Plate 59
Making fuel
Highway 9, Savannakhet province, Laos
21 January 1997

Plate 60 – commentary on p. 177
The *omphalos*, a conical sacred
object made of limestone
Delphi, Greece
February 1984

Plate 61
Demolition of the historic post office
Solothurn, Switzerland
1975

Plate 62
Sheet glass
Haicheng, Liaoning province, China
25 October 1987

Plate 63
The calendar
Porţile de Fier power station
Gura Văii, Romania
4 June 2000

Plate 64
The warden
Cathédrale Notre-Dame, Paris, France
December 1976

Plate 65
Traditional medicaments
Mawlamyinegyun, Myanmar
6 October 2019

Plate 66
Departure at -10°C
Siziwang Banner,
Inner Mongolia Autonomous Region, China
30 December 1987

Plate 67
Cotton Cloth
Maheswari Mills, Ahmedabad, India
24 December 1990

Plate 68
Working a cotton-spinning machine
Asarwa Mills, Ahmedabad, India
21 December 1990

Plate 69
Stone breaker's feet
Narayanganj, Bangladesh
22 January 1992

Plate 70
Condensation trail
Zürich, Switzerland
1 August 1977

Plate 71
High noon
Hpa An, Myanmar
4 December 2018

Plate 72
Looking down on Nanjing Lu
Shanghai, China
27 May 1992

Fig. 39 – commentary on p. 177

Sculptured pillar, Yungang Buddhist Grottos
Waiting for the shift at the Meiyukou mine
Yungang/Datong, Shanxi province, China
16–20 November 1987

Gelatin silver double-exposure print, 2021.
Sheet size 50 × 40 cm (19 3/4 × 15 3/4 in.)

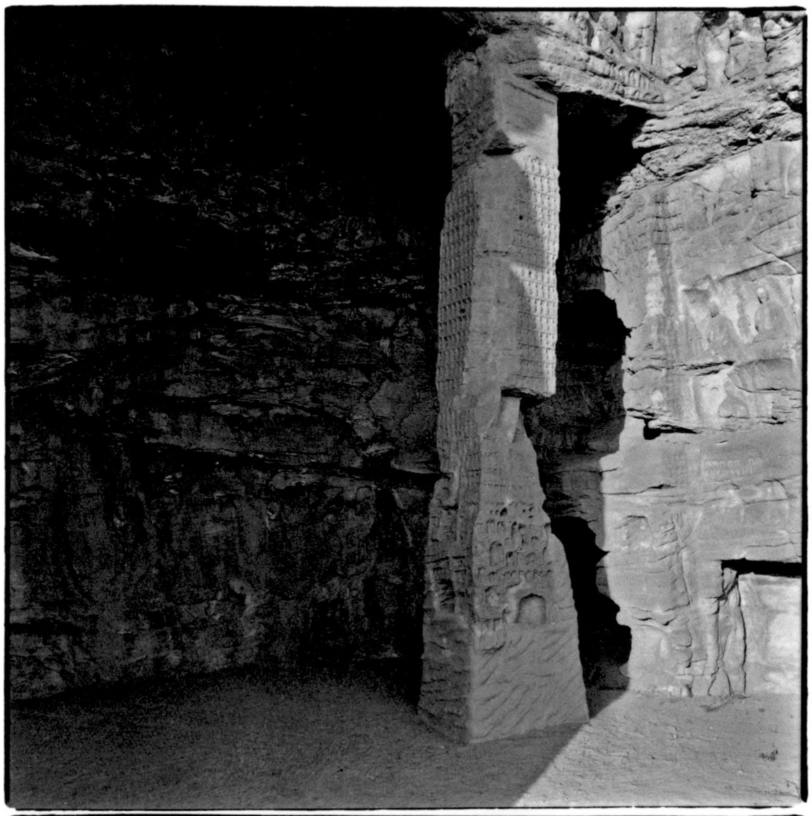

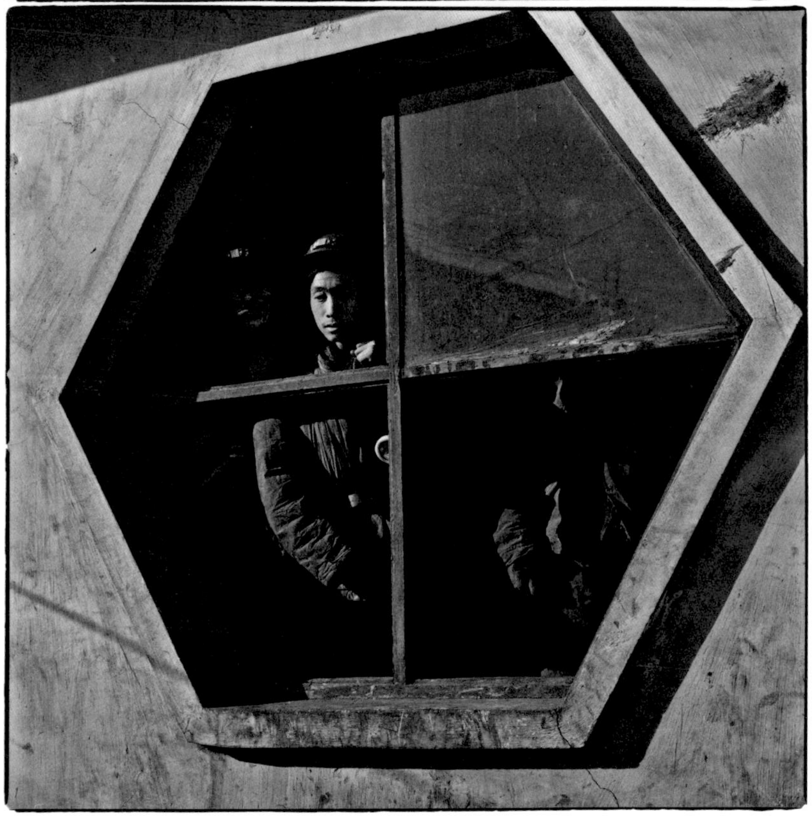

Fig. 39

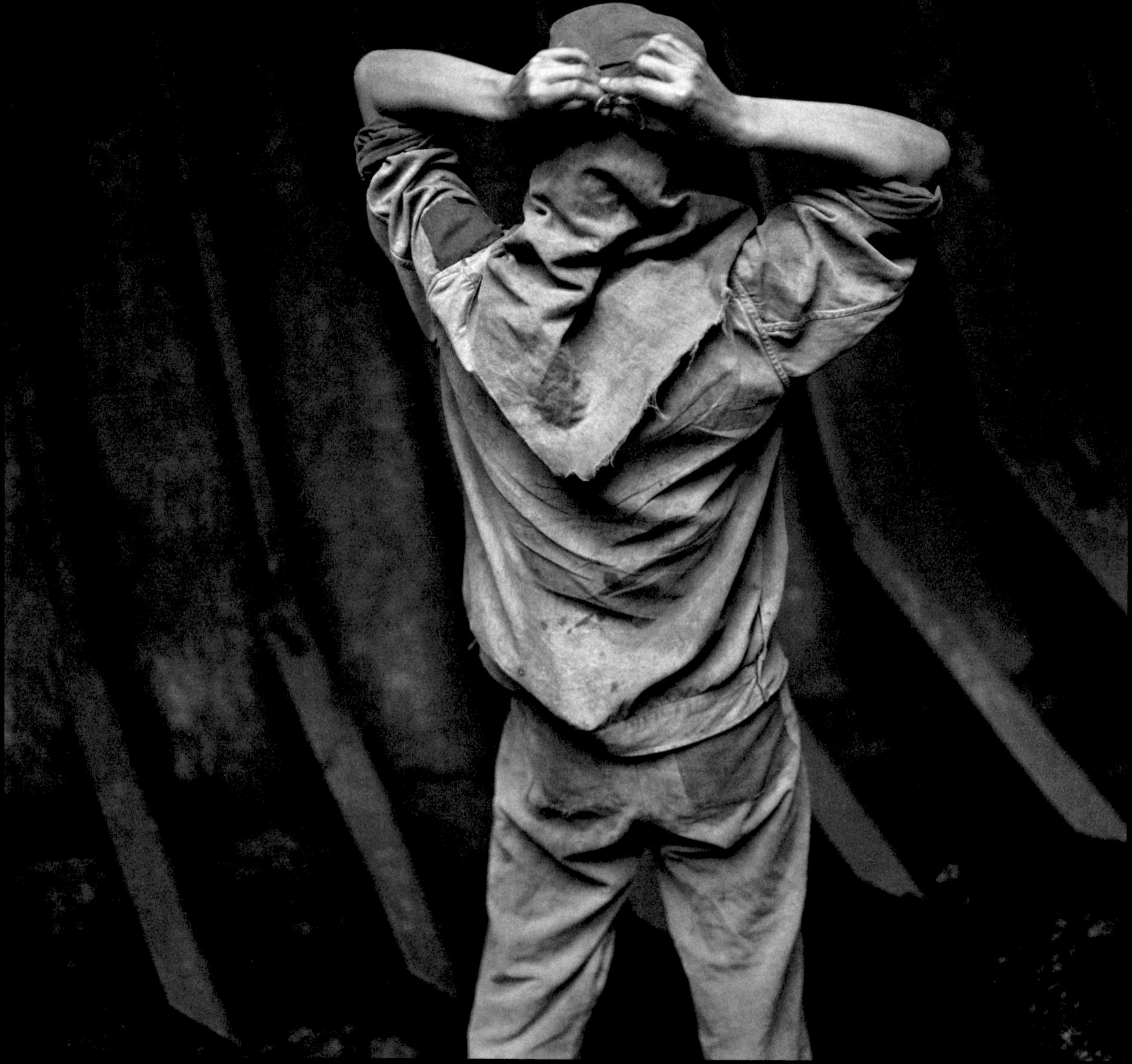

V Observation

Daniel Schwartz has undertaken long journeys to numerous crisis regions for his extensive book projects and reportage assignments. Since the 1990s he has been regarded as an outstanding representative of classic reportage photography, and he is also one of the last in a tradition that has been drawing to a close since that decade – a change that is not only rooted in but hugely accelerated by the displacement of analogue by digital photography, and most recently by mobile phone photography.

It goes without saying, perhaps, that observation is fundamental to reportage, the intention of which is primarily an ambition to educate and, naturally, to create a meaningful image. The photographer has his eye, as the saying goes, on the scene of the crime, whereby the 'scene' can extend over huge areas and regions, and the 'crime' can refer to ongoing processes, to permanent refugee movements in Kurdistan or Afghanistan as well as to the collapsing glaciers at the equator.

The observer's camera has nothing to do with a surveillance camera, the lens of which records comprehensively; instead his eye is concentrated and focused on the moment in which what is observed is bundled and condensed in the picture. The picture of a boy trying to get close to the hot-water pipe network in the icy-cold Mongolian capital (plate 74) speaks of resilience and the will to survive; the shattered leg of a child in a Rohingya refugee camp (plate 79) speaks of cruel injury intentionally inflicted; the portrait of an old Vietnamese man (plate 87) shows an eyewitness's furrowed but beautiful face, which has been etched over many years with traumatic memories of terrible war atrocities. The photographer observes conditions that should not be like this, he records crimes against humanity and does not close his eyes to extreme inequalities.

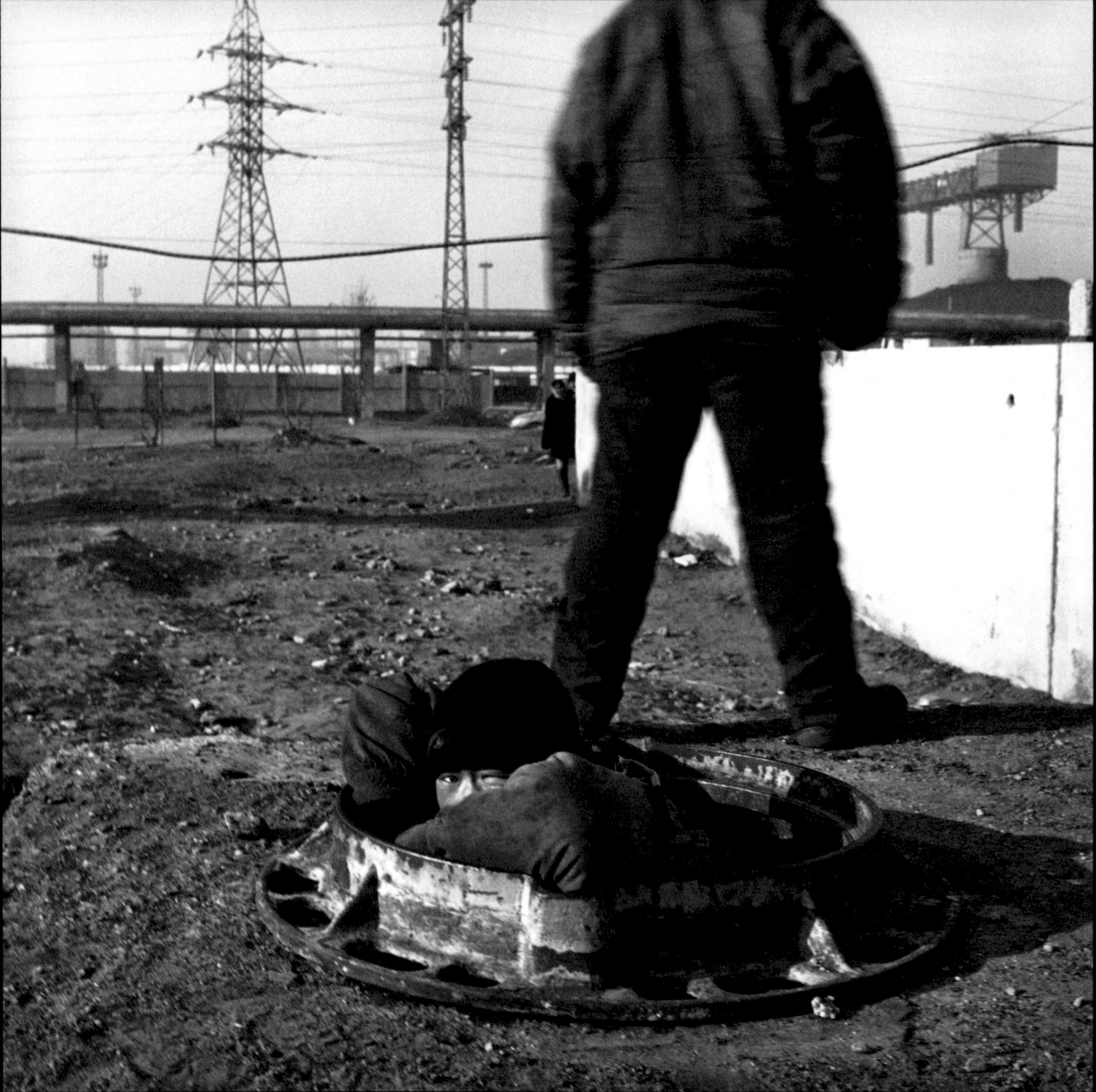

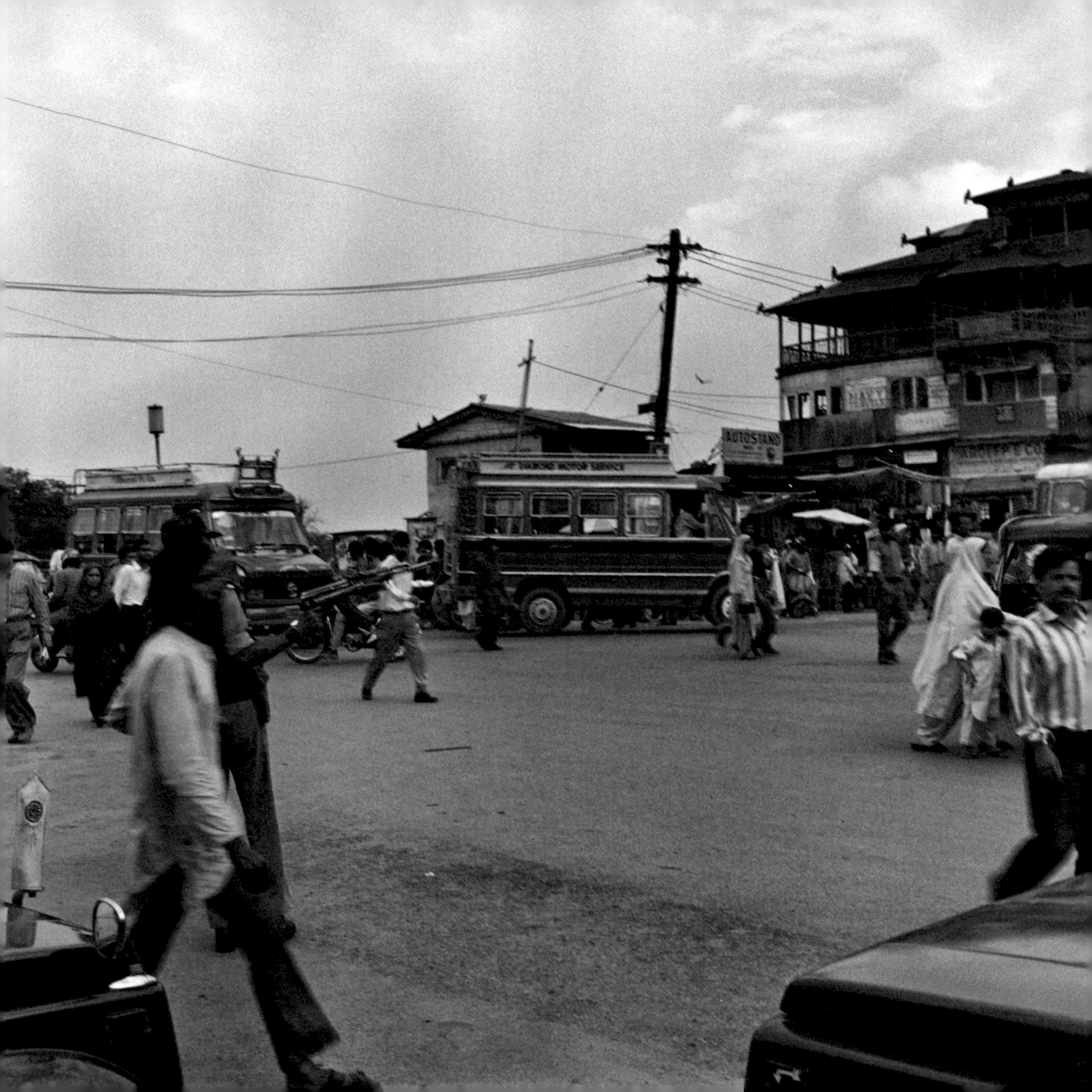
AUTOSTAND

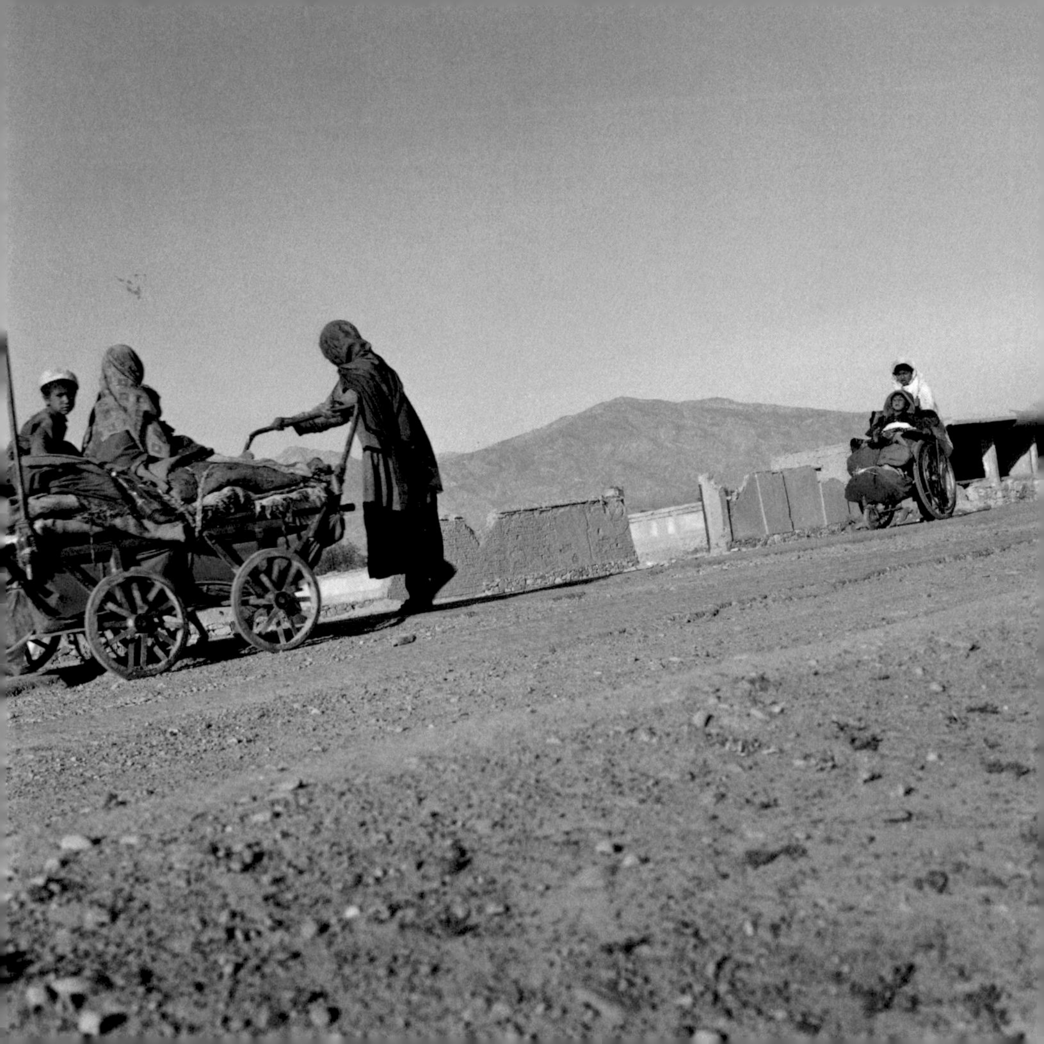

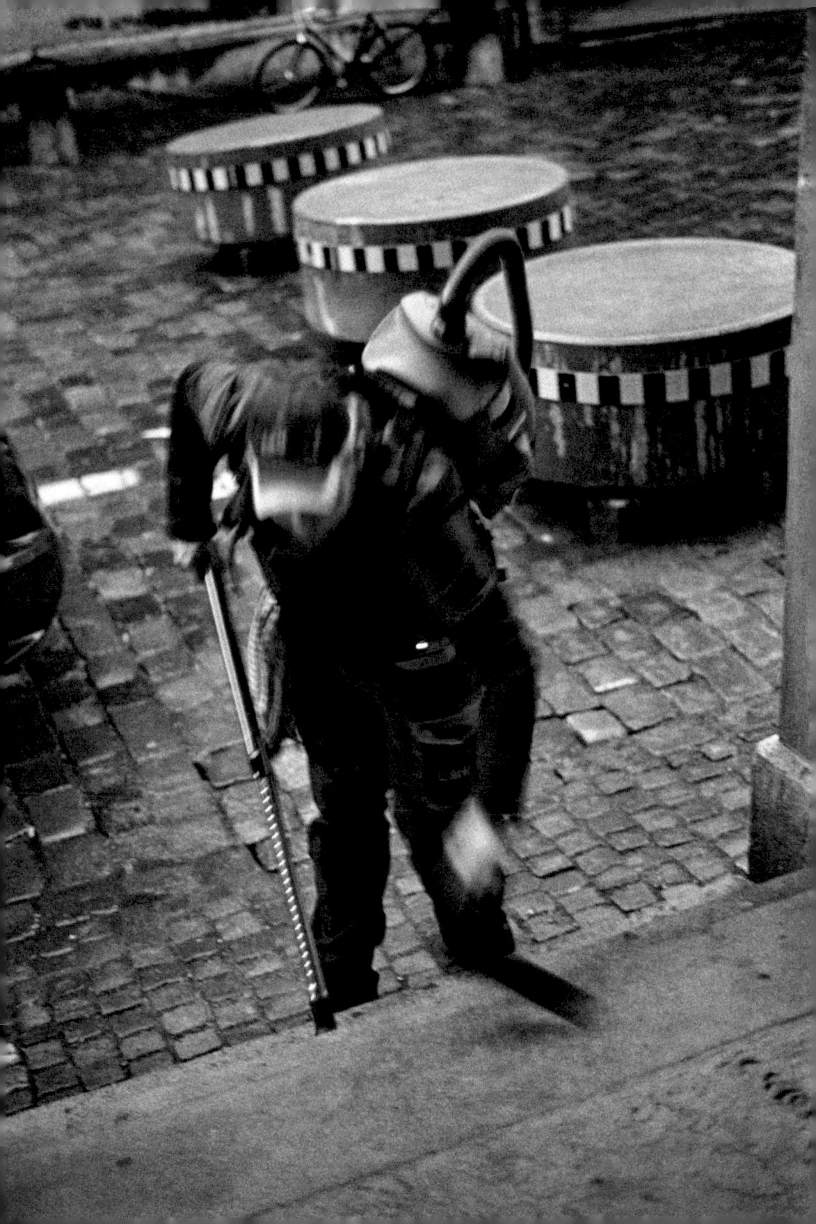

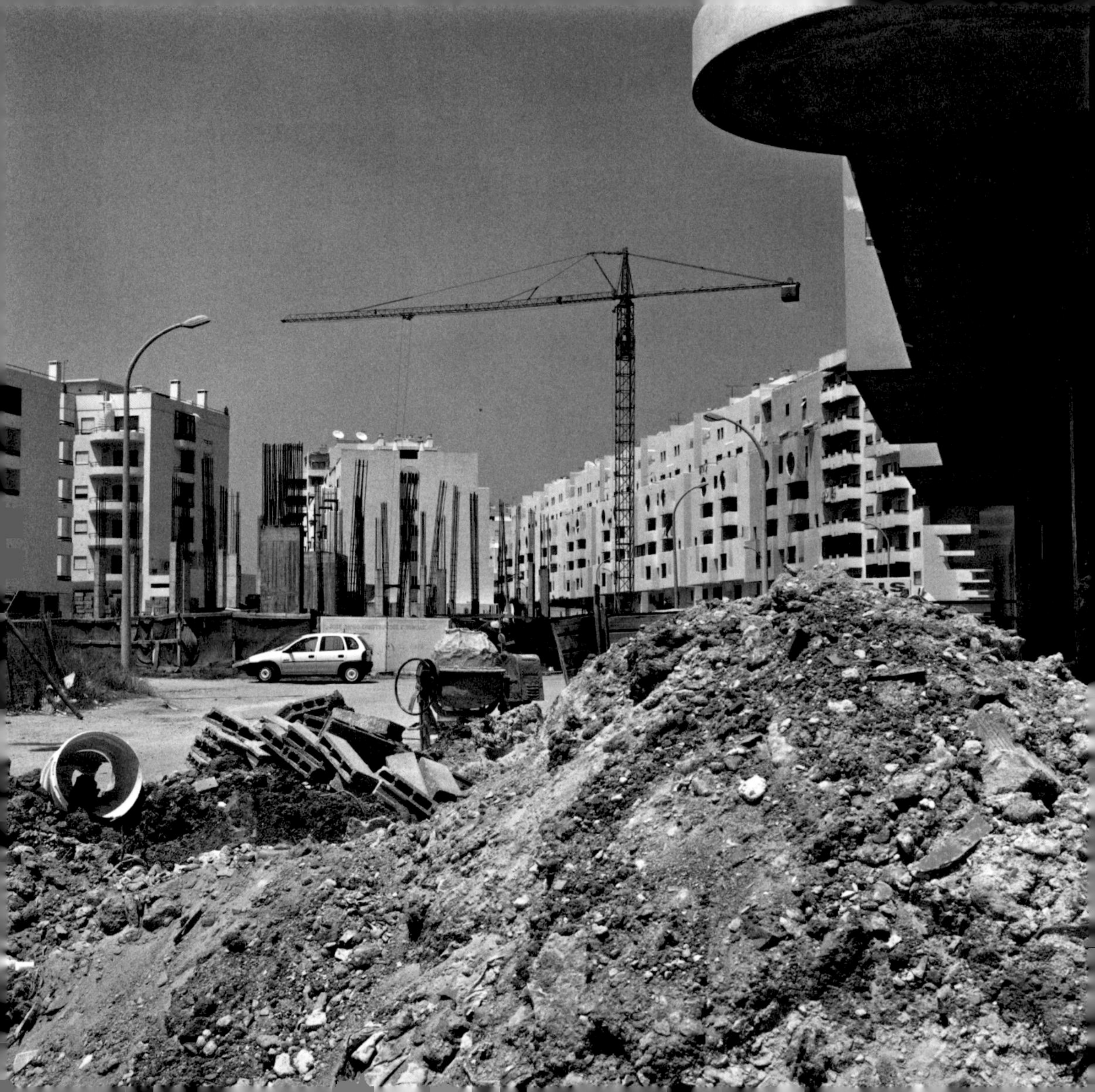

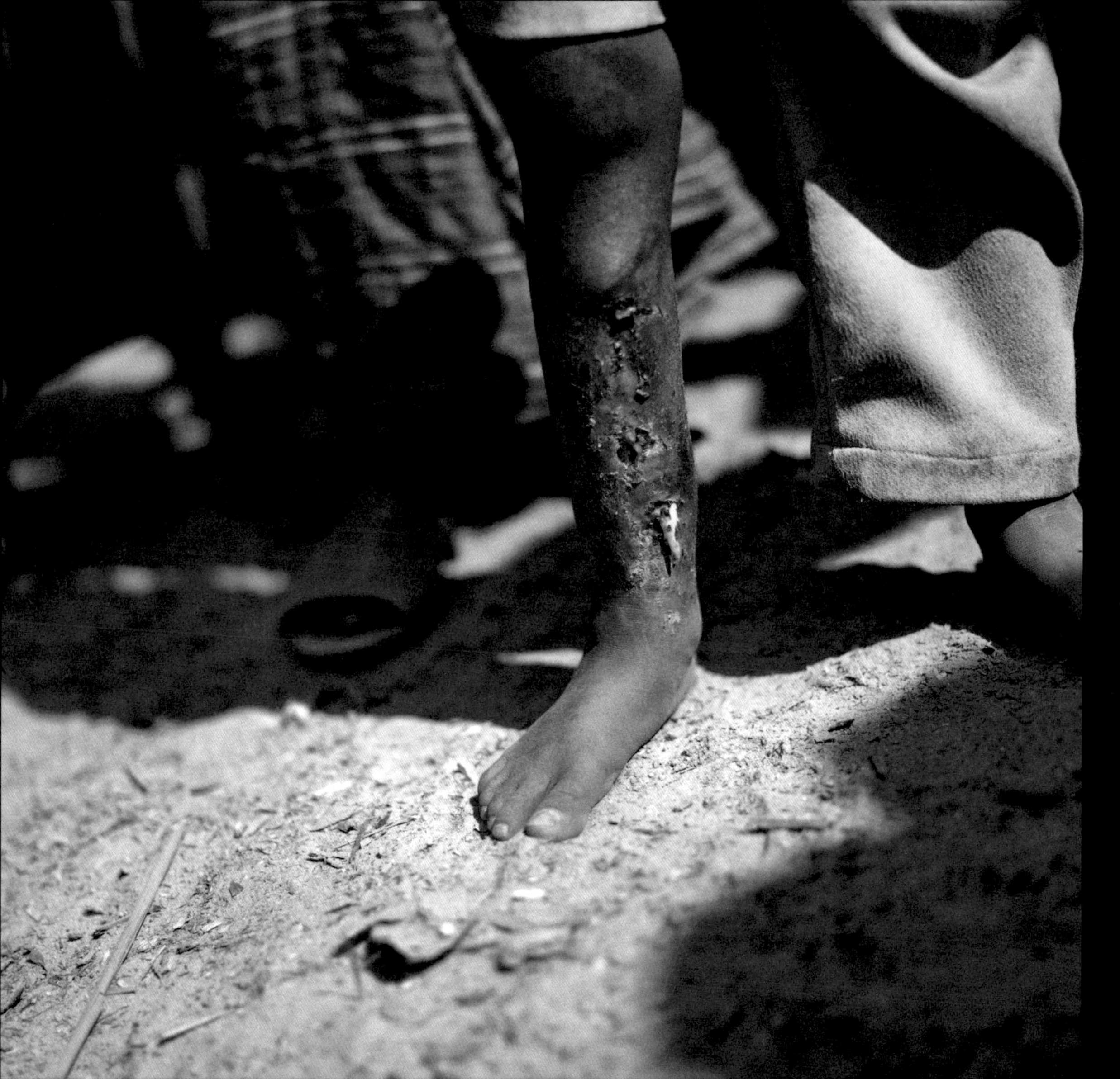

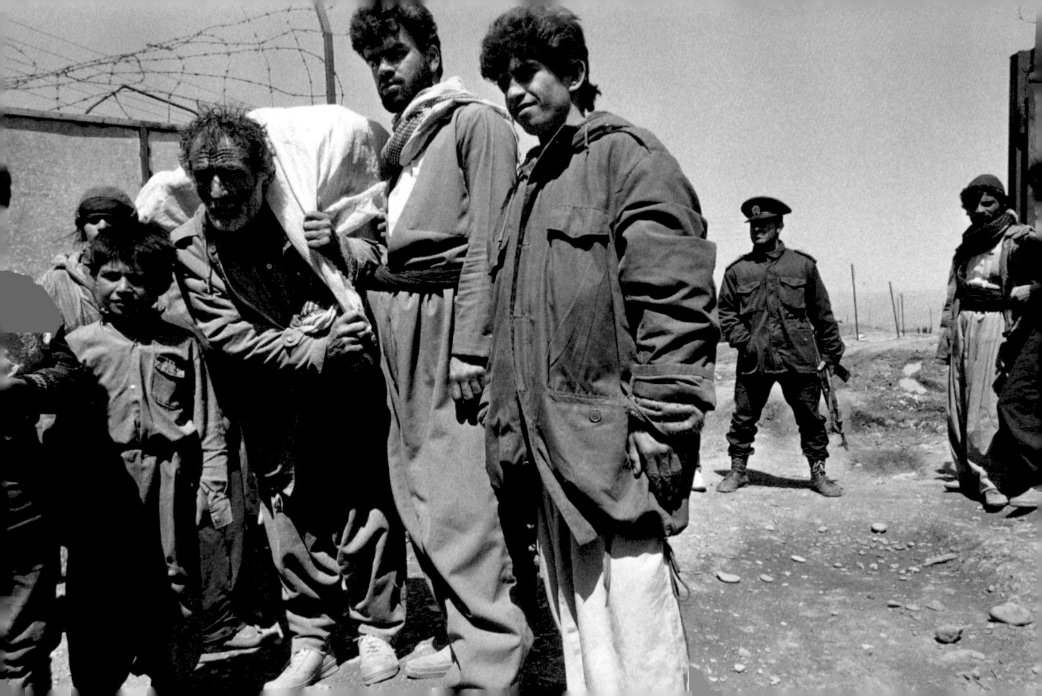

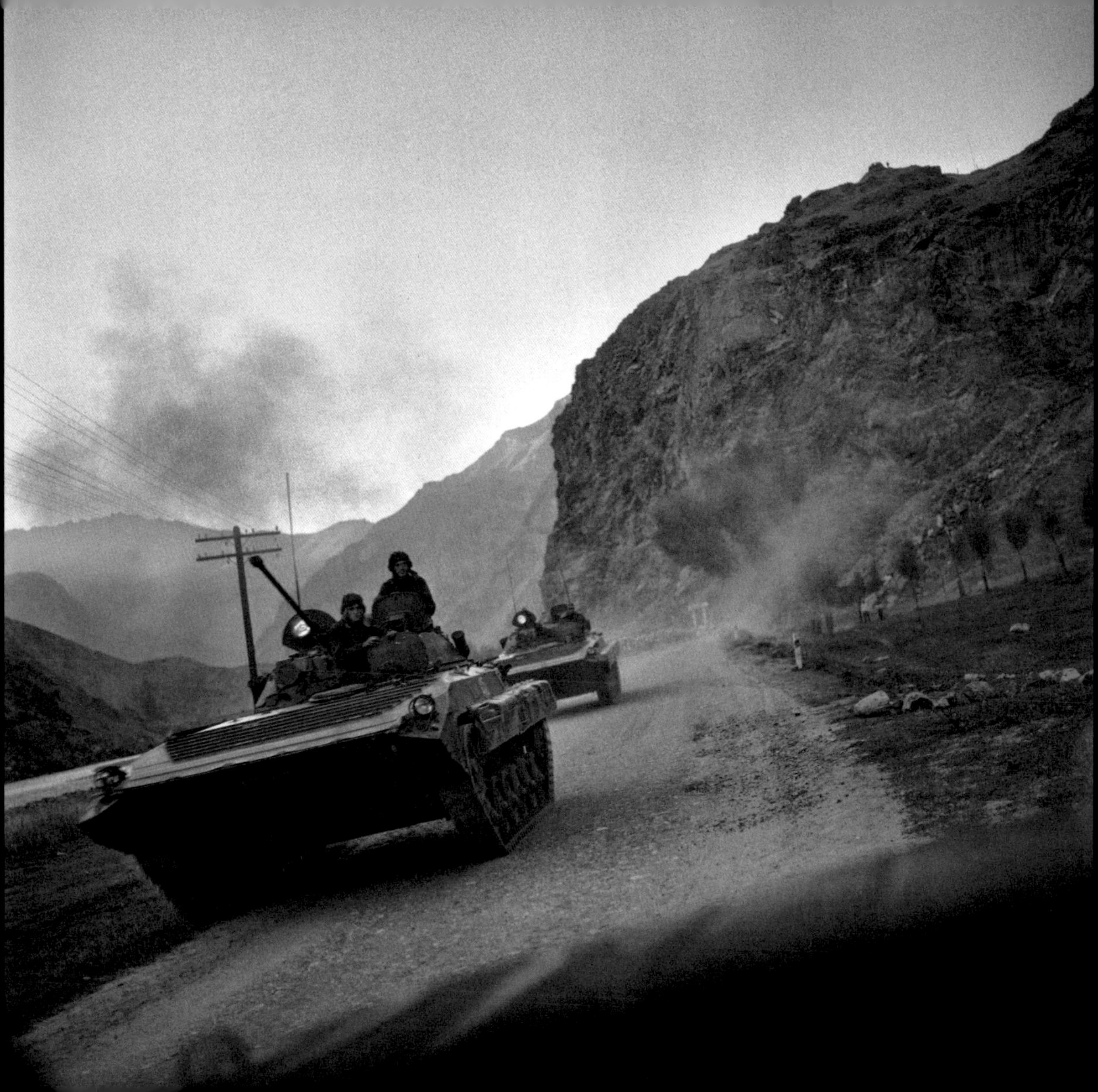

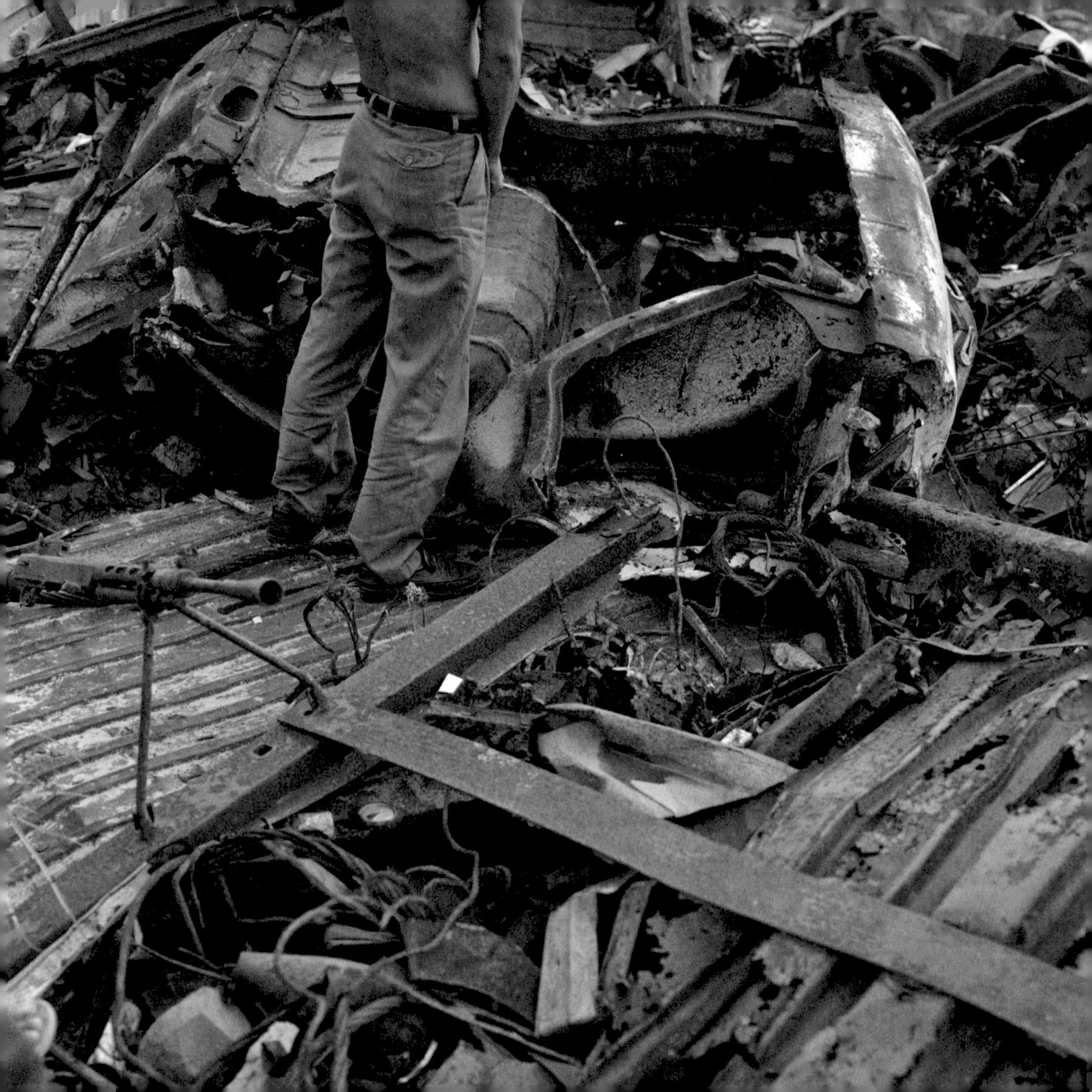

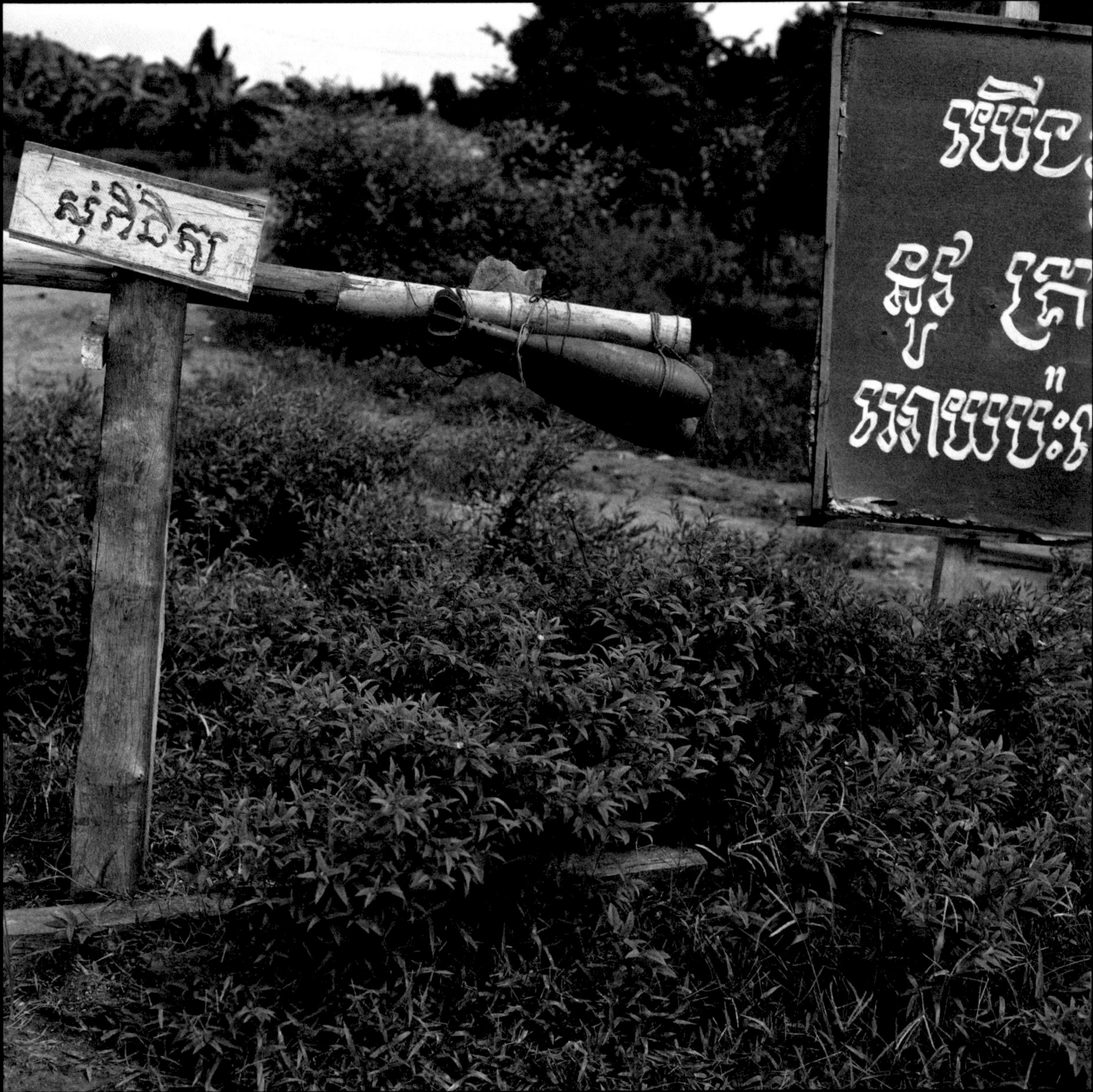

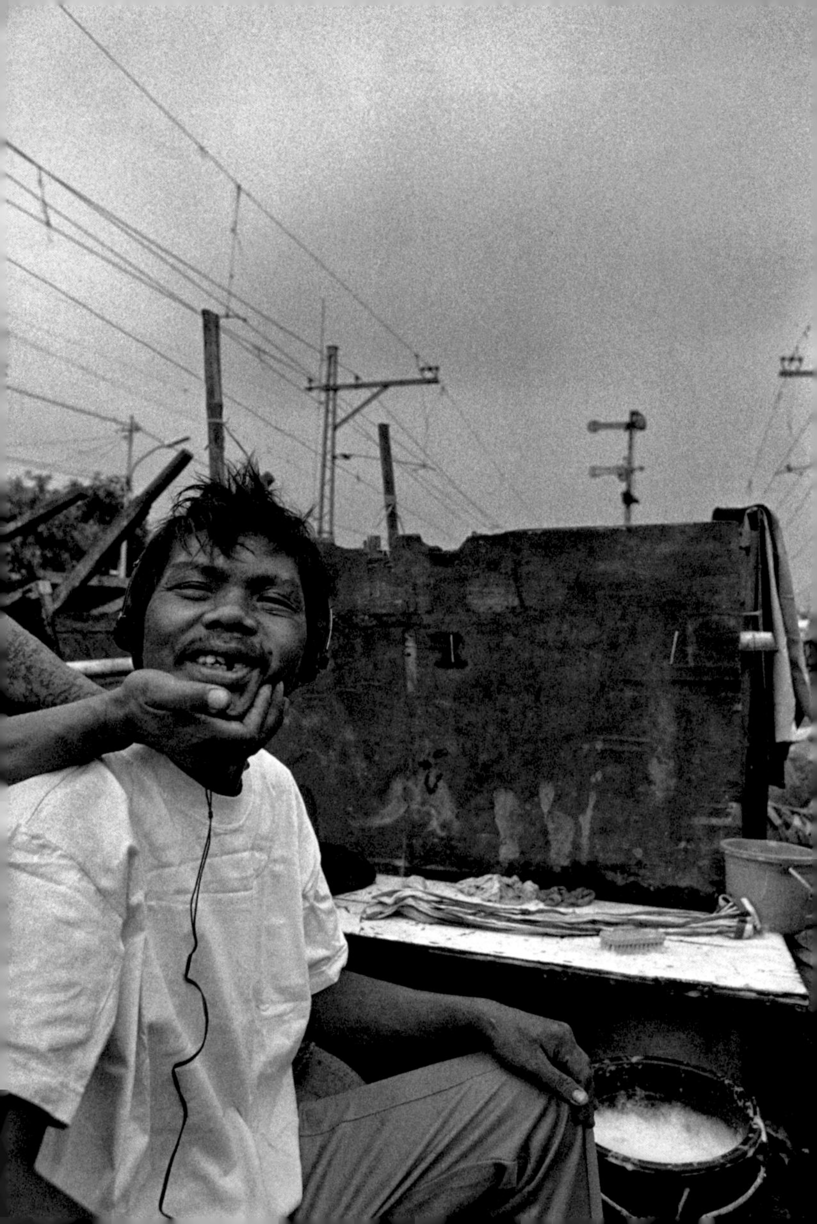

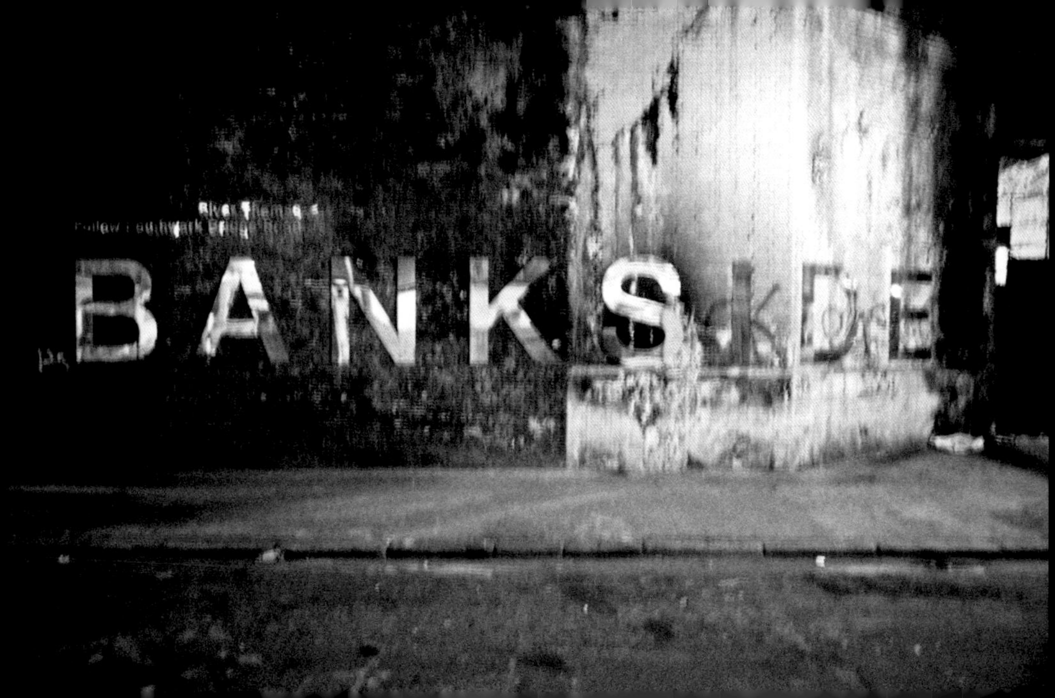
BANKS

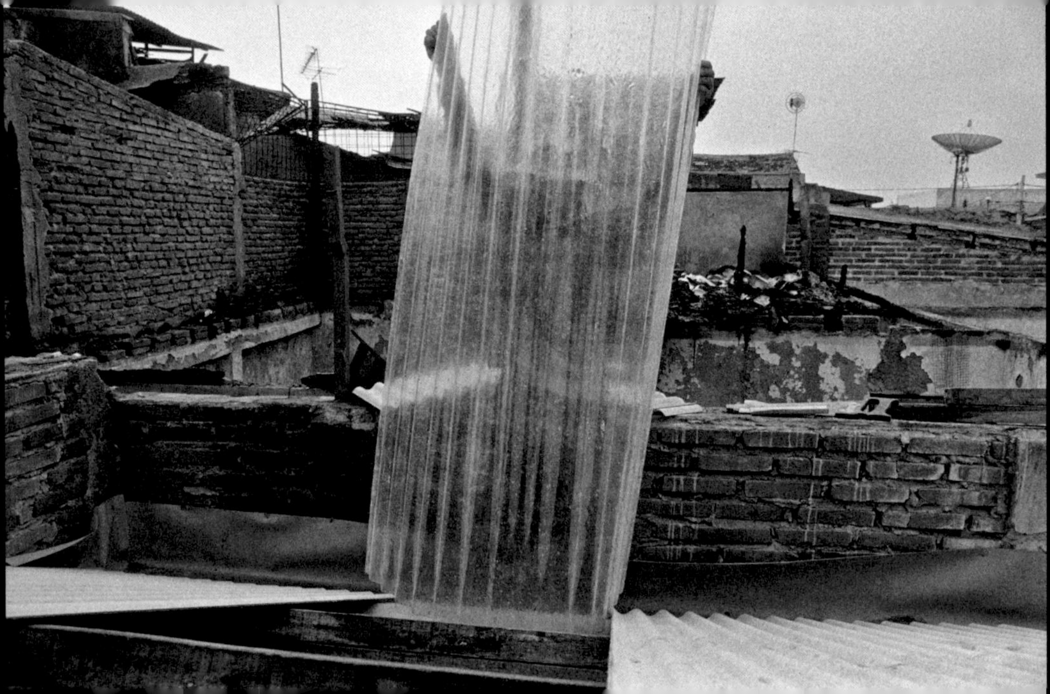

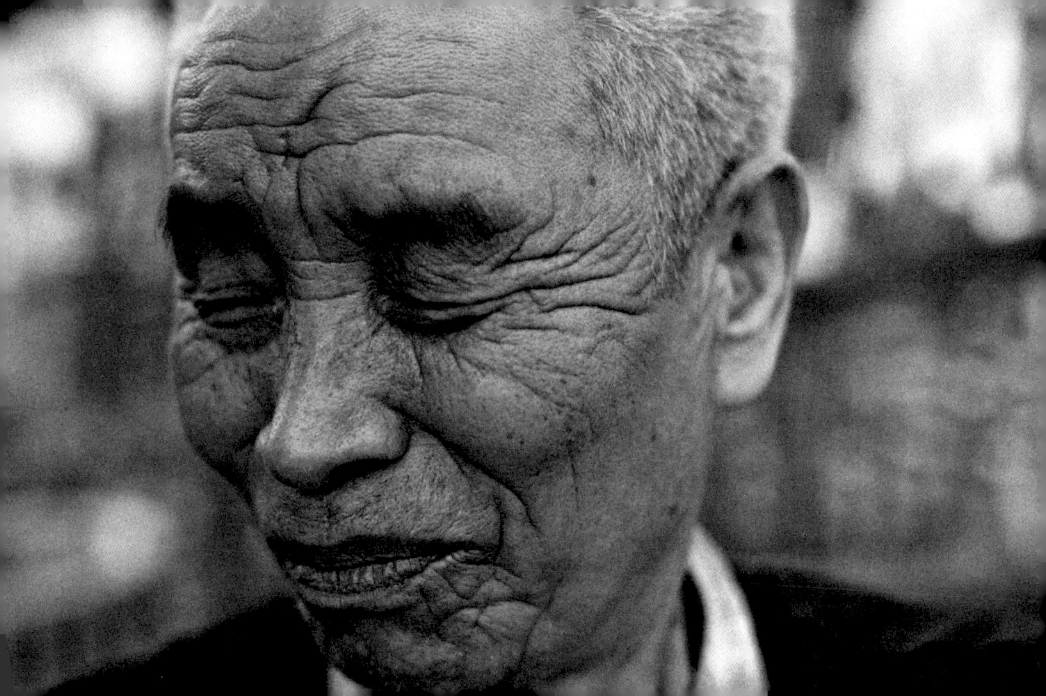

Preceding pages

Plate 73
Female worker in the cargo hold
of a Russian freighter
Bach Dang Shipyard, Haiphong, Vietnam
30 September 1993

Plate 74 – commentary on p. 177
Underground life
Ulaanbaatar, Mongolia
4 March 2000

Plate 75 – commentary on p. 177
Intimidation
Srinagar, Jammu and Kashmir, India
21 May 2000

Plate 76
Displaced by war
Kabul, Afghanistan
21 June 1998

Plate 77
Christmas Eve
Bern, Switzerland
24 December 2019

Plate 78 – commentary on p. 178
Tourist resort in the making
Quarteira, Algarve, Portugal
18 July 1996

Plate 79 – commentary on p. 178
Child's shinbone shattered by soldier's rifle butt
Maricha Palong camp for Rohingya refugees
from Myanmar
Ukhia Upazila, Bangladesh
16 January 1992

Plate 80 – commentary on p. 178
Kurds fleeing the war in Iraq
at the gate of a refugee camp
Sardasht, Iran
19 April 1991

Plate 81 – commentary on p. 178
Russian troops en route to Ishkashim
at the border to Afghanistan
Badakshan, Tajikistan
18 September 1996

Plate 82
Civil war weapons dumping site
Choeung Ek, Cambodia
15 July 1994

Plate 83
En route from the Thai border to Pailin,
the last stronghold of the Khmer Rouge
Cambodia
2 October 1997

Plate 84 – commentary on p. 178
On an ordinary day
Pasar Senen railway station, Jakarta, Indonesia
17 November 1994

Plate 85 – commentary on p. 178
London, United Kingdom
20 February 2000

Plate 86 – commentary on p. 178
Roofing in an informal settlement
Jakarta, Indonesia
15 November 1994

Plate 87 – commentary on p. 178
Memories
Dien Bien Phu, Vietnam
6 March 2011

Fig. 40 – commentary on p. 178

On the Burma Road
Baoshan, Yunnan, China
21 January 1998

Gelatin silver double-exposure print, 2020.
Sheet size 50 × 40 cm (19 3/4 × 15 3/4 in.)

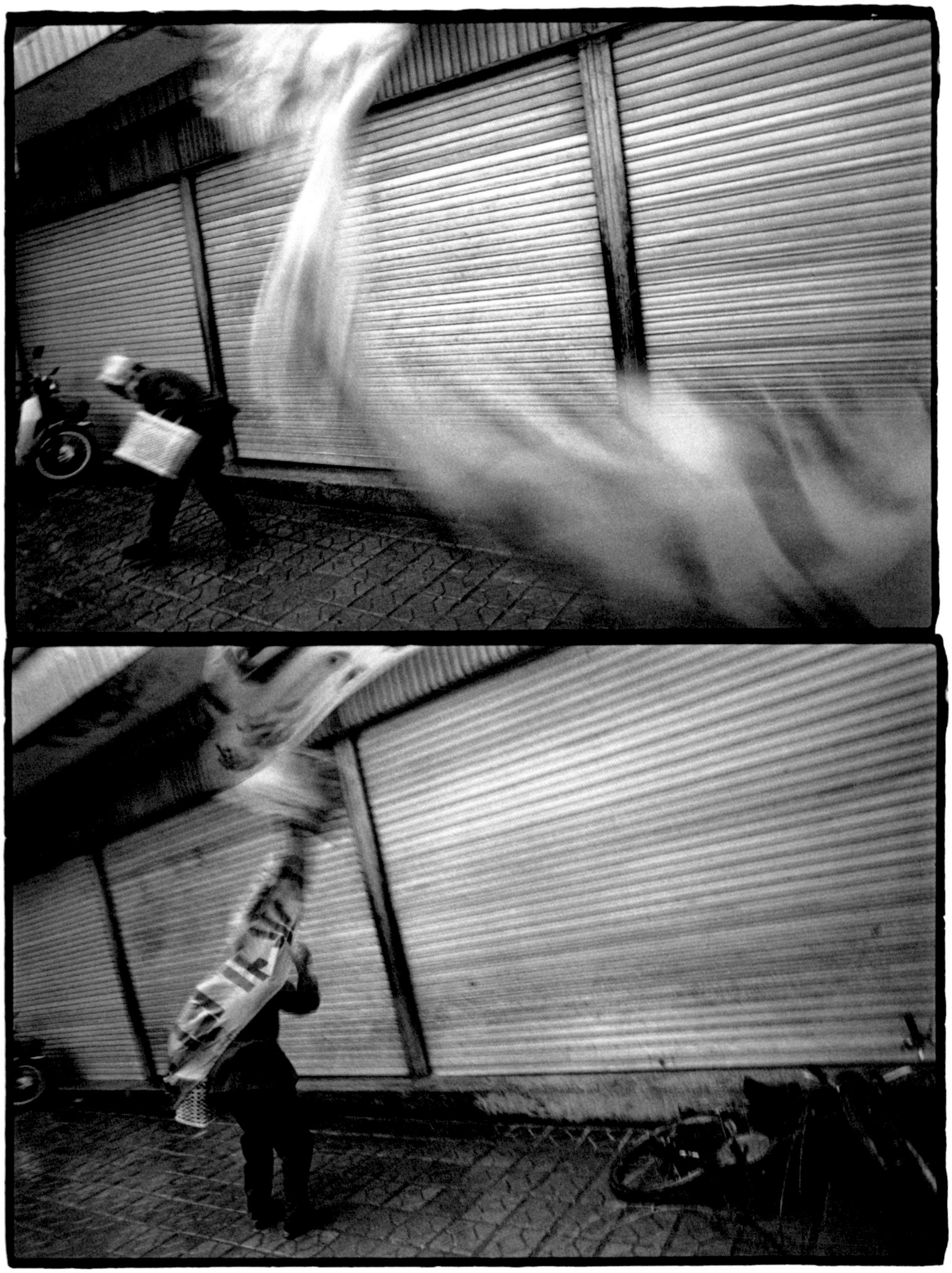

Fig. 40

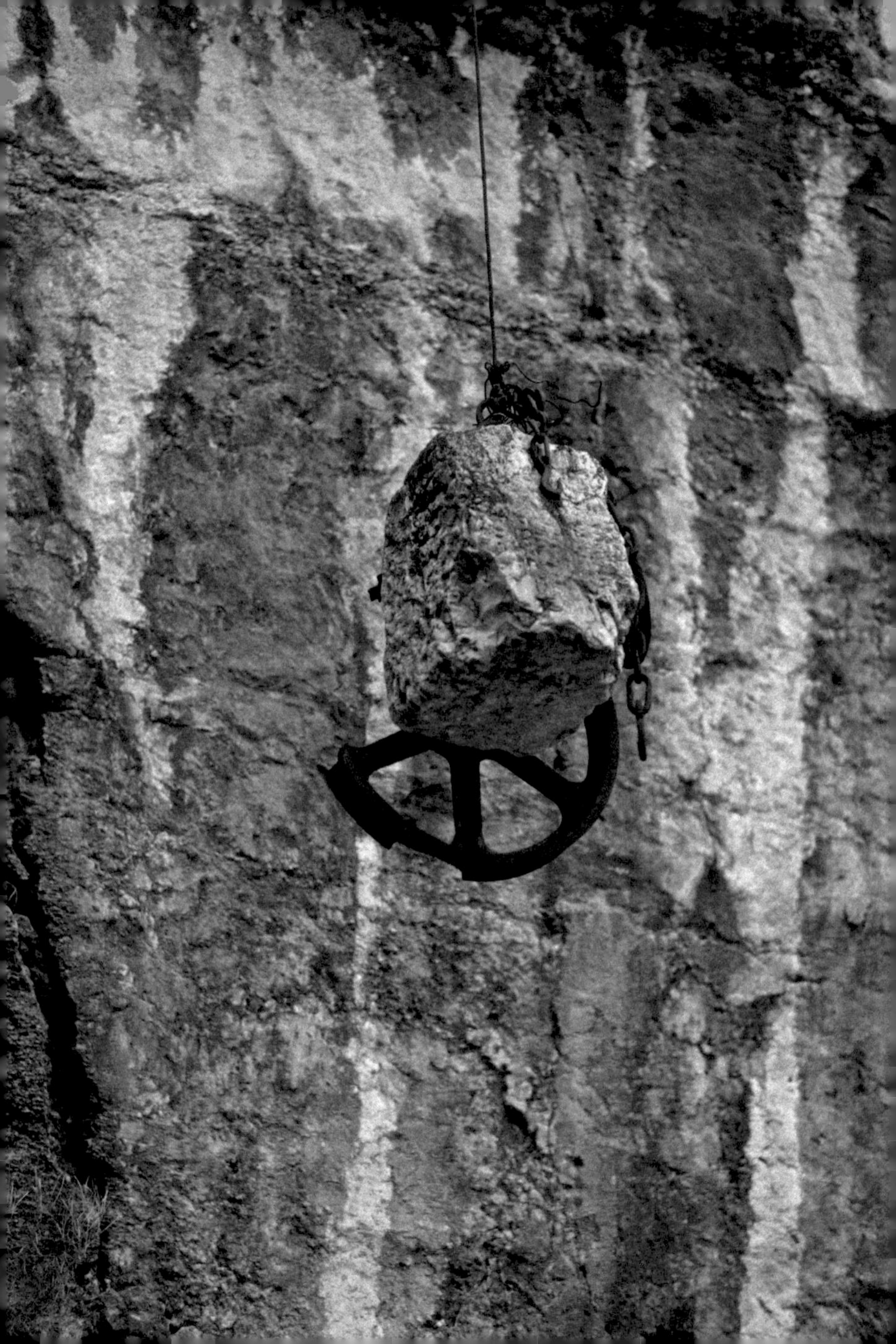

VI Duration

Daniel Schwartz's photographs are often about extended periods of time; but his comprehensive thematic long-term project about the disappearance of the glaciers was explicitly about immense periods of time condensed into the image. The complex reflection on duration and continuity, on the after-effects of the current event and beyond, constantly acts subliminally as a subtext, in the ruthless testimony of a cruel fact from an area of incendiary crisis as well as in images whose content seems superficially rather unencumbered.

An image from a hospital in Cambodia of a young man's leg amputated below the knee (plate 90): the horrific result of stepping accidentally on a landmine. The funeral of a child in Laos (plate 92), killed by unexploded submunitions from a cluster bomb dropped many years earlier in the Second Indochina War. We know the images from the daily news not only from Tigray, but from Ukraine, where again large areas of land will remain as deadly, mined terrain, and where again the disabled victims of war will be encountered in the coming years and decades. History does not stop, nor does it stop being written. An aerial photograph from a helicopter shows a cratered landscape thirty years after the Americans' secret, all-encompassing bombardment of Cambodia: the bomb craters were used as fish ponds after the war (plate 12). Another aspect of ongoing history.

A very early photograph by the young Daniel Schwartz, then a graduate of the Fotoklasse in Zürich, shows a motif from a long-abandoned eighteenth-century quarry above Solothurn (plate 88). More than four decades later, also close to home, he took an almost abstract picture of a waterfall (plate 102). It is said to be inspired by a depiction of the same waterfall by Caspar Wolf, the Swiss pioneer of mountain painting, painted exactly at the time that limestone was being extracted from that quarry in the 1770s for the construction of Solothurn's baroque cathedral. Caspar Wolf's pictures, created almost one hundred years before the first landscape photographs, are important testimonies to the dramatic changes in the Alpine region for scientists today. Similarly, Daniel Schwartz's glacier pictures will be read as testimony by scientists in the future.

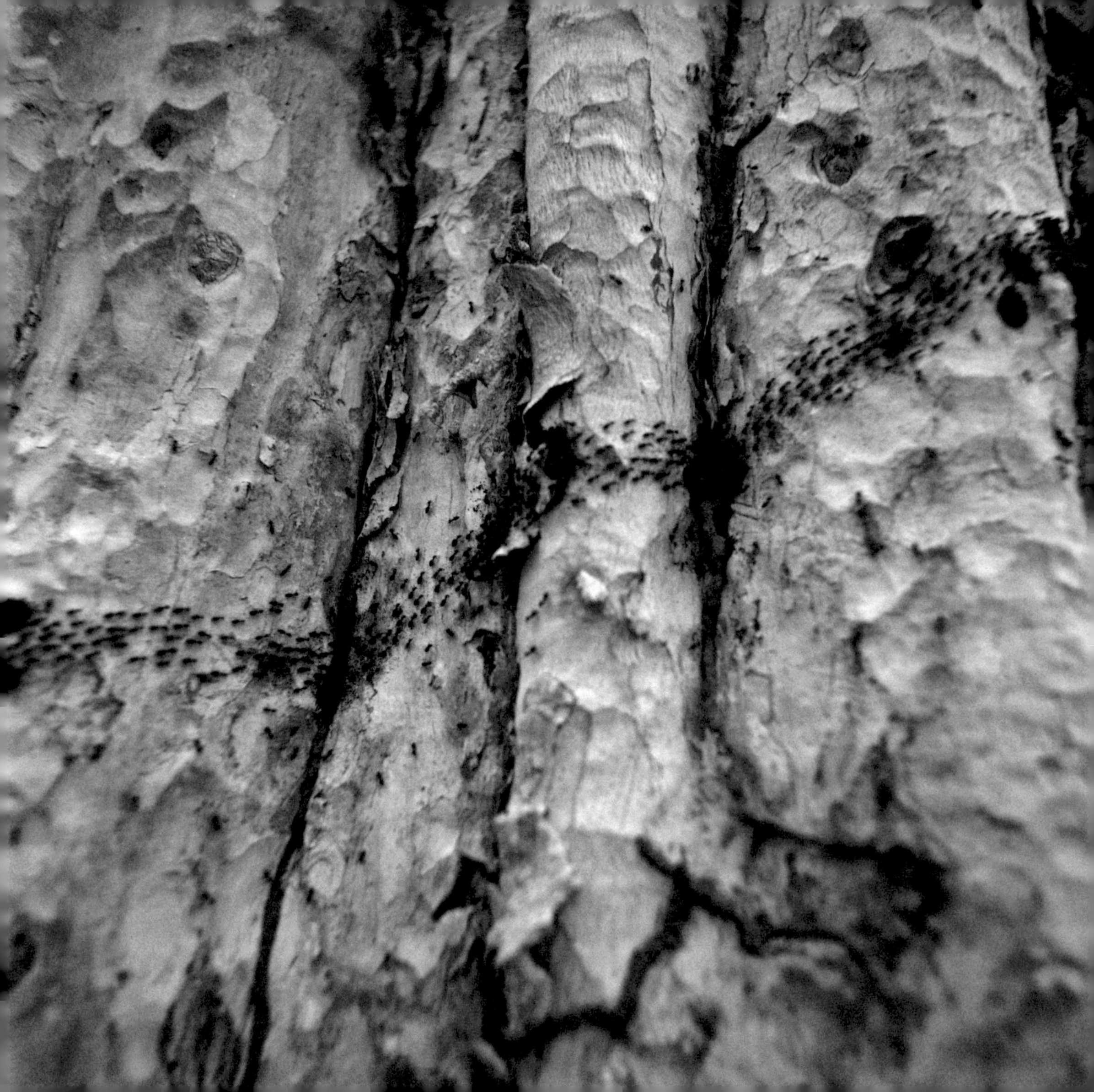

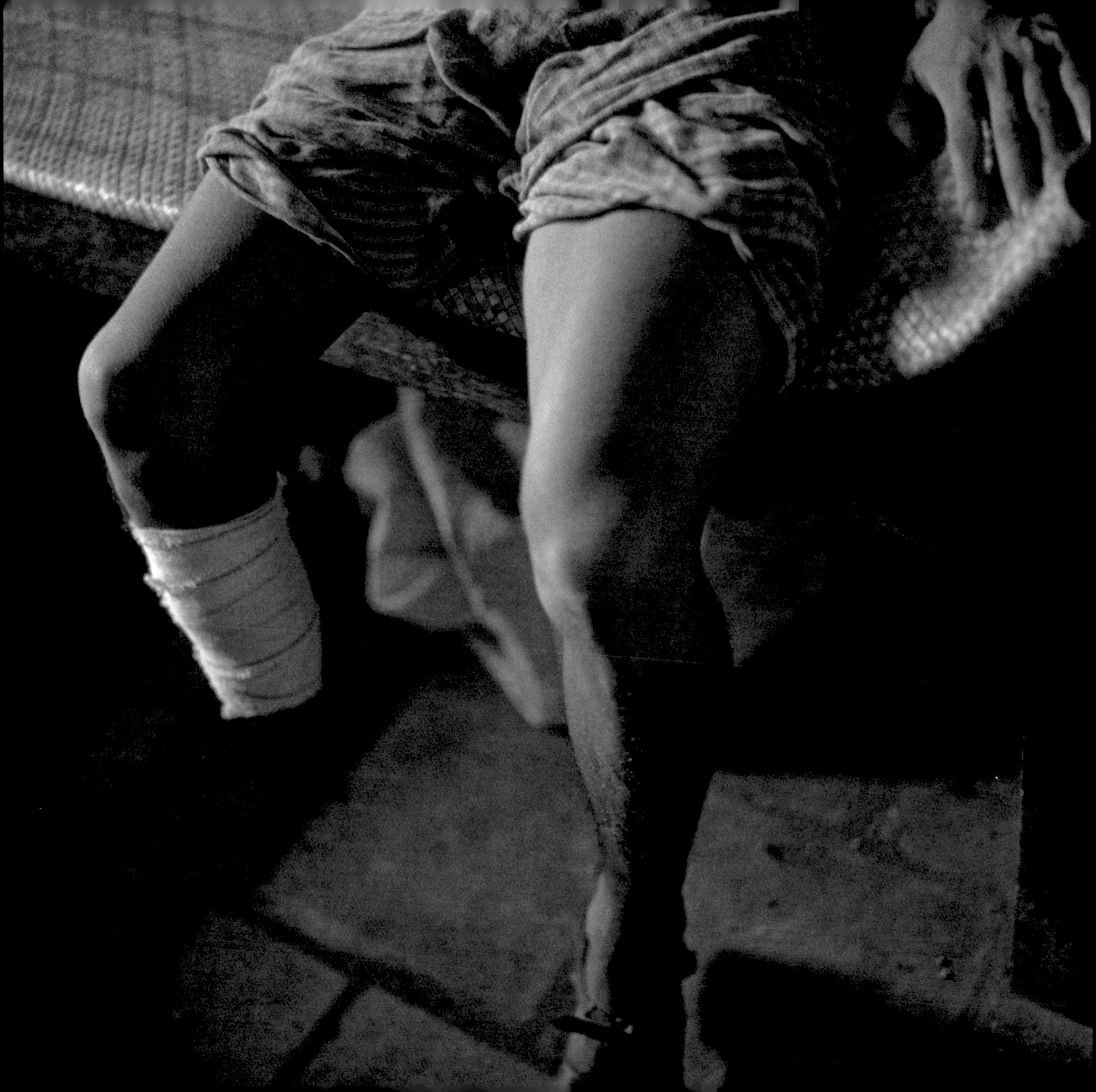

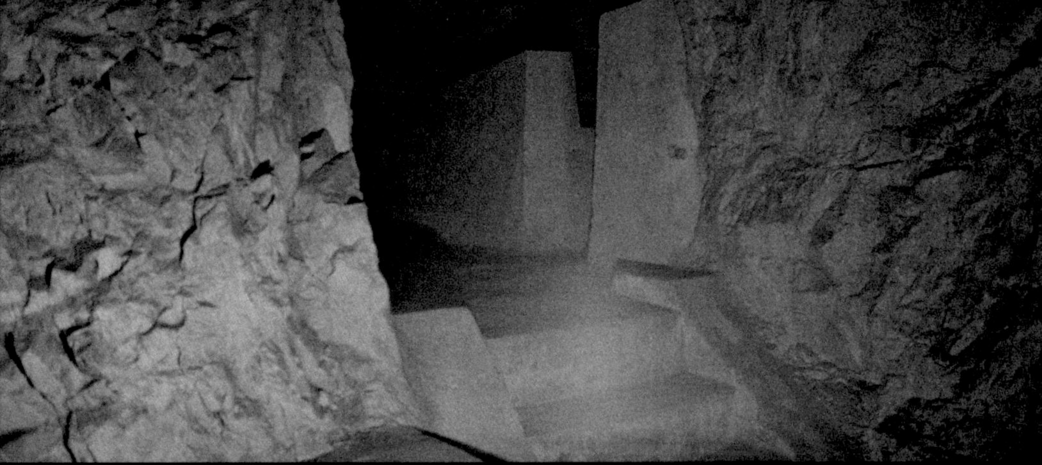
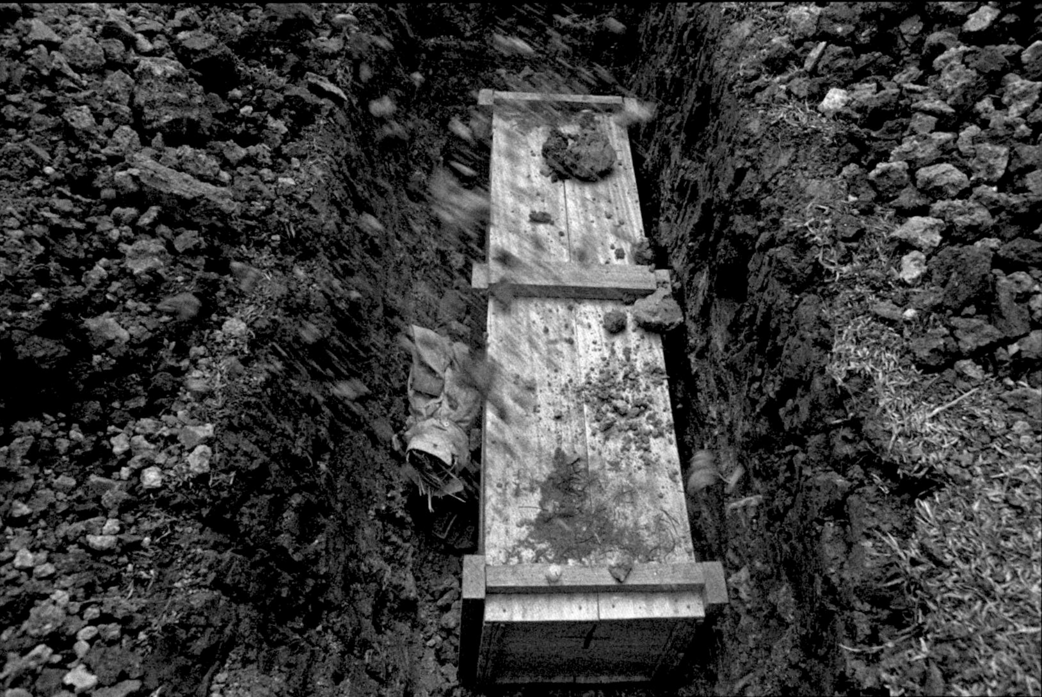

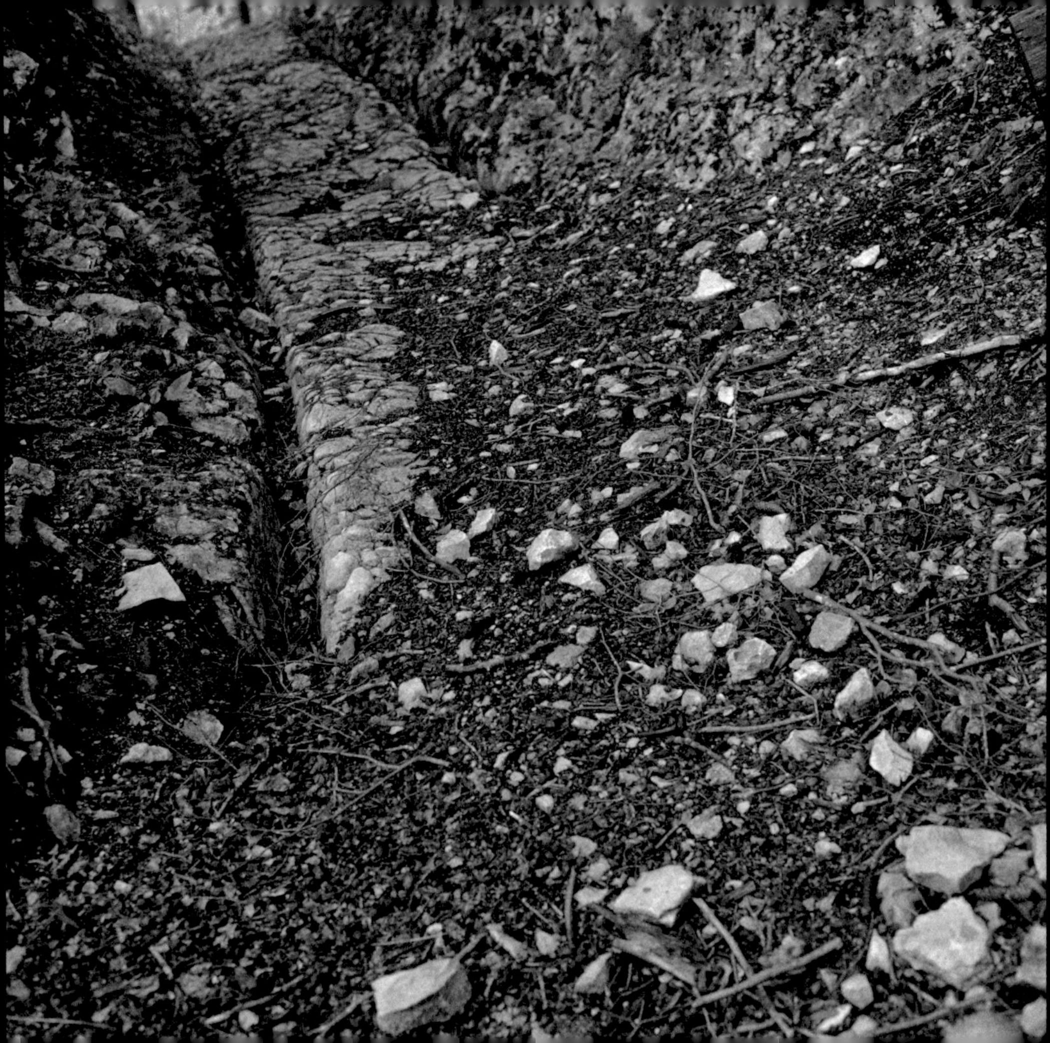

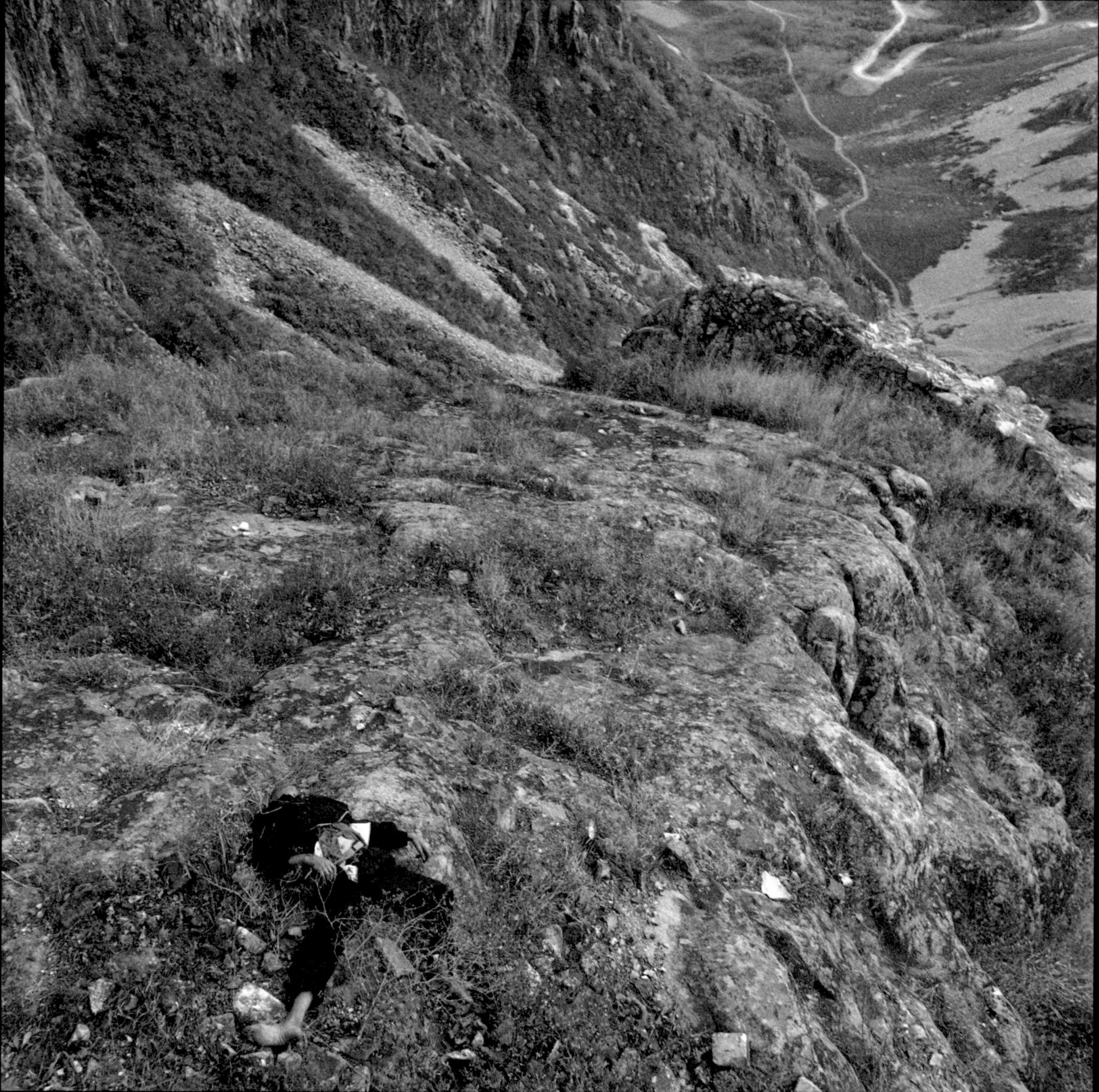

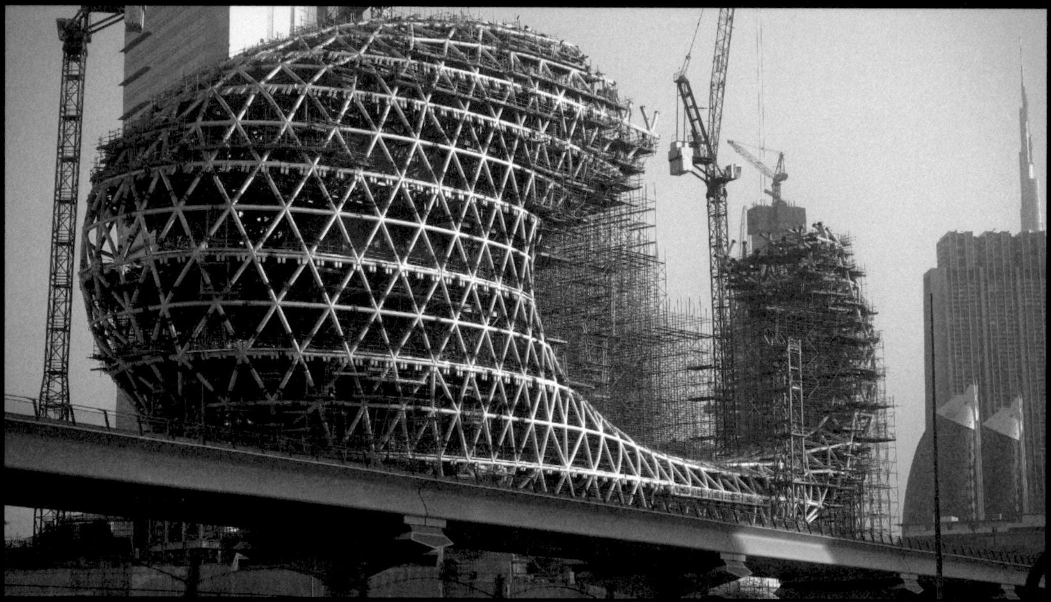

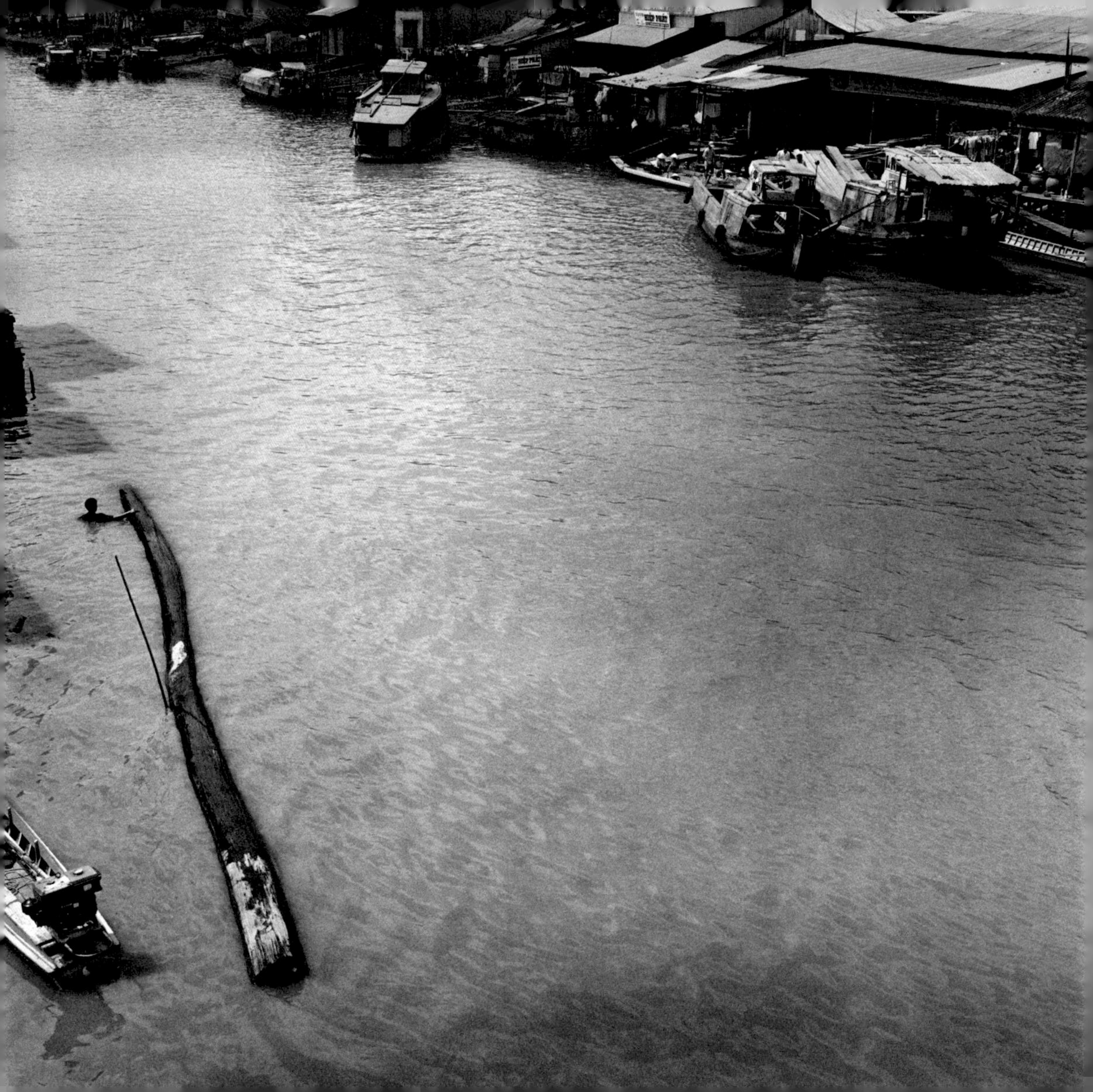

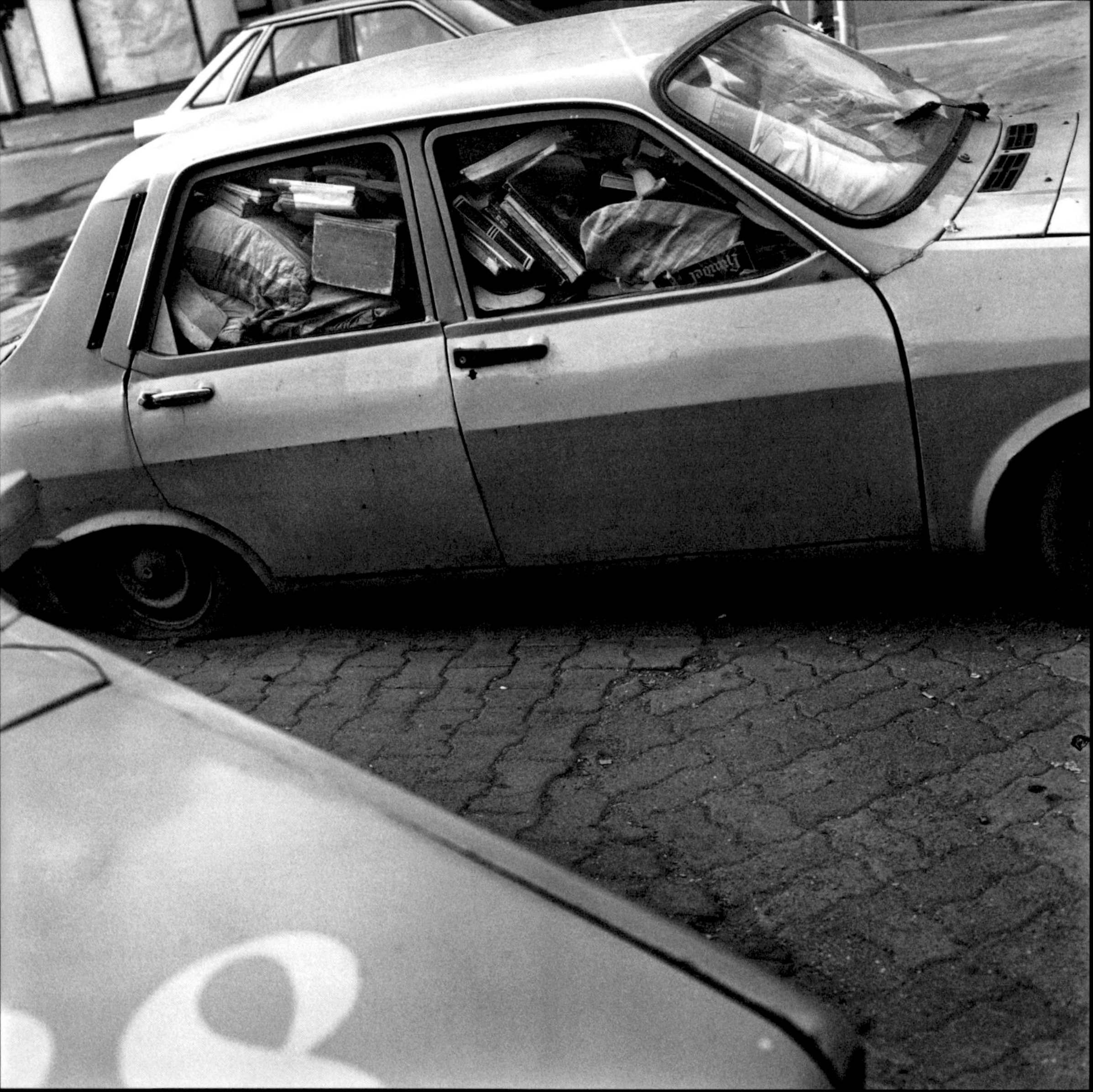

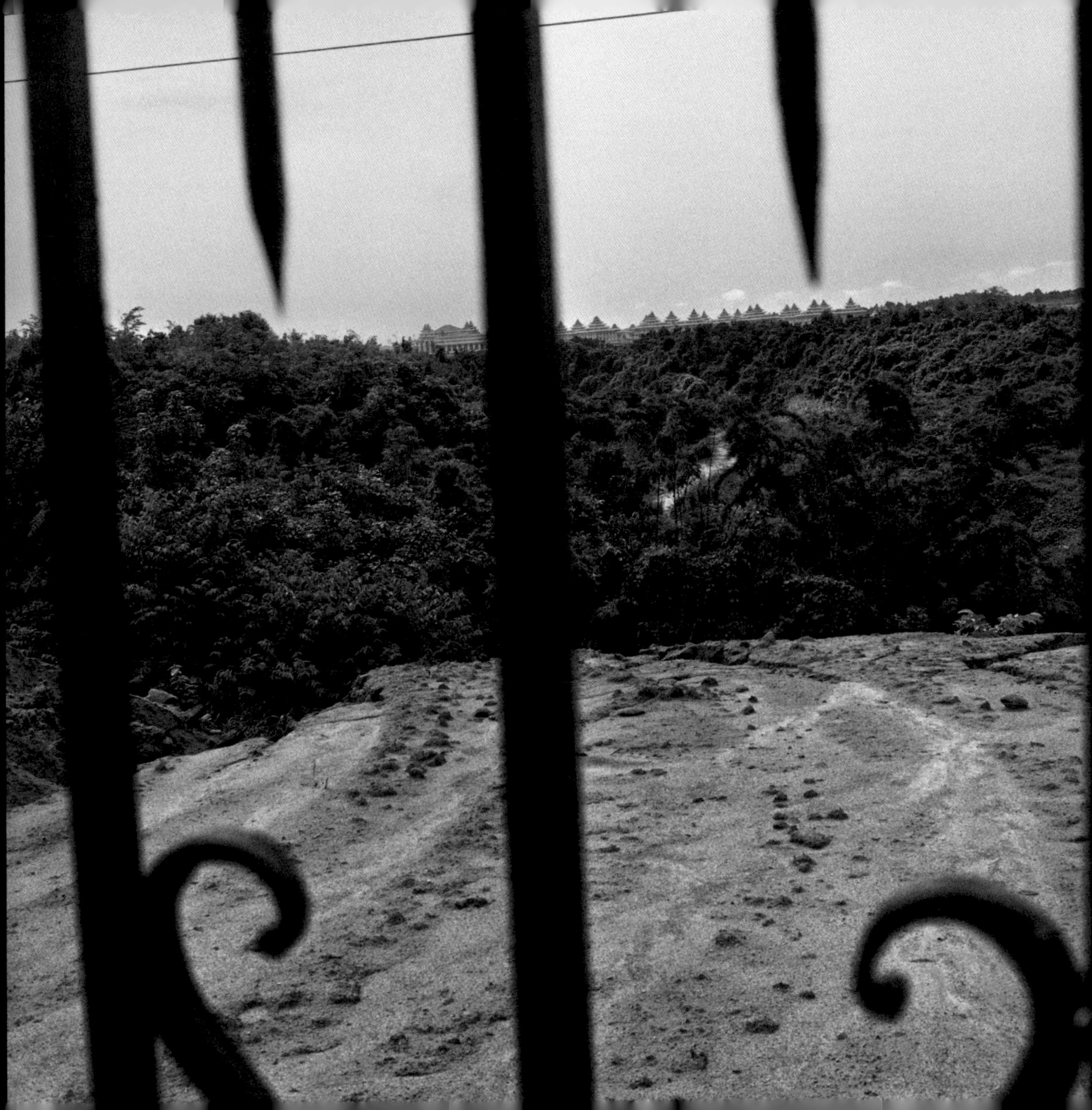

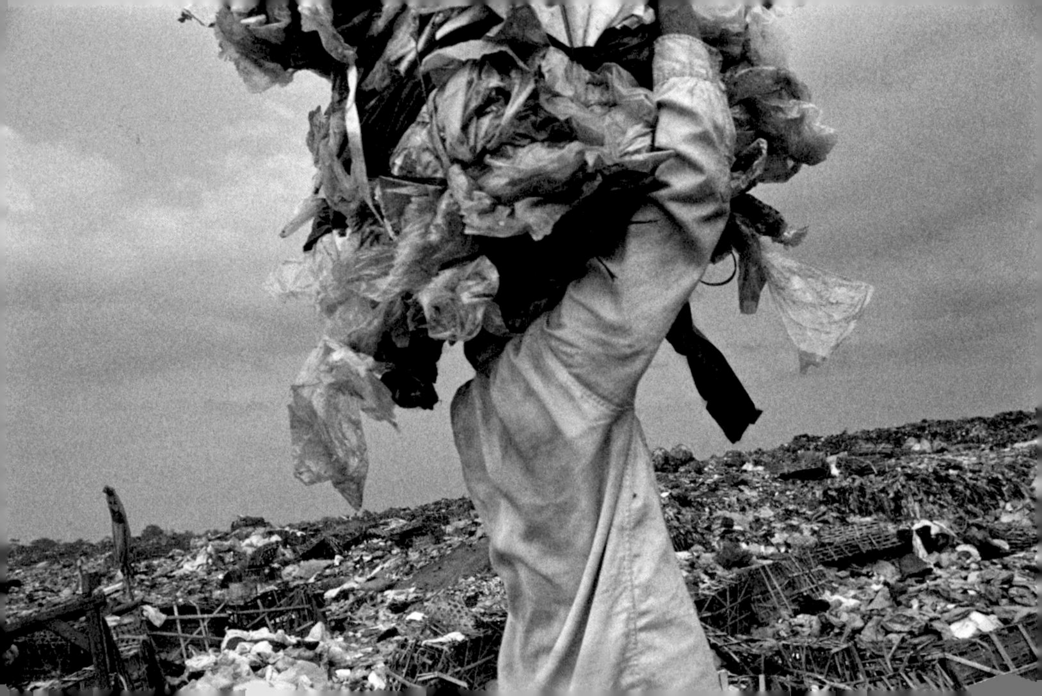

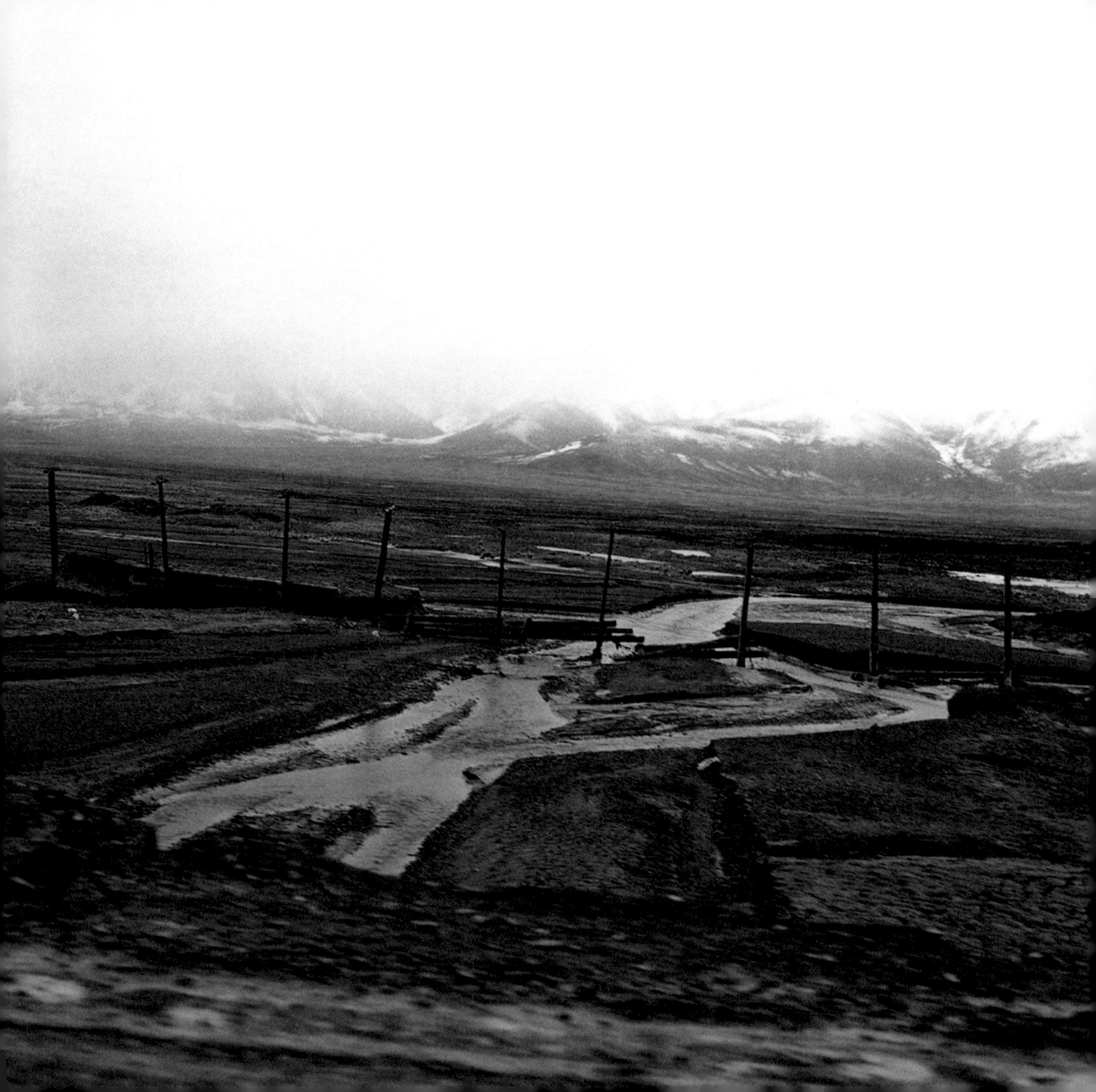

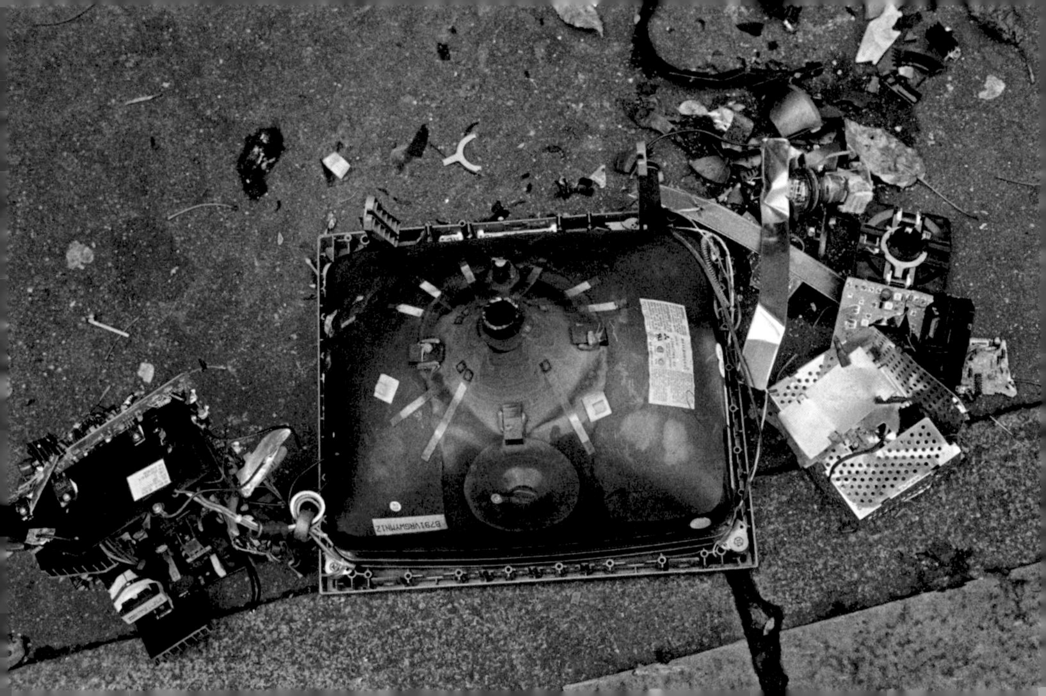

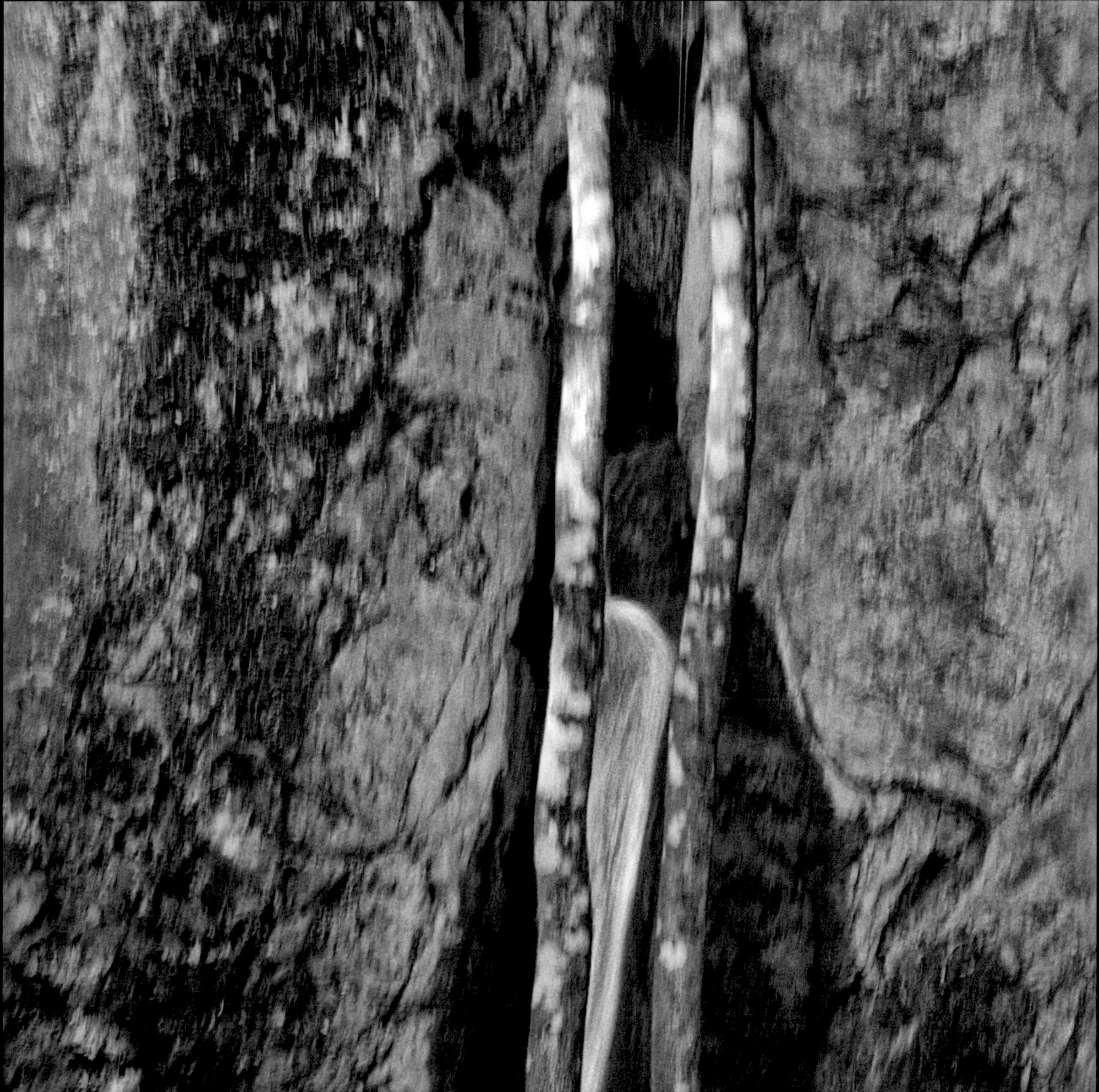

Preceding pages

Plate 88 – commentary on p. 178
Once quarrying had come to a halt
Rüttenen, Switzerland
14 October 1977

Plate 89
Ants on a Sra Lao (*Lagerstroemia calyculata*)
Angkor, Cambodia
2 January 1997

Plate 90
Landmine victim
District Hospital, Kompong Thom, Cambodia
12 November 1992

Plate 91 – commentary on p. 179
Blast wall
Headquarters of the Communist Pathet Lao
Vieng Xai limestone cave complex,
Hua Phan province, Laos
10 March 1996

Plate 92 – commentary on p. 179
Burial of a child killed by an unexploded
remnant of war
Ban Chomtong, Xiangkhouang province, Laos
8 March 1996

Plate 93
Wheel tracks of the Roman road
Langenbruck, Switzerland
22 June 2021

Plate 94 – commentary on p. 179
Dead man lying at the foot of the Great Wall
Sandaoguan, Hebei province, China
16 October 1987

Plate 95 – commentary on p. 179
The Museum of the Future
Dubai, United Arab Emirates
1 September 2018

Plate 96 – commentary on p. 179
River road
Mekong Delta, Vietnam
17 February 2001

Plate 97
Bucharest, Romania
8 June 2000

Plate 98 – commentary on p. 180
The Parliament
Nay Pyi Taw, Myanmar
30 September 2012

Plate 99 – commentary on p. 180
Scavenger on the Bantar Gebang dump
Bekasi, Java Barat province, Indonesia
14 November 1994

Plate 100
Crossing no-man's land, Torugart Pass, Tian Shan
Xinjiang Autonomous Region, China/
Naryn region, Kyrgyzstan
19 July 2004

Plate 101
Paris, France
18 November 2010

Plate 102 – commentary on p. 181
Siggern waterfall
Balm bei Günsberg, Switzerland
23 September 2021

Fig. 41

Lime escarpment covered by the Rosenlaui Glacier until the late 1980s. Glacially carved meltwater channels in the Rosenlaui gorge
Bernese Oberland, Switzerland
11 August 2014

Gelatin silver double-exposure print, 2019.
Sheet size 50 × 40 cm (19 ¾ × 15 ¾ in.)

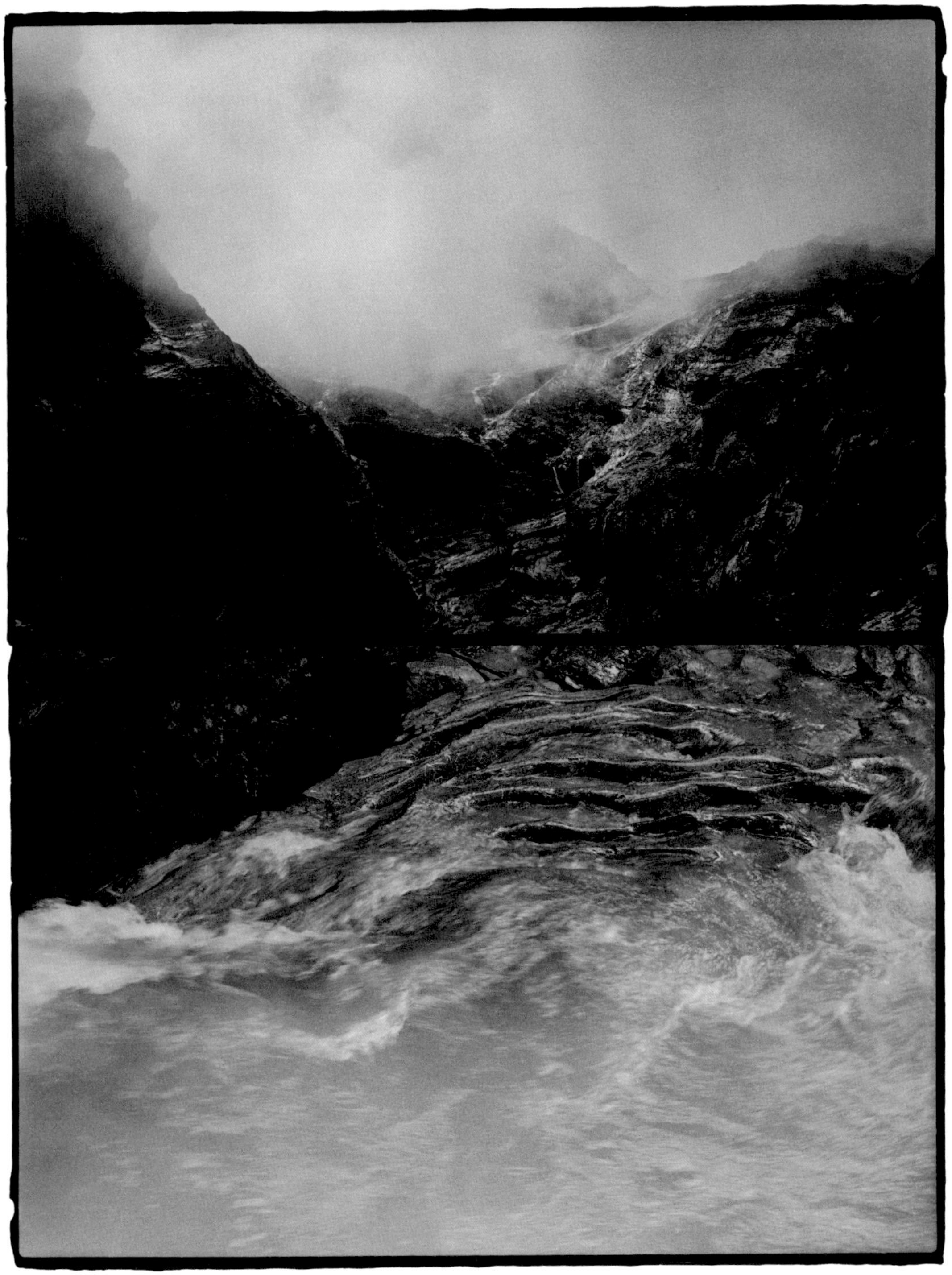

Fig. 41

Selected commentaries

Plate 6

The World Economic Forum was established in 1971 as a non-profit foundation, until 1987 named the European Management Forum. Its mission as the 'International Organization for Public–Private Cooperation', 'independent, impartial and not tied to any special interests', is to 'engage the foremost political, business, cultural and other leaders of society to shape global, regional and industry agendas': the Davos World. Its annual gathering in Davos, Switzerland transforms the Swiss Alpine resort into a fortress, which seems at odds with the WEF's belief that 'progress happens by bringing together people from all walks of life who have the drive and influence to make positive change'. The WEF's honesty of purpose is an issue to this day. Riot police in disproportional armour, even auxiliary forces from Austria, have not been the ideal way to meet those who wish to shed light on, for instance, societal issues affecting the global South, or the destructive forces of globalization. Blocking the valley's entrance has only led to escalation, exploited by others seeking excitement from the destruction of public property as far away as Zürich or Bern.

An uneasy feeling lingers when a WEF statement such as 'moral and intellectual integrity is at the heart of everything we do' is read against the list of invitees who have graced the annual gathering over the years. This feeling was present in 1990, the year the global banking and investing elite met those who claimed to dismantle the old administrative economies, and in 2002, when the 'Spirit of Davos' resided in New York in solidarity with the wounded city on the Hudson, a decision that former mayor Rudolph Giuliani saw as a message that 'New York is back in business'. It was there in 2003, when President George W. Bush's no-show in Davos was a consequence of his imminent, premeditated war against Saddam Hussein, as well as in 2012, the year that Myanmar's generals pitched themselves as champions of democracy. Today's humanitarian crisis in Europe and the unprecedented financial and economic penalties against Russia are viewed as a watershed by the WEF, as its website (as of 14 December 2022) emphasizes 'Better Business' – a notion as noncommittal as it is unfathomable.

Plate 11

The break-up of the Socialist Federal Republic of Yugoslavia during the early 1990s led to separate though related ethnic conflicts affecting the former constituent republics of Slovenia, Croatia, Bosnia and Herzegovina, Kosovo and North Macedonia. The break-up of the former Yugoslavia figures prominently in *Le Monde "Ex": Confessions* by Predrag Matvejević (1932–2017), as the author spends his years of emigration travelling from the Mediterranean through post-Communist Europe.

Plate 12

Seen from one of the ex-USSR Russian Air Force MI17 helicopters serving UNTAC (United Nations Transitional Authority in Cambodia, 1992–93, then the UN's largest peacekeeping operation) are craters resulting from President Nixon and his security adviser Henry Kissinger's attempted destruction by carpet bombing of North Vietnamese installations and sanctuaries in southern Cambodia. In 2000, twenty-five years after the end of the Second Indochina War, a still-incomplete database revealed that from 4 October 1965 to 15 August 1973, during what became to be known as the 'sideshow'[1] to America's war in Vietnam, 2,756,941 tonnes worth of ordnance was dropped against a supposedly heterogeneous insurgency.

Plate 15

After the defeat in December 1978 of the Khmer Rouge by Vietnamese forces, who had invaded Kampuchea in retaliation against border-region assaults, Pailin became the stronghold of the China-backed Communists and, in the mid-1990s, the capital of the breakaway faction led by Ieng Sary, one of the three leaders accused and convicted of genocide and war crimes before the Extraordinary Chambers in the Court of Cambodia (ECCC). Pailin is rich in natural resources, particularly gemstones. Ruby miners there are prone to fall ill with malaria and to be injured or killed by landmines.

Plate 16

The Taliban came to the world's attention in the 1990s in part because of the geostrategic implications of their rise and expansion. American and Brazilian oil companies negotiated with them in an effort to secure a safe pipeline corridor through embattled Afghanistan. Then came 9/11. The prize, however, remained the same: access to Central Asian oil and gas fields and transit routes for pipelines. In the twenty-first century, Kazakhstan (in 2019 the producer of an all-time high of 1,587.252 barrels per day average) had become the heart of a so-called New Great Game for oil in Central Asia. The fields and pipelines that the republic had inherited from the Soviet Union, developed by Canadian and German companies, soon changed ownership. Russia tried hard not to lose its primacy as a supplier of Europe and America to China, the aggressive new player, which operates in the Tarim oil fields in Xinjiang and began building pipelines to both Kazakhstan and Turkmenistan in the early 1990s.

Azerbaijan, whose capital Baku had been the centre of an epic quest for oil, money and power between Standard Oil, Nobel, Rothschild and Shell in the last decade of the nineteenth century, combined its on- and offshore drilling with naval ambitions. Its position on the Caspian Sea allowed it to transport oil straight to Europe and Scandinavia from the Kazakh steppes, bypassing Russia. The 'Georgia corridor' is an incredibly complicated route that involves detours, tanker trucks, tank cars, supertankers, pipelines and an often-stormy sea. By 2010, such geographical and logistical factors, as well as political turmoil in eastern Turkey and West Asia, had led to the construction of the Baltic Nord Stream 1 pipeline, aimed at pumping Siberian gas to Germany. A controversial project, the direct link between the Russian and Western European networks circumvented traditional overland routes through Ukraine, Belarus and Poland, which are often beset with payment disputes and vulnerable to sabotage. Incidents of the latter in 2022 – only months after the completion in September 2021 of Nord Stream 2, financed by Gazprom and several European energy companies – would remove any remaining doubts that Europe's critical dependence on Siberian fossil fuel and the long-lasting politics of appeasement towards Moscow, propagated especially by Germany, had been a devil's pact. Long before the Russian invasion of Ukraine in February 2022, the perception that the two Baltic pipelines would ensure the long-term security of Europe's supplies had been exposed as a chimera. Nord Stream 2 had been conceived by Vladimir Putin as a geopolitical tool to strengthen political and military pressure over Ukraine without endangering Moscow's gas business with the EU.

Plate 18

After the conquest of Constantinople in 1453, a decree removed the ancient tanneries and the slaughterhouses to Kazlıçeşme, a location outside the Theodosian Wall near the Golden Gate. They remained there until 1993, when the poisonous leatherware industry was moved to an industrial zone on the Asian side of the Bosphorus and the maze of buildings was demolished.

Plate 30

The infrared and colour video cameras mounted in American helium balloons were supposed to detect black-market trade in Allied forces' fuel, but they could not see members of the armed resistance or terrorist organizations infiltrating Afghanistan's capital. The population feared that the 'eyes of the immoral foreigners' were spying on women and children sleeping on the rooftops of their homes.

Plate 33

In the run-up to the plebiscite in 1999 that brought the independence of East Timor from Indonesia, attacks by pro-integration militias, operating under the eye of the Indonesian Armed Forces, sought to intimidate and kill inhabitants of pro-independence neighbourhoods in East Timor's capital, Dili. The bloodbath, looting and what appears to have been a planned campaign of destruction killed hundreds and drove some 300,000 people to flee to West Timor before an Australia-led UN force managed to halt the chaos.

The tragedy that came along with the democratic transition and the birth of the world's youngest nation shed light on the events that had been determining factors. For decades, East Timor, impossible to reach for outsiders, was marked by the hidden horrors of the genocide committed under General Suharto's regime. In April 1974, the Carnation Revolution had brought the collapse of the Portuguese fascist regime and the dissolution of Lisbon's colonial empire. On the island in the Indonesian archipelago, the vacuum was filled by the leftist movement FRETILIN (Revolutionary Front for an Independent East Timor), with a strong popular base in the Catholic Church. Indonesia's ensuing infiltration of its regular units was the beginning of an expansionist policy of attrition and subversion on Timor. One-sixth of East Timor's population, 100,000 people, are said to have perished during the resistance to the illegal proclamation of their homeland as a part of Indonesia. The figure is an understatement. In the years since the full-scale invasion on 7 December 1975, which was launched from the western half of Timor – Suharto had the full approval of US President Ford and his Secretary of State, Henry Kissinger, who had met Junta members that same day – tens of thousands more died conflict- and abuse-related deaths, as well as from hunger and illness.

Plate 36

Tokai, a street urchin aged about eight, is a Bangladeshi cartoon character who has become a popular outlet for people's feelings about their country's political and socio-economic conditions. His name has become a colloquial synonym for street children, who often find themselves trapped in the vicious cycle of pilferage, the sex trade and the crime world.

Plate 38

The collapse of the ruble was one of the consequences of a financial crisis that had begun in Thailand, Indonesia and South Korea, and exposed what was behind the myth of the 'Asian Tiger': unreliable legal systems, inadequate bank regulation and supervision, lack of corporate transparency and widespread corruption and cronyism. As the crisis spread globally, it engulfed Eastern European markets, alarming the stock markets of the Western capitals of capital. There was fear that the emerging markets' collapse could lead to a deep worldwide recession. The notion that global market capitalism was in retreat undermined the vision that this same global market capitalism would secure worldwide prosperity and, ultimately, democracy. Twenty years later, the Covid-19 pandemic and Moscow's war on Ukraine would expose the profound structural deficits of globalization as well as the West's fossil-fuel dependence upon Russia.

Plate 39

The old Caucasian nation of Georgia arose out of kingdoms both ancient and medieval. The Early Modern period saw it struggle to maintain autonomy against Ottoman and Persian domination, a status it at last gained as a constituent republic of the Union of Soviet Socialist Republics, though only after being annexed by the Russian Soviet Federative Socialist Republic in 1921 (and before it by the Russian Empire in 1801). This journey took place at the time that the country renamed itself the Republic of Georgia and declared its sovereignty over Soviet law (which it did on 15 November 1990; on 31 March 1991 it formally declared its independence from the Soviet Union, which would itself be dissolved on 26 December 1991) – a time of uncertainty. Near Sukhumi, the photographer's driver, a Georgian from Tbilisi, had argued with drunken Abkhaz, and when about to break away they tried to set light to the car. Two years later, a war broke out between Abkhaz separatists and Georgian government forces.

Plate 44

Gümüşhane (in Greek, Argyroupolis) was the capital city of the historic province of Chaldia. The name refers to the silver that was first discovered there in around 700 BCE by Ionian Greeks, who established the city as the settlement of Thyra. In Byzantine times, the region was ruled by the Byzantine's last refuge of Trebizond, which fell in 1461. Under Ottoman rule, Argyroupolitans, among other Pontic Graecophones, superficially adopted Turkic Islam but remained crypto-Christian in private. Income from mining and riches extracted from the churches led to the foundation of educational institutions. During the Russo-Turkish war (1829–30) many Greeks collaborated with or welcomed the Russian army and joined its withdrawal to Georgia. After the Ottoman Greek Genocide (1914–23) and the forcible exchange of populations between Greece and Turkey in 1923, no Greek Orthodox population remained in the region.

Plate 46

Roughly 2 million Kurds were displaced after the suppression by Saddam Hussein's loyalist forces of ethnic and religious uprisings following the ceasefire at the end of the (Persian) Gulf War (1990–91). Iran and Turkey only reluctantly allowed the refugees to cross the mountainous borders.

Plate 47

Shortly after the collapse of the ruble, a consequence of the financial and capital crisis that began in East Asia in August 1997 and spread globally, the scariest repercussion of all was the fall of Wall Street in the early days of September 1998. The question became how long the European and American economies, cornerstones of the global economy, could remain immune to the turmoil. A dispute emerged over the increasing interest being shown by politicians and economists in market intervention and capital controls as the right solution to the crisis. During the 1998 crisis it became evident that global capitalism, with its deregulation of trade and free capital flows, had destabilized the economies of poor countries and inflicted large losses on investors in rich countries. Some had suffered more than others.

'Dynamic markets periodically engender large defaults', said Alan Greenspan, Chairman of the Federal Reserve Board, in his testimony before the Committee on Banking and Financial Services, US House of Representatives, on 1 October 1998, in which he reported on the private sector refinancing of the large hedge fund Long-Term Capital Management, and continued: 'Officials of the Federal Reserve Bank of New York facilitated discussions in which the private parties arrived at an agreement that both served their mutual self-interest and avoided possible serious market dislocations. Financial market participants were already unsettled by recent global events. Had the failure of LTCM triggered the seizing up of markets, substantial damage could have been inflicted on many market participants, including some not directly involved with the firm, and could have potentially impaired the economies of many nations, including our own.'

Plate 49

Glaciers didn't figure at all during the twenty years of failed peace-enforcing and attempts at nation-building in Afghanistan by the international community after 9/11. Fighting increasingly took place outside the traditional climatic season – a sign that factors driven by climate change might have contributed to the precarious situation in the drought-prone Hindu Kush, where glaciers are a source of the water needed for irrigation, meaning that their retreat and fluctuations have implications for the rebuilding effort and, most notably, for food security. Glaciers have indirectly become a variable in the course of war. Here, armed men sit on a glacier table. The boulder is perched on a pedestal of ice and protects the ice from ablation (melting) during sunny weather. Around the boulder, the ice ablates and its surface is lowered, whereas the boulder itself remains at the original level. As the pedestal becomes higher and higher in relation to the surface of the glacier, the sun shines further under the boulder from the south (in the northern hemisphere). The greater ablation on the southern side will eventually cause the boulder to fall off the pedestal. After this, a new cycle of table growth and destruction may begin. From a regional perspective, the photograph foreshadows the prospect of further war over a finite resource: water. Redolent of nineteenth-century images of tourism in the Alps, it is also a metaphor. The 'Glacier Walk in Times of War', an exploration of the glaciers of Mir Samir (5809 MASL), situated on the border of the Panjshir Valley and Nuristan, was inspired by Eric Newby's classic *A Short Walk in the Hindu Kush* (1958); it took place sixty years after its first publication and against the background of the ongoing war.

Plate 54

There is a historical Swati belief that smashing statues will bring the thrower rewards; to preserve or sell them is a sin.[2] In the eleventh century the Islamic Ghaznavid dynasty rule brought under their control ancient Gandhara, the birthplace of Buddhist art of Indo-Greek origin, which largely flourished during the Kushan dynasty (1st century BCE–7th century CE) in what is today eastern Afghanistan and northwestern Pakistan, including Swat, a district that between 2007 and 2009 was controlled by the Tehrik-i-Taliban.

Plate 55

What was the source of the money that financed the Parthenon and Athens's navy? Who extracted, crushed and melted the silver ore providing the material for the drachm (standardized at 4.32 grams) and the tetradrachm with Athena and her owl (17.28 grams of silver) – the global currency that had a democratizing effect on the city state of Athens in the sixth and fifth centuries BCE, that under Alexander was minted even in Egypt, and that circulated as far as Bactria and Britain? The answers are to be found in the Lavreotiki area at the southeastern tip of Attica, in the hinterland of Cape Sounion. There, systematic exploitation began as the Neolithic gave way to the Bronze Age and the Cycladic, Minoan and Mycenaen civilizations had to be supplied with silver, lead and copper. In this ancient industrial landscape of mining and metallurgy, with roads and trails, galleries and shafts, cisterns and tanks, washing plants that used the difference in gravity to separate heavy ore from lighter rock, as well as kilns, workshops and living quarters for tens of thousands of slaves, lies the ancient quarry where the columns of the Temple of Poseidon at Sounion were cut. On one of them an oversized signature is to be found: Byron. The hero of the Greek war of liberation from Turkey had stayed in Athens in 1810–11, but if the graffiti is indeed by his own hand, he would not have been the first to commemorate a visit to the promontory.

Plate 56

An estimated 132,000 people vanished in the cyclone of 29–30 April 1991 in Bangladesh. Most were swept to the Bay of Bengal. Only 75,528 bodies were reported to have been buried by teams of volunteers. Nearly half a million people were injured. In the following decades, cyclones have caused fewer deaths due to improved adaptation strategies combined with the use of satellite imagery. The global climate crisis, however, affects both the severity of tropical storms and their path, and thus the locations where they hit the land increasingly differ. In Bangladesh, the Sundarbans mangrove belt acts as a natural wall against storms and cyclones, salinity intrusion, tidal surge, sea-level rise and other natural hazards.

Plate 57

Ice loss from Swiss Alpine glaciers in 2021 amounted to 3.1 cubic kilometres, 6 per cent of their volume, and surpassed the 2003 summer record of 2.9 cubic kilometres; three minor glaciers vanished altogether. As glaciers split up, their number increases but so does their vulnerabilty. Five factors contributed to the record loss: a winter with little snowfall, Saharan dust in spring colouring the ice and reducing its albedo radiation, a heatwave in May, dry summer months and only a few centimetres of snow until mid-September. A consequence of this continuing, climate crisis-induced trend is the movement of the equilibrium line that marks the altitude of the boundary between a glacier's zones of accumulation and of ablation. The equilibrium line altitude (ELA) is the elevation at which the net accumulation in a given year is zero. When annual snow and ice accumulation exceeds the loss by melting and other processes such as the calving of icebergs, the glacier has a positive mass balance and increases in mass. When the snow and ice loss exceeds the mass gain, the glacier has a negative mass balance. Generally the head part of the glacier, the accumulation area, has a net gain, and the lower part of the glacier, the ablation area, has a net loss. The state of health of a glacier can be defined by its mass balance.

Towards the end of the Little Ice Age, around 1850, Alpine glaciers threatened pastures and settlements, and religious processions sought to stop their advance. In the twenty-first century the Pope in Rome was asked to give permission to the community of Fiesch, in the Valais canton, to reverse these petitions. Tales circulate in the Matter Valley that once upon a time there was no Findel Glacier at all, that it emerged from the Strahlhorn and overran the forest of larches, the trunks and rhizomes of which can now, as the ice retreats, be found in the moraines left behind. Unstable as they become, they are occasionally sliced by mudslides originating from higher altitudes due to thawing permafrost. As the cryosphere continues to collapse unabated, science, religion and circulating popular belief increasingly converge. Once, lamenting souls and the peening of scythes of those who ventured beyond cornerstones were said to have been heard during very silent days under the ice.[3] Today, entire sets of bones together with pieces of equipment found on glaciers help the understanding of glacial movements and allow mortal remains to be laid to rest, many decades after the missing were last seen.

Figs 3, 26 and 27
In 2001, as Afghanistan endured its worst drought in thirty years, 4 million people were forced to leave their homes in Badghis province. The cumulative effect of three rainless years, the extreme cold of the previous winter and the war in the northeast had made a humanitarian disaster inevitable. With its refusal to extradite Osama bin Laden, the Taliban had effectively sealed the Emirate of Afghanistan's isolation. One consequence of the unilateral UN sanctions against Afghanistan was the ban on Ariana flights, which in turn affected the transport of relief goods and desperately needed medical supplies. While the sanctions forbade members of the international community, the EU and ASEAN from providing any economic or military help at all, the Northern Alliance, the Taliban's opponent, continued to enjoy the support of Russia and Iran. In Herat, a transit camp for displaced people was located in the vicinity of the last minarets of the Musalla Complex, designed and built under Queen Gawhar Shad's long tenure (1405–1447) during the Timurid Renaissance, after the capital of the empire had been moved from Samarkand. From there people were moved to Mashlak camp, in the desert outside Herat. Contrary to their normal policy, the Taliban leadership allowed photographs of people, in distress and dying, to give the drought a face. At a time when international media interest was focused on the destruction of the Bamiyan Buddhas, the answer to the question posed by Wakil Ahmed Mutawakil, then the Taliban's Foreign Minister, as to why the West cares more for stones than for humans, was not an easy one. The infamy of the Taliban was evident, as was the indifference of the international donor community towards the WFP and ICRC's predictions that a famine was imminent.

Fig. 13
A general assumption is that wars – not hybrid wars, but wars by land, air and sea – are decided in battle. But since the design and manufacturing of the Colt Single Action Army handgun (a.k.a. the Peacemaker), which from 1873 to 1892 was the standard-issue pistol of the US Army, wars are won in factories, including insurgent wars, where the indestructible and reliable AK-47, deliberately not protected by a patent until 1997, was and still is the weapon of choice. The party that produces more would eventually win over its adversary. Industrial mass-production of weapons and ammunition was the signature of the First World War. The nature of the 'War to end all Wars' was shaped by industrialization and technology – aviation, motorized transport and modern weapons such as machine guns and artillery, battleship guns, submarines and zeppelins, which launched the first strategic bombing campaigns. As it became a war of attrition, it was hoped that the stalemate of trench warfare would be broken by introducing the world's first tank, the British Mark I, into combat in August 1916. A tracked and armoured vehicle, it crawled across the burnt and churned dystopian landscape of Flanders Fields at a speed of 4 mph, crushing barbed wire fences and hedgerows alike. Because ground affects military operation, armed conflicts cannot be kind towards nature. The influence of geography, per Carl von Clausewitz (*On War*, 1832), is 'always active', in degrees varying 'according to the nature of the country'. Because this influence is always felt, nature must be overcome 'as an obstacle to the approaches, as an impediment to visibility, and as a cover from fire'.

Figs 20 and 21
The withdrawal of Vietnamese forces in September 1989 ended Vietnam's ten-year commitment to Kampuchea (renamed Cambodia in April of that year) and paved the way for the Paris Agreements on Cambodia, which established the United Nations Transitional Authority in Cambodia (UNTAC), of 1992–93. The UN's largest peacekeeping operation to date combined the repatriation of the Khmer refugees, disarming the warring parties, de-mining the country and establishing a peaceful environment for the 1993 elections, but many returnees soon found themselves on allocated land that was still heavily mined, or were again displaced by fighting.

Fig. 23
Each dry season during the military regime of the State Law and Order Restoration Council (SLORC), which assumed direct power in Burma in 1988 and subsequently renamed the country Myanmar, ethnic minority populations' struggle for autonomy in the border regions intensified, as did the campaigns of the Tatmadaw, the Burmese Armed Forces. After the military coup of 1 February 2021, young citizens whose pro-democracy demonstrations were met with brutal force began to seek refuge in the jungle, joining the various insurgent armies as their parents had done thirty years before.

Fig. 31

While waiting in a hotel room for the next interrogation by the County Public Security Bureau, tracing the trajectory of the Great Wall across the Ordos on Operational Navigation Chart sheet ONC G-9 (1:1.000.000, prepared by the Defense Mapping Agency Aerospace Center, USA) was the only escape from boredom and incertitude in the face of the authorities' arbitrariness. It also served to plot tactical side trips in case of detours enforced by the security authorities, or ways to make good the hundreds of kilometres they put between Wall and photographer. The self-critical letters written while a police officer huddled next to his small stove, spitting onto the tile floor whenever the photographer looked around in search for words, might still be stuck in the Bureau's filing cabinets.

Plate 60

For the ancient Greeks the *omphalos* (or *baetylus*, Semitic *bet el*, 'house of god') was the navel or centre of the Universe, where two eagles sent out by Zeus met.

Fig. 39

The Yungang sanctuary (Northern Wei dynasty, 460–534 CE) comprises 252 caves and niches and more than 50,000 statues within a carved area of 18,000 square metres, including pillars at the entrance. The cave sanctuary is located in the suburbs of Datong, the city which became 'China's coal capital' during the Second Sino-Japanese War (1937–45). The mass grave in the Meiyukou mine contains the remains of more than 150,000 workers, killed by occupying forces. Following nationalization in 1949 and reforms in the 1970s, in the 1980s, under a new policy officially called 'letting water flow as fast as possible', hundreds of small local mines began to operate, dominating land once used for agriculture. During the 'Golden Decade' (2003–12), when marketization and 'rationalization' contributed to the evolution of coal production, work safety, which had formerly been neglected because coal bosses could count on the complicity of local cadres (mining accidents happened frequently), was one of the reasons to eventually limit private and collective mines in favour of large publicly owned coal bases. At the same time, mining-induced land-subsidence led to the implementation of massive displacement and relocation measures, together with the demolition and rebuilding of Datong. In 2001, the Yungang caves were added to the UNESCO World Heritage List. The infiltration of rainfall water polluted by atmospheric particles, which affects the weathering process of the sandstone cliff that houses the Buddhas, is now an issue of scientific study.

Plate 74

To be childless in the traditional herding society of Mongolia is devastating. Children are treasured, and they help with herding, looking after the young animals. In the mid-1990s, street children were a new phenomenon in Mongolia, especially in Ulaanbaatar, the capital. The majority of the children had been driven out of school by poverty. They began to work the streets, earning money by begging, prostitution or theft. Some had left home to escape alcoholism and domestic violence, travelling to the capital along the railway corridor. The government at first thought it best to deny the issue, and so removed the children from the streets and locked them up in prisons and youth detention centres. By leaving the covers of Ulaanbaatar's many manholes unlocked, the government finally acknowledged that the sewers or heating ducts to which they afford access can serve as life-savers in the world's coldest capital city, where temperatures regularly drop below -30°C. While the retreats are fetid places with a high risk of tuberculosis, urinary infections and sexually transmitted diseases, they are at least warm.

Plate 75

Truth is a distorted matter in Kashmir. Ever since its annexation by the Mughal Empire in 1586, Kashmiris have never enjoyed independence. After the Mughals, the region was ruled by the Afghan Durrani Empire until 1819, when the Sikhs annexed Kashmir. Under Sikh rule, the discrimination that Kashmir's Muslim majority still faces to this day came to the fore. On 5 August 2019, India's Hindu nationalist Bharatiya Janata Party (BJP) government issued a legally disputed executive decree stripping away the autonomy that had been granted to the princely state of Jammu and Kashmir in 1947 in exchange for joining the Indian Union after the conclusion of British rule on the subcontinent.

Since 1947, India and Pakistan have fought multiple wars over Kashmir (latterly the Kargil War in 1999). Each has come to control different parts of the Himalayan territory, with an agreed 'Line of Control', a ceasefire line that extends as far as the India-occupied Siachen Glacier, the world's highest battlefield, adjacent to Chinese-administered Aksai Chin. Both Pakistan and India claim to have the best interests of the local population in mind. But in saying that Kashmir is fully theirs, they jointly suppress Kashmiri voices that criticize their actions and do everything they can to control the narratives of Kashmir. India has not only resorted to brutal methods of oppression such as physical violence, torture, fake encounters, rape and unlawful prosecutions, it has also concocted an alternative history, twisting data and facts to turn Indian public opinion against the plight of Kashmiri Muslims. Pakistan, meanwhile, has been no champion of the Kashmiri separatist insurgency, as it supported and trained armed groups active in the valley such as Lashkar-e-Taiba (LeT) in the 1990s. As both Delhi and Islamabad went nuclear in 1998, Kashmir, a paradise lost, has been said to be the most dangerous place on earth.

Plate 78
The Algarve is a 'transition region' and therefore the recipient of structural funds from the European Regional Development Fund. As tourism counts as strategic economic development, planning on the ground pays little heed to the industry's sensitivity to fluctuations in the global economy and to changing tastes and lifestyles. Between Faro and Ponta de Sagres, an unbroken string of white elephant projects and overbuilding reveals the wanton disregard for the environment.

Plate 79
Atrocities against civilians are a hallmark of the Tatmadaw, the Armed Forces of Myanmar (formerly Burma). Practices used during the campaign against the Rohingya Muslim population of Rakhine State in 1991 and 1992 were repeated in 2017 in what the UN called 'a textbook example of ethnic cleansing'. Then, as in the previous exodus, more than a million Rohingya fled to neighbouring Bangladesh, where they continue to live in the precarious conditions of sprawling refugee camps.

Plate 80
Following the end of the (Persian) Gulf War (1990–91), ethnic and religious uprisings against Saddam Hussein's rule resulted in the displacement of almost 2 million people, the majority of them Kurdish. Iran and Turkey only reluctantly allowed the refugees to cross the mountainous borders.

Plate 81
The Russian troops are part of the Forces of the Commonwealth of Independent States. With roots in the Tsarist Empire, the CIS was declared on 8 December 1991 in lieu of the dissolving Soviet Union. Following the Russo-Georgian war, Georgia withdrew its membership in 2008, and Ukraine ended its participation in 2018 due to prolonged tensions with Russia, which annexed Crimea in 2014 as a prelude to its invasion of the country on 24 February 2022.

Plates 84 and 86
Java is the world's most populous island, its c. 150 million people constituting about half of Indonesia's population. The informal settlements that sprawl along the railway tracks leading into Jakarta are built by rural migrants. As Indonesia's overcrowded capital of 10 million inhabitants is sinking at an alarming rate due to over-extraction of groundwater, in 2022 the government announced construction of a new capital city named Nusantara in East Kalimantan, one of Indonesia's two provinces on the island of Borneo – itself an ecological disaster zone.

Plate 85
The development and changes in the urban design of the London Borough of Southwark, and its ongoing gentrification, might be said to have begun with the 1998–2000 renovation of the Tate Modern art gallery, a former power station, by Swiss architects Herzog and de Meuron.

Plate 87
Some of the elderly in the Valley of Dien Bien Phu are haunted by things they saw in their childhood during the siege of the garrison of the French Union's colonial Far East Expeditionary Corps, the capture of which by the Vietminh in May 1954 brought an end to the First Indochina War (1946–54).

Fig. 40
At the outset of the Second World War, when all Chinese seaports were closed under Japanese aggression, the Burma Road, which connected Yunnan's capital Kunming with Lashio, Shan State, in the British colony of Burma (now Myanmar), was China's sole international conduit for goods. After 1942, combined with the Ledo Road into northeast India, it served as an Allied military supply route to Chiang Kai-shek's nationalist government of China, and was thought of as a hypothetical overland route towards the Korean peninsula and a springboard to Japan. The road was built in 1937 and 1938 by 200,000 Chinese forced labourers. In the mid-1990s, as China started to encroach on its South and Southeast Asian neighbours, a new Burma Road highway was dynamited through the mountains, and bridges were built over the Mekong and Salween rivers.

Plate 88
In Switzerland, Jura chalk had been mined since Roman times. The 'bey Creützen' ('near the Cross') quarry in the vicinity of the St Verena hermitage was one of eleven extraction sites which opened in the boom years after the construction of Solothurn's Vauban entrenchments (1667–1727) and the baroque St Ursen cathedral (1762–73).

Plate 91
The Pathet Lao (Lao Country, or Lao Nation), a left-oriented nationalist group, took control of Laos in 1975. Founded in 1950, the movement joined with the Vietminh, the Communist-oriented Vietnamese nationalist organization, in armed resistance to French rule in Indochina. In 1956 a legal political wing, the Lao Patriotic Front, was founded and participated in several coalition governments. The Laotian Civil War (1953–75) was a classic Cold War conflict, during which the Pathet Lao fought the US-backed Vientiane regime. In May 1975 the group consolidated its power throughout the country, formed a new government in the capital and subsequently renamed the country Lao People's Democratic Republic. During the civil war, the Pathet Lao was effectively organized, equipped and even led by the People's Army of Vietnam (PAVN). The most important source of military aid to the movement, under direct orders from Mao Zedong (as was also the case for the Vietnamese Communists), was China. Close ties between Laos and Vietnam were formalized via a treaty signed in 1977, and in 1979 50,000 PAVN troops were stationed in Laos. Hanoi has since provided direction for Laotian foreign policy and provides the basis for Vietnamese involvement at all levels of political and economic life in Laos. In 1979 Laos was asked by Vietnam to end relations with the People's Republic of China, leading to isolation in trade by China, the United States and other countries. In 2021, China opened its Boten–Vientiane railway, thus returning to and incorporating Southeast Asia's only landlocked country in Beijing's controversial and much-debated global 'Belt and Road Initiative'.

Plate 92
Xiangkhouang is said to be the most heavily bombed place on earth. Pockets of the province, together with the Xaisamboune Closed Military Zone near Vientiane province, are still living with the legacy of the Second Indochina War, the conflict between Washington's former ally, the Hmong, and the Vientiane. Given the neighbouring conflict in Cambodia and Vietnam, Laos was of key geostrategic interest for the US in the mid-twentieth century, but its intervention remained hidden from the public. The US bombing campaign in Laos, one of the most intensive in human history, was designed to interdict North Vietnamese supply lines that ran through the country. The bombing also supported Laotian government forces fighting against the Communist Pathet Lao and their North Vietnamese allies. Cluster munitions were considered the weapon of choice because they penetrated jungle canopy, covered large areas and could successfully attack convoys and troop concentrations hidden by the trees. Bombings in the northeast were intended to deny territory, particularly the Plain of Jars, to Pathet Lao and North Vietnamese forces and, in the South, to sever the Ho Chi Minh Trail, which crossed the border into eastern Laos. The northeastern part of Laos was also used as a 'free drop zone', where planes that had taken off from bases in Thailand and had been unable to deliver their bombs could dispose of them before returning to Thailand.

During this 'Secret War', run by the CIA from 1964 to 1975, 580,000 bombing runs were reportedly flown and over 270 million cluster bombs dropped on a country forty-two times smaller than the US – more than the amount dropped on Germany and Japan combined during the Second World War. An estimated one-third of these munitions failed to explode. The Lao government claims that between 75 and 80 million submunitions or bomblets released from the cluster bombs remain in over one-third of the country's area. Conflicts during the French colonial period and the Laotian Civil War during the 1960s and 1970s also contributed to the problem of UXO/ERW (Unexploded Ordnance / Explosive Remnants of War). It is estimated that around 50,000 Laotians, most of them civilians, and especially children, have been killed or injured by American bombs. Fewer than 1 per cent of these munitions have been cleared and at the current pace it could take more than 100 years to clear the country of this long-term legacy, making this the number one development issue in Laos.

Plate 94
On 4 June 2006, Xinhua Agency reported the discovery of two game boards at this location, noticed by the photographer in 1987. The two boards, the dispatch stated, were probably used by soldiers guarding one of the Sandaoguan passes of the Great Wall. One board was for Chinese chess and the other for the ancient game 'Tiger Eats Sheep'. They were engraved in the rock next to a watchtower possibly during the Song dynasty (960–1279).

Plate 95
The Museum of the Future, designed by Killa Design of Dubai, is made of 2,400 diagonally intersecting steel frames. It opened in 2022, and the architectural term for its shape is 'torus with an elliptical void'.

Plate 96
Never has anything been built on solid ground in the Mekong Delta. The delta that is by nature and by definition 'land in the making' is now, in essence, 'land in the sinking', as the effects of sea level rise and coastal erosion are combined with those of land subsidence, the latter happening faster than the former. Findings published in 2019, based on digital elevation models collected in 2000 by the Endeavour orbiter

and lidar-corrected to measure the ground and not the canopy, put 20 million people, almost a quarter of Vietnam's current population, at risk. By 2050, the country's entire south, along a line from Ho Chi Minh City to Rach Gia on the Cambodian border, will be lost to flooding. This outcome, two hundred years after the first French inroads into the Mekong Delta following their occupation in 1859 of Saigon (renamed Ho Chi Minh City in 1975), will be the result of both the climate crisis and the technological transformation of the delta.

Opening the delta to economic progress and, with the construction of two spanning bridges in the twenty-first century, to fleets of container trucks that began to replace the wooden barges with black eyes on their bows to confront the water spirits, destroyed a tradition that had evolved over centuries. During the pre-Khmer civilization of Funan or Oc Eo (*c.* 300 BCE–600 CE) the canals, settlements and warehouses of the delta had connected sea-based trade between India and China, and thus had made it a vital link in the maritime Silk Road. When the Portuguese arrived after 1516, in the wake of an upsurge in Indian Ocean commerce (of which their presence was a consequence, not a cause), the north of the Mekong Delta peninsula was a contested borderland between a Cambodian kingdom in decline and the Vietnamese state centred on Huê. As the French embarked on the modernization of their colonial possession, their canals, water-gates, bridges and railways were partly financed by opium sales and carried out by private monopoly contractors out of government reach. They were portrayed as a manifestation of a *mission civilisatrice* and an example of French Revolutionary ideas about labour reform put into practice. In fact, until 1881 the colonial bureaucracy relied on *corvée*, a form of forced labour practised under the Nguyen, the last Vietnamese imperial dynasty. In 1929, mechanized dredging was introduced to battle siltation and to secure the constant movement of water between coastal and hinterland river zones, in the face of seasonal flooding and the tidal pulses that reach up to 100 kilometres upstream and are responsible for the delta's extremely flat, ever-changing aquatic landscape. The following year, in 1930, mobilization of the poor peasants in the delta began. This was the basis of the rural revolution and resistance to come, the last chapter of which the Vietcong, Hanoi's Communist ally in South Vietnam, would write during the American War (1960–73).

During the First Indochina War (1945–54), as many of the colonial waterways fell into decay, the unintended regeneration of the pre-colonial waterscape and the simultaneous liberation of French-controlled zones by the Vietminh had strategic implications. The *dos d'âne*, the donkey's-back bars of silt that formed where opposing water currents converged, once again became the traditional local meeting points for the exchange of goods and information, and thus of intelligence. To the French technocrats these bars had been dead points. Neither they nor the speculators in Paris sufficiently understood the complex hydroecology upstream from the *Bouches du Mekong*, as they took water management away from the farmers. Instead, the ambitious engineered transformation of vast parts of the wetland ecosystem they had set in motion would foreshadow the delta's tragic environmental narrative, with its apocalyptic culmination of a dioxin-induced ecocide during the American War in Vietnam.

Two postscripts to be added: first, prolonged periods of deeper inland seawater intrusion and the Mekong turning salty, a result of its hydraulic interplay with Cambodia's lung, the Tonle Sap Lake, being broken by a dozen dams in China, and second, the over-exploitation and ban-ignoring export of alluvial sand, which depletes riverbeds and which the country will run out of in the next few years.

Plate 98

The Parliament is the heart of Nay Pyi Taw, the 'Royal Capital'. Built into cleared jungle, Nay Pyi Taw is a planned city that officially replaced Yangon on 6 November 2005 as the administrative capital of Myanmar (formerly Burma). It was here that the coup of 1 February 2021, which deposed the democratically elected members of the National League for Democracy (NLD), took place, thus ending an interlude of few years of relative freedom during which the military establishment enriched itself as the country became Asia's last investment front. By 2022, the Myanmar junta, with few friends left in the world and desperate for legitimacy, embraced deeper ties with Russia. In this relationship of unequals, each side has something to gain. Myanmar gets resources, ammunition and a powerful partner to back them at the United Nations, while Russia gets another customer at a time when it is struggling to find sources of revenue. And both can use the other to undermine the Western sanctions imposed on them – Myanmar for launching a coup, and Russia for invading Ukraine. In Nay Pyi Taw and the Kremlin's vision, they are part of a new world order, two countries led by strongmen ideologically opposed to democracy.

Plate 99

In 2019, Indonesia became the latest Asian country to return waste to be recycled to the West. Among the consignments were 100 tons of Canadian paper waste, imported via the United States, because it was contaminated with material including plastic, rubber and diapers. The spike in imports from Western countries occurred after China banned imports, thus disrupting the global flow of millions of tons of waste each year. The change of policy happened as the country, which produces approximately 7.8 million tons of waste annually, remained locked in a battle against its own uncollected waste, which contributes more plastic waste discharges than leakages from final disposal sites. Rivers carry and discharge 83 per cent of the annual plastic debris that leaks into the marine environment from land-based sources, while only 17 per cent is directly discarded or washed off from coastal areas.

Plate 102

The photograph of the Siggern waterfall is inspired by the work *Chûte d'eau près du rocher de Balm dans le Canton de Soleure* (1777) by Swiss artist Caspar Wolf (1735–1783), a coloured engraving in the possession of the photographer. Wolf, most famous for his dramatic paintings of Alpine scenery with glaciers, as well as of caves, of which he was especially fond, is regarded as a pioneering landscape painter between the Enlightenment period and Romanticism. Initially inspired by Albrecht von Haller's poem 'Die Alpen' (1729), the artist's growing interest in geology came from excursions between 1773 and 1776 with his publisher Abraham Wagner and the naturalist Jakob Samuel Wyttenbach, both of Bern. The latter's collection of Alpine stones was praised by Goethe, but there is no evidence that during his halt in Bern in October 1779 the poet paid a visit to Wagner's cabinet of Wolf's paintings. The *Chûte d'eau* engraving was realized during a brief residency in Solothurn and must be one of Wolf's last works before his departure to Paris in 1779. There his depictions of what was imagined as Alpine Cythera were too dramatic, too frightening to be fully esteemed, but served as templates for series of aquatints. On his home-bound journey, Wolf died lonely in a Heidelberg hospital. The *Alpen-Kabinett*, as the series of Swiss paintings was known, ended up in Keukenhof Castle in the Netherlands; discovered after the Second World War, they were repatriated to Switzerland in 1948, becoming part of the collections of the Aargauer Kunsthaus, Aarau, the Kunstmuseum Basel and the Kulturstiftung in Muri, birthplace of Wolf.

Chûte d'eau does not depict the real situation of the chalk cleft near the village of Balm. Instead it is an assembly of diverse existing natural elements that creates the illusion of a view from the interior of a cave across the great Swiss plain towards the distant silhouette of Bernese Oberland peaks. Two figures, seen from the back, are shown in conversation and pointing a walking stick at what lies before them. Just seven kilometres away from the real Siggern waterfall, beyond the Balmberg Pass in the second Jura fold-thrust belt, a pair of intricately shaped caves is to be found, the geological source of Wolf's *Kleine Bärenhöhle bei Welschenrohr* (1778). Whereas *Chûte d'eau* provides no certainty about the two onlookers – the artist and his assistant, perhaps – the speleological masterpiece, executed a year later, leaves no doubt. The interior of the cave is dominated by an outcrop, hugely enlarged compared to its actual mass and dimensions, on which a minuscule figure stands – the artist, backlit, sketchpad in hand, a baroque trick that heralds the lonely figures of Caspar David Friedrich and other painters of Romanticism. The piece is only in part result of geological fieldwork; rather it displays the artist's aesthetic immersion in geology as a way towards cognition of nature. Caspar Wolf has disentangled himself from the naturalists' and his employer's life-like expectations, from the task to paint recognizable scenery. But so topographically accurate were these earlier paintings that today they exhibit inestimable value as visual historic documents for scientists studying the dramatic changes of the Alpine environment since the Little Ice Age, the peak of which Wolf witnessed during his arduous walks.

Notes on the text

Beat Wismer: Tracings

1 William A. Ewing has described Daniel Schwartz 'as a photographer, author, editor, journalist, photojournalist, explorer, historian, or (he'd be embarrassed to hear it) sage'. William E. Ewing, 'Unassuming Places', in *Parkett*, no. 89, 2011, pp. 216–32 (p. 216). This text is exceptional in that it was the first and one of only a very few to have been published in a magazine dedicated exclusively and programmatically to contemporary art.

2 See Paul Vionnet, *Pierre à Bot, Neuchâtel*, 23 August 1869, albumen print, 18.9 x 25.2 cm (7½ x 10 in.). In Martin Gasser and Sylvie Henguely (eds), *Nach der Natur. Schweizer Fotografie im 19. Jahrhundert*, with Peter Pfrunder, Fotostiftung Schweiz, Winterthur, Photo Elysée, Lausanne and Museo d'arte della Svizera italiana, Lugano; Göttingen, Steidl, 2021, fig.10.34, p. 349.

3 Richard McClure, 'Images which speak louder than words', in *Financial Times*, Weekend, 13–14 December 1997.

4 Daniel Schwartz, *Schnee in Samarkand. Ein Reisebericht aus dreitausend Jahren*, Frankfurt/M., Eichborn-Berlin, Eichborn AG, 2008.

5 Daniel Schwartz, *While the Fires Burn. A Glacier Odyssey*, London, Thames & Hudson, 2017, p. 7.

6 Photographs of the glacier project were first shown at the Kunsthaus Langenthal in an exhibition entitled 'Ice Age Our Age. Ballads and Enquiries Concerning the Last Glacial Maximum' (2012). They were then shown in the 'theatrum Alpinum' and 'de glacierum natura' exhibitions at the Kunstraum Medici in Solothurn in 2016 and 2018, and finally the 'Gletscher-Odyssee' (Glacier Odyssey) exhibition at the Bündner Kunstmuseum in Chur in 2018–19.

7 Peter Levi, Introduction to Daniel Schwartz, *Metamorphoses. Greek Photographs*, London, Thames & Hudson, 1986, p. 5.

8 Dieter Bachmann and Daniel Schwartz (eds), *So Many Worlds. A Photographic Record of Our Time,* Thames & Hudson, London, 1996 (German edition: *Der geduldige Planet. Eine Weltgeschichte. 255 Fotografien aus der Zeitschrift „Du“*, du Verlag, Zürich, 1996); Daniel Schwartz (ed.), *Tales from a Globalizing World*, London, Thames & Hudson, 2003.

9 Hans Finsler, 'Das Bild der Photographie', *DU*, Heft 277, March 1964.

10 Urs Franger, 'The Family of Man', in *ZHdK. A Future for the Arts: Zürich University of the Arts Inaugural Publication*, Zürich, Scheidegger & Spiess, 2007, p. 158.

11 Tim Page, Introduction to Daniel Schwartz, *Delta. The perils, profits and politics of water in South and Southeast Asia*, London, Thames & Hudson, 1997, p. 19.

12 Hugo Loetscher, 'The Concerned Photographer: A Witness of his Time', in Marco Bischof and René Burri (eds), *Werner Bischof, 1916–1954*, Boston, Little, Brown, 1990, p. 9.

13 Daniel Schwartz, Statement on 7 March 2016, in response to Peter Pfrunder's question on the subject of 'Werner Bischof et son influence'. Musée de l'Elysée, Lausanne, 30 April 2016. Unpublished.

Fanni Fetzer: Persistence

1 Albert Camus, *The Myth of Sisyphus, and Other Essays*, New York, Vintage Books, 1991, p. 123.

2 'Landslide' and 'debris flows' are familiar terms for those who live in regions affected by the phenomenon. Extreme weather causes material to be removed from the steep mountains (erosion) and transported via the streambed into the valley, where it is deposited in the form of an alluvial fan (accumulation). Understanding this principle makes it possible to read the landscape, such as the gently sloping, uniform cones located at the side of a main valley, where villages, fields and pastures are situated slightly above the changing level of the main river. According to the dictionary, landslides are an event – mudslides, mudflows, sand avalanches – but in fact the term is frequently used to denote the mark left on the landscape, the trail that points to past and future debris flows, mudslides and avalanches. The landslides are a constant physical presence, and occasionally they are still happening, too – that is, when they are actually in progress.

3 This image has a counterpart: a diptych with one vertical and one horizontal line. A rock face towers upwards, then stops abruptly in roughly the middle of the picture and seems to transition into an infinite expanse. In fact, the shadow is what suggests the depth of a vertical drop here. Once again, the question arises: Where does the photographer actually stand? Once again, one might think this was a photographic study of organic material, were it not for scale provided by the camels – four and five of them, respectively – walking through the image in the faraway distance and minuscule as a result. Where do camels with one hump live? Why are they clearly walking in file, but so far apart from each other? Who is leading them? Why are they passing through the image from the right in one case and from the left in the other? These animals would appear not to be free, but they are certainly wilful. Once again, the barely there colour of the photograph provides no further clues.

4 The curator and author Beat Wismer describes the occasional colour photographs to be found in Daniel Schwartz's oeuvre as *knapp farbig*: barely colourful.

5 Albert Camus, *The Myth of Sisyphus, and Other Essays*, New York, Vintage Books, 1991, p. 123.

Giovanna Calvenzi: The Anatomy of Books

1 Giovanni Battista Piranesi's copperplate etchings were displayed alongside modern-day images of the urban landscape on the initiative of the Fondazione Giorgio Cini in Venice to celebrate the exhibition and the publication of the book *Le arti di Piranesi: Architetto, incisore, antiquario, vedutista, designer*, Venice, Marsilio, 2010. This was followed later by the publication of the book *Piranesi Roma Basilico: L'arte di vedere*, Rome, Contrasto, 2019, www.archiviogabrielebasilico.it.

2 'Ero troppo occupato a fotografare e non ho guardato' is the title of a lecture given by Umberto Eco at the 38th Convention of the Italian Association of Semiotics (Associazone Italiana di Studi Semiotici) entitled 'La fotografia: oggetto teorico e pratica sociale' (Photography. Theoretical Object and Social Practice) held in Rome between 8 and 10 October 2010. The papers from the conference were published by Vincenza Del Marco and Isabella Pezzini in 2011.

3 Tim Page, introduction to Daniel Schwartz, *Delta. The perils, profits and politics of water in South and Southeast Asia*, London, Thames & Hudson, 1997. Tim Page (1944–2022) achieved worldwide acclaim for his photographs of the Vietnam War. Just eighteen when he first saw combat, he was wounded several times, once almost fatally. A striking presence in Michael Herr's *Dispatches*, New York, Alfred A. Knopf, 1977, he is said to be the model for the photographer in Francis F. Coppola's film *Apocalypse Now* (1979). He is author of *Tim Page's Nam, Ten Years After* and *The Mindful Moment*, London, Thames & Hudson, 1983, 1987 and 2001, and co-author with UPI/AP photographer Horst Faas (1933–2012) of *Requiem*, New York, Random House, 1997, which features the work of local and foreign photographers killed during the Indochina wars between 1945 and 1975 and accompanied a travelling exhibition that found a permanent home in the War Remnants Museum in Ho Chi Minh City. Before these titles, the memoirs *Page After Page*, London, Sidgwick & Jackson, 1988, and *Derailed in Uncle Ho's Victory Garden*, New York, Touchstone, 1995, established the so-called gonzo photographer as a gifted writer.

4 John Thomson was born in Edinburgh in 1837. He opened his own photography studio in Singapore in 1862. In later years he visited Sri Lanka (then Ceylon) and India, where he photographed the cyclones, as well as Thailand (then Siam), Ho Chi Minh City (then Saigon) and Cambodia. He published his first book, *The Antiquities of Cambodia*, in 1866. During his travels through China between 1870 and 1871, Thomson produced material for two more publications: *Foochow and the River Min*, London, Autotype Company, 1873, and *Illustrations of China and Its People*, London, Sampson Low, Marston, Searle & Rivington, vols I & II, 1873, vols III & IV, 1874. Back in London in 1872, he collaborated on the book *Street Life in London*, London, Sampson Low, Marston, Searle & Rivington, 1878, with journalist Adolphe Smith. Thomson was appointed as the Royal Family's official photographer in 1881. He died in 1921.

5 Leone Nani was born in Albino (Bergamo, Italy) in 1880. He left for China as a missionary in 1903, where he joined the Catholic Mission in Hanzhong and remained until 1914. He travelled across the various regions of the Shaanxi province during this time, combining his religious work with photography, mostly on glass plates. On returning to Italy, he gave up photography to pursue a career in teaching. He died in 1935. Nani's archive is held by the Pontifico Istituto Missioni Estere (PIME) (Pontifical Institute for Foreign Missions) in Milan.

Selected Commentaries

1 William Shawcross, *Sideshow: Kissinger, Nixon and the Destruction of Cambodia*, London, Hogarth Press, 1986.

2 Muhammad Salman Khan and Sarah De Nardi, 'The Affectual-Social Ecology of Cultural Artefacts: Illegal Markets and Religious Vandalism in Swat Valley, Pakistan', *Forum for Social Economics*, Abingdon, Taylor & Francis, 2022.

3 Karl Lehner, *Zermatter Sagen und Legenden*, Visp, Buch- und Offset-druckerei Mengis, 1974, p. 173

Tabula

This list is set out as a concordance of each photograph reproduced in this volume and its origin. The information sheds light on the intertwined publication history and the genesis of the photographer's archive. The numbers preceding each entry refer to plate and figure numbers. Ninety-nine photographs of the 136, reproduced as 102 plates and 24 figures (as individual illustrations, in fig. 11 as a triptych and in figs 1, 2, 3, 39, 40 and 41 as a component of six multi-exposure composite prints) are published here for the first time.

Bold type indicates origin and first publication in *Tracings*
Bold italic type indicates entry of first publication
Regular type indicates origin without publication at the time or in the respective entry
Regular italic indicates primary literature inclusion
*Regular italic** with asterix indicates additional secondary literature inclusion

The list is organized as follows:

I Primary literature
I.1 Books and related assignments
I.2 Limited editions
I.3 Publication assignments
I.4 Independent press assignments

II Peripatetic
II.1 Projects
II.2 Themes
II.3 Solitaires

III Secondary literature: Portfolios
III.1 Miscellaneous volume publications
III.2 Exhibition publications
III.3 Press publications

IV Secondary literature: Illustrations
IV.1 Miscellaneous volume publications
IV.2 Critique and reviews
IV.3 Press publications

V Selected additional references

Selected exhibitions are added in the list when related to major publications.

I Primary literature

I.1 Books and related assignments

Plate – *57*
Figures – ***11*** – *14* – ***41 (both images)***

2009–16
While the Fires Burn. A Glacier Odyssey
London, Thames & Hudson, 2017
Afterword by Daniel Schwartz

Bündner Kunstmuseum, Chur (10 November 2018–17 February 2019)

Plates – *16* – **37** – *74* – ***76*** – *81*
Figures – ***3 (top right;*** colour version*)* – *26* – ***27*** – *28*

1991/95–2007
Travelling Through the Eye of History
London, Thames & Hudson, 2009

San Francisco Museum of Modern Art (Excerpt in 'Face of our Time', group exhibition; 2 July–16 October 2011)
Martin-Gropius-Bau, Berlin (23 June–12 September 2011)
Helmhaus, Zürich (17 April–14 June 2009)

Plate – *16*

1991/95–2007
Schnee in Samarkand. Ein Reisebericht aus dreitausend Jahren
Frankfurt/M., Eichborn-Berlin, Eichborn AG, 2008

Related assignments

Plates – ***16*** – **52**

'Der Chinese dreht am Geldhahn'
Text by Marcus Bensmann
Neue Zürcher Zeitung (*Zeitbilder*), Zürich; Nr. 14, 18 January 2008

Figure – **36**

'Trostlose Normalität'
Text by Navid Kermani
Neue Zürcher Zeitung (*Zeitbilder*), Zürich; Nr. 16, 20–21 January 2007

Plate – **100**
Figure – ***28***

Die Seidenstrassen. Vom Lauf der Welt
Texts by Paul Kennedy, Andreas Nentwich, Olivier Roy, Daniel Schwartz
Du, Zürich; Heft 753, February 2005

Figures – **3 (top left, bottom images)** – ***26*** – 27

'Afghanistan. Der leise Tod'
Additional photograph by Alexandra Boulat; text by Kurt Brandenberger
FACTS, Zürich; Nr. 16, 19 April 2001

Plate – **75**

'Kashmir. Im Tal des Todes'
Text by Kurt Brandenberger
FACTS, Zürich; Nr. 27, 6 July 2000

Plate – 74

'Überleben in Ulaanbaatar'
Text by Ulrich Schmid
Neue Zürcher Zeitung (*Zeitbilder*), Zürich; Nr. 90, 15–16 April 2000

Plates – **41** – **50** – *76*

'Ökonomie des Überlebens in Afghanistan'
Text by Bernard Imhasly
Neue Zürcher Zeitung (*Zeitbilder*), Zürich; Nr. 217, 19–20 September 1998

Plate – ***81***

'Die Raubvögel vom Pamir'
Text by Marcus Bensmann
FACTS, Zürich; Nr. 1, 31 December 1996

Plate – **4**

Iran. Drei Wege nach Isfahan
With Thomas Kern and Samer Mohdad
Texts by Houchang Chehabi, Navid Kermani a.o.
Du, Zürich; Heft 658, March 1996

Plates – ***12*** – **23** – **25** – **36** – **45** – **56** – *69* – *73*

1991–95
Delta. The perils, profits and politics of water in South and Southeast Asia
Introduction by Tim Page
London, Thames & Hudson, 1997

Scalo. Books & Looks, Zürich (8 October–20 November 1999)

Related assignments

Figure – **18**

'Die "tanzenden Flüsse" von Bangladesh'
Text by Bernard Imhasly
Neue Zürcher Zeitung (*Wochenende*), Nr. 223, 24–25 September 1994

Plate – **90**
Figure – **21**

'Kambodscha. Rückkehr in ein verlassenes Land'
Text by Jutta Lietsch
Das Magazin, *Tages-Anzeiger*, Zürich; Nr. 10, 13 March 1993

Plates – **48** – **79**
Figure – **23**

Burma 1992. Eine Reportage
Text by Bertil Lintner
Du, Zürich; Heft 620, November 1992

Plate – **72**

'Shanghai. Auf den Frühling bauen'
Additional photographs by Frédéric Meyer
Text by André Kunz
Das Magazin, *Tages-Anzeiger*, Zürich; Nr. 37, 11–12 September 1992

Plate – **1** – **35**

'Wasserpolitik am Ganges'
Texts by Usha Rai and Parveen Anwar
Das Magazin, *Tages-Anzeiger*, Zürich; Nr. 17, 24–25 April 1992

Plate – *94*
Figure – *17*

1987–2000
The Great Wall of China
Revised edition (with additional photographs taken in 1990, 1993, 2000)
London, Thames & Hudson, 2001
Preface by Daniel Schwartz
Texts by Jorge Luis Borges, Franz Kafka and Luo Zhewen

Plates – **9** – **62** – **66** – *94*
Figures – 17 – **31** – 38 – **39 (top)** – 39 (bottom)

1987–88
The Great Wall of China
London, Thames & Hudson, 1990
Introduction by Daniel Schwartz
Texts by Jorge Luis Borges and Luo Zhewen

Selected venues:
Imperial Palace Museum, Beijing (10–20 December 1993)
Château des Ducs d'Epernon, Cadillac; Arret sur l'Image, Bordeaux '92 (1–30 April 1992)
Musée de l'Elysée, Lausanne (8 February–14 April 1991)
Museum am Ostwall, Dortmund (12 August–11 November 1990)

Related assignment

Plate – ***94***

Die Grossen Mauern Chinas – eine Idee
Text by Dieter Bachmann
Du, Zürich; Heft 580, June 1989

Plates – **55** – **60**
Figure – *16*

1977–85
Metamorphoses. Greek Photographs
London, Thames & Hudson, 1986
Introduction by Peter Levi

Selected venues:
Instituto Aleman, Madrid (8 May–15 June 1990)
Moore College of Art, Philadelphia (25 May–6 July 1988)
Barbican Centre, London (8–31 July 1987)
Kunsthaus Zürich, Zürich (20 September–23 November 1986)

I.2 Limited editions

Plates – ***28*** – *73*

Turning Away and Other Apparent Affections
Folder in a box, with 20 pages, three in colour; 17 screenprinted photographs
Edition of 30, with 20 artist's copies
Daniel Schwartz (Concept)
Commissioned by the Regierungsrat Kanton Zürich, Zürich, 2010

Plates – ***2*** – ***46*** – ***74***
Figure – ***14***

Le Monde de Candide
Folder in a box, with 24 pages; 20 screenprinted photographs
Edition of 200
Daniel Schwartz (Concept)
Roswitha Schild (Project realization); Kunstverein Solothurn, Solothurn 2007

Kunstmuseum Solothurn (22 September 2007–6 January 2008)

Plates – **44** – *94*

Wieviel Erde – Ce qu'il faut de terre – How Much Land – Quanta Terra
Folder with 28 pages; 23 offset-printed photographs
Texts by Dieter Bachmann, Adrian Budge, Lanfranco Colombo, Charles-Henri Favrod, Hugo Loetscher and Martin Schaub
Daniel Schwartz (Concept)
Schweizerische Stiftung für die Photographie, Zürich, 1989

Galleria Il Diaframma, Milano (8 January–2 February 1991)
Photoforum Pasquart, Biel-Bienne (2 June–1 July 1990)

Photographers' Gallery, London (12 April–19 May 1990)
Nikon Galerie, Zürich (2 December 1989–16 January 1990)

I.3 Publication assignments

Plates – 28 – ***38*** – **40** – **42** – **51**

1998
'From Burma Road to Wall Street'
Die Kunst der Reportage
Texts by Lieve Joris, James Hamilton-Paterson, Peter Mathiessen, Abdelwahab Meddeb, Laszlo Krasznahorkai, Jan Stage
Lettre International, Berlin; Heft 42, 1998

Haus der Kulturen der Welt, Berlin (5–25 October 1998)

Plate – **78**

1996
'Algarve – Landscape under Siege'
In: Albano Silva Pereira and Siza M. Tereza (eds), *Sul*
Coimbra, Encontros de Fotografia, 1997

Galeria de Exposições Temporarias do Museo Antropológico da Universidade de Coimbra, Coimbra (9–24 November 1996)

Plates – 2 – **27** – **84** – **86** – **99**

1994
Down and Out in Jakarta
Commissioned by SDC – Swiss Agency for Development and Cooperation, Bern (unpublished)

I.4 Independent press assignments

Plate – **49**

'Der Freund'
Text by Navid Kermani
Das Magazin, *Tages-Anzeiger*, Zürich; Nr. 3, 19 January 2019

Plate – ***98***

Burma 2012. Eine Reportage
With Philip Blenkinsop and Gary Knight
Text by Bertil Lintner
Du, Zürich; Nr. 832, December 2012–January 2013

Plate – ***30***

'Zwischen Afghanistans Kriegen'
With Lara Studer
Text by Daniel Schwartz
WOZ. Die Wochenzeitung, Zürich; Nr. 6, 11 February 2010

Figure – **20**

'Angkor – wo Apsara tanzt'
Text by Hugo Loetscher
Neue Zürcher Zeitung (*Zeitbilder*), Zürich; Nr. 51, 2–3 March, 2002

Plates – 3 – 43 – 96

'Schwimmende und andere Märkte – Notizen aus Vietnam'
Text by Christoph Neidhart
Neue Zürcher Zeitung (*Zeitbilder*), Zürich; Nr. 64, 17–18 March, 2001

Plate – **97**

'Die Last der dunklen Jahre – Bericht aus Rumänien'
Text by Therese Obrecht
Neue Zürcher Zeitung (*Zeitbilder*), Zürich; Nr. 216, 16–17 September 2000

Plates – **8** – **63**

'Zwischen Leiterwagen und Mercedes – Bericht aus dem Grenzgebiet Rumäniens'
Text by Therese Obrecht
Neue Zürcher Zeitung (*Zeitbilder*), Zürich; Nr. 157, 8–9 July 2000

Plate – **85**

Tate Modern von Herzog & de Meuron
With Gabriele Basilico
Text by Alix Sharkey
Du, Zürich; Heft 706, May 2000

'Herzog & de Meuron: In Process' (group exhibition)
Walker Art Center, Minneapolis (5 November 2000–11 February 2001)

Plate – **33**

'Osttimor auf dem Weg in die Eigenstaatlichkeit'
Text by Peter Sidler
Neue Zürcher Zeitung (*Zeitbilder*), Zürich; Nr. 181, 7–8 August 1999

Figure – **40 (both images)**

'Hanoi-Mandalay via Burma-Strasse'
Text by Peter Sidler
Neue Zürcher Zeitung (*Ausland*), Zürich; Nr. 38 & 47, 16 & 26 February, Nr. 50 & 54, 2 & 6 March 1998

Plates – **15** – **83**

'Pailin. Wildwest im Dschungel'
Text by Andreas Lorenz
Frankfurter Allgemeine Magazin, *FAZ*, Frankfurt/M.; Heft 933, 16 January 1998

Plate – **59**

'Von Hué nach Angkor'
Text by Peter Sidler
Neue Zürcher Zeitung (*Zeitbilder*), Zürich; Nr. 206, 6–7 September 1997

Plates – **58** – **91** – **92**

'In Laos unterwegs'
Text by Peter Sidler
Neue Zürcher Zeitung (*Zeitbilder*), Zürich; Nr. 109, 11–12 May 1996

Plates – **67** – **68**

'Ahmedabad. Anatomie einer Krise'
Text by Kirtee Shah
Du, Zürich; Heft 601, March 1991

II Peripatetic

II.1 Projects

Plates – **10** – **95** – **102**

Since 2017
Governed Prospects

Plates – 54 – **87**

Since 2009
Failure in the East
'Afghanistan. The Endless War'

Bayeux Award for War Correspondents, Bayeux (7–13 October 2019)
The History Museum of Bosnia & Herzegowina, Sarajevo (8–31 July 2019)

Plates – 46 – **80**

1991
Global Migration

II.2 Themes

Figure – **25**

2020
The pandemic – As Switzerland became part of the world

Figure – 1 (both images)

2009
Japan – Random entries going north

Plates – **20** – **21**

1993
Kolkatta – Recycling gods

Plate – **39**

1990
Georgia – Journey through the end of an era

Plate – **18**

1989
Istanbul – Tanneries

Plates – **6** – **26**

1986–2010
Zürich – Brief encounters

Plates – **31** – **70** – **88**
Figures – **5** – 14

1977–80
Formation – Fotoklasse, Kunstgewerbeschule Zürich

Plates – **11** – **17** – **22** – 24– **29** – **32** – **61** – **64**

1972–76
First Exposures

II.3 Solitaires

Plates – **5** – **7** – **13** – **14** – **19** – **34** – **53**
Figures – **2 (both images)** – **10** – **30**
Plates – **65** – **71** – **77** – **82** – **89** – **93** – **101**

III Secondary literature: Portfolios

III.1 Miscellaneous volume publications

Plate – ***96***

Daniel Schwartz, *Das Wasser steigt*
In: Dieter Bachmann, *Archipel. Expeditionen, Begegnungen, Schauplätze (Band 3)*
Wädenswil, Nimbus. Kunst und Bücher AG, 2022

Plate – *57**

—, *Aufnahmen aus dem Zyklus theatrum Alpinum*
In: Patrick Hegglin (ed.), *In den Gletschern der Erinnerung. Literarische Gletscherbilder aus drei Jahrhunderten*
Luzern, edition bücherlese, 2020

Plates – *2** – ***3*** – ***24*** – *28*
Figure – ***1*** (both images)
Plate – *69**

—, *30 ganzseitige Fototafeln*
In: Georg Brunold (ed.), *Nichts als der Mensch. Beobachtungen und Spekulationen aus 2500 Jahren*
Berlin, Verlag Galiani Berlin, 2013

Figure – ***38***

—, *Über das Fotografieren des sogenannten Anderen – gerade in China*
(photographs and text)
In: *At Eastern Gates*, SCRIPT 5, Wolfsberg.
Ermatingen, The Platform for Executive and Business Development, 2012

Schloss Wolfsberg, Ermatingen (4 September–7 December 2012)

Plates – *38** – ***47***

—, *De Burma Road a Wall Street*
In: *Realidades Ajenas*
Madrid, Trama editorial, 2000

Plates – ***73*** – *94**

—, *Sur la route du photographe étranger*
In: *Dédale*, Paris; nos 9 & 10, autumn 1999

III.2 Exhibition publications

Plate – ***57***

Daniel Schwartz, *de glacierum natura*
Roberto Medici and Brigitte Plüss-Medici (Project and exhibition curators)
USM Münsingen, 2016

Kunstraum Medici, Solothurn (25 January–31 March 2018)
USM Showrooms Hamburg, Düsseldorf, Berlin, Munich, Paris, New York, Stuttgart and Tokyo (2016–18)

Plate – *30**

—, Afghanistan
In: Andreas Fiedler and Simon Maurer (eds), *Weltbilder 5*
Nürnberg, Verlag für moderne Kunst, 2013

Helmhaus Zürich, Zürich (group exhibition; 6 December 2013–26 January 2014)

Figure – *14**

—, *Ice Age Our Age. Ballads and Enquiries Concerning the Last Glacial Maxium*
Eight single photographs and one as concertina including a carthographic artwork and a textwork
Boxed set of screenprints, Edition of 50

Kunsthaus Langenthal, Langenthal (29 November 2012–27 January 2013)

Plate – ***69***

—, *Dhaka, Bangladesh*
In: 'Über Sicht. Fotoförderung im Kanton Solothurn seit 1973'
Solothurn, Kantonales Amt für Kultur und Sport, Kantonales Kuratorium für Kulturförderung'

Palais Besenval, Solothurn (group exhibition; 3–25 September 1994)

Figure – ***17***

—, 'Viaggio alla muraglia cinese'
In: Arturo Carlo Quintavalle, *Muri di carta. Fotografia e paesaggio dopo le avanguardie*
Milan, Electa, 1993

Pavilion of Italy, 45th Venice Art Biennale, Venice (group exhibition; 13 June–10 October 1993)

III.3 Press publications

Plate – *54**

Daniel Schwartz, 'Von der doppelten Last des Erbes' (photographs and text)
SoRock. Kulturmagazin Solothurn, Solothurn; 1, 2018

Plates – *30** – ***54***

—, 'Afghanistan – Unser Dreissigjähriger Krieg'
Lettre International, Berlin; Heft 100, 2013

Plate – *47**

—, 'Wir sind das Geld'
Fotogeschichte, Vienna; Heft 105, Jg. 27, 2007

Plate – *38**

—, 'Desde Burma Road a Wall Street'
Letra Internacional, Madrid; 61, 1999

Figure – ***39*** (bottom image)

—, 'Buddha in den Minen'
Neue Zürcher Zeitung, Zürich; Nr. 248, 25–26 October 1997

Plate – *69**

—, 'Bittere Steine'
Neue Zürcher Zeitung, Zürich; Nr. 96, 26–27 April 1997

IV Secondary literature: Illustrations

IV.1 Miscellaneous volume publications

Plate – *54**

In: John Falconer, 'Photography in Central Asia', in: Susan Whitfield (ed.), *Silk Roads: Peoples, Cultures, Landscapes*
London, Thames & Hudson, 2019

IV.2 Critique and reviews

Figure – *41** (both images)

Annabelle Seubert, 'Da stimmt was nicht'
Die Tageszeitung (*Wochenende*), Berlin; 5–6 January 2019

Plate – *57**

Roman Bucheli, 'Daniel Schwartz. Die Dunkelkammer ist die andere Küche'
Neue Zürcher Zeitung (*Feuilleton*), Zürich; 27 December 2017

Plate – *47**
Figure – *28**

William Ewing, 'Unassuming Places'
Parkett, Parkett Verlag AG, Zürich; Nr. 89, December 2011

Figure – *26**

'Ich lasse die Bilder zu mir kommen'
Daniel Schwartz in conversation with Nanni Baltzer and Thilo König
Photonews, Hamburg; Nr. 7–8, 2011

Plates – *73** – *94**

'Fotografie ist eine gut gemachte Lüge'
Daniel Schwartz and Jules Spinatsch in conversation with Brigitte Ulmer
Du, Zürich; Heft 800, October 2009

Plate – ***43***

In: Urs Fanger, 'Bilderkosmos mit Porträts und Werken', in: Hans-Peter Schwarz (ed.), *ZHdK. Publikation zur Gründung der Zürcher Hochschule der Künste*
Scheidegger & Spiess, Zürich 2007

Plates – *38** – *47**

Roger Nickl, 'Daniel Schwartz. Vom Verschwinden des Geldes'
uni-maganzin. Die Zeitschrift der Universität Zürich, Zürich; Nr. 4, December 2001

Figure – *17**
Plate – *94**

Anna Swan, 'Daniel Schwartz. Behind the Wall'
The Peak Magazine, Hong Kong; October 1990

Figure – ***16***

Hugo Loetscher, 'Der Traum der Karyatiden'
Du, Zürich; Heft 515; January 1984

IV.3 Press publications

Plate – *12**

Christopher Hitchens, 'Die Akte Henry Kissinger. I. Teil: Kriegsverbrechen; II. Teil: Verbrechen gegen die Menschlichkeit'
Lettre International, Berlin; Heft 53, 2001

Plate – *38**

Klaus-Helge Donath, 'Machtkampf im Kreml', and Marina Rumjanzewa, 'Russlands Mittelschicht in der Krise'
Weltwoche, Zürich; Nr. 37, 10 September 1998

Plate – *12**

Vietnam. Dossier Erinnerung
Du, Zürich; Heft 674; July–August 1997

'Mémoire du Vietnam: Vietnam People's Army/Vietnam News Agency Photographers, Don McCullin, Philip Jones Griffiths, Tim Page, Daniel Schwartz'
Bieler Fototage/Journées photographiques de Bienne (20 September–26 October 1997)

V Selected additional references

What follows is a list of further reading with photographs of the same origin as those reproduced in this volume, but which were not included in these pages.

Daniel Schwartz, *Cotton field and fibre optic cable post, Uzbekistan 2002*
In: Marti Guixé and Inga Knölke (eds), *Intertwingled. The Role of the Rug in Arts, Crafts and Design*
Mantova, Maurizio Corraini Edizioni Srl, 2022

Galleria Nazionale d'Arte Moderna e Contemporanea, Rome (22 March–4 September 2022)

—, *Garbage truck, 1993*
In: Kathrin Frauenfelder, *Die Kunstsammlung des Kantons Zürich*
Zürich, Scheidegger & Spiess, 2019

—, *Embedded, 2013/2014*
In: Céline Eidenbenz, *En Marche/Unterwegs*
Bern, Till Schaap Edition, 2017

Musée d'Art, Sion (group exhibition; 3 June 2017–18 March 2018)

—, *Alexander-Geschichten. Vietnam und Afghanistan* (Photographs and text)
Leukerbad, Leukerbad International Literature Festival, 2016

Galerie St.Laurent, Leukerbad (1–3 July 2016)

–, *WAR IS A MISERABLE BUSINESS, 1996/2000*, Triptych with textwork
In: Huang Du (ed.), *Ansiedad de la imagen / Image Anxiety*
Madrid, La Fabrica Editorial, 2012

Photo Espagna, Madrid (group exhibition; 6 June–22 July 2012)

–, *Bangladeshi selling newspapers on Wall Street, New York, 1998; New York Stock Exchange brokers, Wall Street, New York, 1998 (Diptychon I)*
In: Christoph Doswald (ed.), *Press Art. Die Sammlung Annette und Peter Nobel*
Bern, Stämpfli Publikationen AG, 2010

Pera Museum, Istanbul ('And Now the Good News. Works from the Nobel Collection', group exhibition; 13 April–7 August 2022)
Museum der Moderne, Salzburg (group exhibition; 3 July–24 October 2010)
Kunstmuseum St. Gallen, St. Gallen (group exhibition; 30 January–20 June 2010)

–, illustrations opp. pp. 76, 77 and 333
In: Julia Lovell, *The Great Wall. China against the World. 1000 BC–AD 2000*
London, Atlantic Books, 2006

–, *1992 Daniel Schwartz, Burma*
In: Mary Panzer (ed.), *Things as they are. Photojournalism in Context since 1955*
Amsterdam, World Press Photo, and London, Chris Boot Ltd, 2005

—, *The Great Wall of China*
In: Nanni Baltzer, *Nature of Artifice*, in: Kurt W. Forster, *Metamorph. Trajectories*
Venice, Fondazione di Biennale di Venezia, 2004

9th International Architecture Exhibition, Venice (group exhibition; 12 September–7 November 2004)

—, *Timor-Leste, 1999. Tempo de Agonia*
In: *Dia di Bai*
Coimbra, Centro de artes visuais, 2003

Colégio das Artes, Patio da Inquisiçao, Coimbra (group exhibition; 27 June–30 September 2003)

—, *Gran Muralla China*
In: Matthias Bärmann, *The spirituality of void. Khmer sculptures and modern Western art*
Valencia, Fundación Bancaja, 2001

Centre Cultural Bancaja (group exhibition; 2 October 2001–6 January 2002)

—, *Vom Verschwinden des Geldes. Der Foto-Essay*
In: Peter Pfrunder and Martin Gasser (eds), *Hugo Loetscher. Durchs Bild zur Welt gekommen. Reportagen und Aufsätze zur Fotografie*
Zürich, Scheidegger & Spiess, 2001

Kunsthaus Zürich, Zürich (group exhibition; 31 August–18 November 2001)

—, *Diadoumenos, Paris, 1976; Marmorköpfe und Mosaiken, Mytilene 1983; Relief von Phaleron, 1983*
In: Erika Billeter (ed.), *Skulptur im Licht der Fotografie. Von Bayard bis Mapplethorpe*
Wabern-Bern, Benteli Verlags AG, 1997

Selected venues:
Musée d'art et d'histoire, Fribourg (group exhibition; 27 March–1 June 1998)
Wilhelm Lehmbruck Museum, Duisburg (group exhibition; 6 December 1997–22 February 1998)

—, *Burma und Kambodscha in den Medien*, and *Thomas Kern und Daniel Schwartz, Iran 1991–1997*
In: Martin Gasser and Urs Stahel (eds), *Weltenblicke. Reportagefotografie und ihre Medien*
Zürich, Offizin Verlag, 1997

Fotomuseum Winterthur, Winterthur (group exhibition; 14 June–17 August 1997)

—, *Il mondo, la carne, il diavolo*
Giovanna Calvenzi, in: Walter Guadagnini and Filippo Maggia (eds), *Modena per la Fotografia, catalogo generale*
Milan, Edizione Gabriele Mazzotta, 1995

Foro Boario, Modena per la Fotografia, Modena (group exhibition; 15 October 1995–7 January 1996)

—, *Vierzehn Fotografien*
In: Albert Lutz and Huang Qi (eds), *Chinesische Szenen 1656/1992. Die 13 Meter lange Bildrolle des Malers Xiao Yuncong, 1656. Fotografien von Daniel Schwartz, 1992*
Zürich, Museum Rietberg, 1992

Museum Rietberg, Zürich (22 October 1992–31 January 1993)

—, *Das Mass aller Dinge, Teil I & Teil II*
In: Guido Magnaguagno, 'Neue Wahrnehmungen. Über die Schweizer Photographie der letzten Jahre'
Du, Zürich; Heft 534, August 1985

—, *Über ein Heilbad auf der Insel Nysiros, Griechenland, 1978*
In: Walter Binder, Hendel Teicher and David Streiff, *Junge Schweizer Photographen. Reportagen, Konzepte, Experimente*
Zürich, Stiftung für die Photographie, 1981

Kunsthaus Zürich, Zürich (group exhibition; 29 August–25 October 1981)

—, *Peperoni, 1977/1978*
In: *Visuelle Kommunikation 1878–1978: 100 Jahre Kunstgewerbeschule Zürich Wegleitung* Nr. 319
Zürich, Kunstgewerbemuseum Zürich

Kunstgewerbemuseum der Stadt Zürich, Zürich 1978 (group exhibition; 23 September–12 November 1978)

Biographies

Daniel Schwartz is one of the most internationally renowned photographers of his generation. From 1990 to 2005, he was photographer and editorial contributor for the cultural magazine *Du*. He made his debut as an author with *Snow in Samarkand. A Travelogue of Three Thousand Years* (2008), and his photographic monographs include *Travelling Through the Eye of History* (2009) and *While the Fires Burn. A Glacier Odyssey* (2017). His work has been exhibited at Martin-Gropius Bau, Berlin (2011), San Francisco Museum of Modern Art (2011) and Bündner Kunstmuseum (2018). In 2010 he received the Culture Prize of the Canton of Zürich and in 2019 the Art Prize of the Canton of Solothurn. He has been a member of VII Photo Agency since 2017, and in 2018 his work to date was honoured in Vadim Jendreyko's artist documentary *Beyond the Obvious*. www.danielschwartz.org

Giovanna Calvenzi is a curator, researcher and editor. From 1985 to 2019 she was photo editor for publications including *Vanity Fair* and *Corriere della Sera Sette*. She has edited books on contemporary photography and realized exhibitions including 'Il mondo, la carne, il diavolo', an exhibition of Daniel Schwartz's work for Modena per la Fotografia (1995), the Rencontres Internationales de la Photographie, Arles (as Artistic Director, 1998), PhotoEspaña, Madrid (2002) and Mois de la Photo, Paris (as Artistic Director, 2004). She is the director of the Archivio Gabriele Basilico, archiviogabrielebasilico.it

Carolin Emcke is a philosopher and writer. From 1999 to 2014 she worked as an international reporter focusing on human rights and war crimes. Since 2004 she has moderated the monthly discussion series *Streitraum*, held at the Schaubühne, Berlin. Her books include *When I Say Yes* (2020), *Against Hate* (2016), *Because We Can Speak: On Witnessing and Justice* (2013) and *Echoes of Violence: Letters from a War Reporter* (2007). In 2016, she was awarded the Peace Prize of the German Book Trade.

Fanni Fetzer is an author and curator. Since 2011 she has been director of Kunstmusuem Luzern, where she has realized exhibitions with, among others, Betye Saar, David Hockney, Candida Höfer, Thomas Schütte, Taryn Simon and Vivian Suter. She has received several awards from the Swiss Federal Office of Culture for her work as a curator and museum director. In 2022, she received the prize of the Central Switzerland Cultural Foundation.

Beat Wismer is an art historian. He was director of the Aargauer Kunsthaus, Aarau, from 1985 to 2007, and from 2007 to 2017 was general director of the Museum Kunstpalast, Düsseldorf. He has organized and curated many exhibitions of historical and contemporary art, edited numerous publications and written widely on modern and contemporary art. In 2003 he was awarded the inaugural Max von Moos Prize for his 'extraordinary services to the mediation of Swiss art'. Since his retirement, Wismer has lived in Zürich as a freelance curator and author. In 2019 he was co-curator of 'Turner. The Sea and the Alps', realized by Kunstmuseum Luzern and Tate, London.

Credits

Text

p. 19 Hannah Arendt, *The Human Condition* (Chicago: University of Chicago Press, 1958). © 1958 University of Chicago. By permission of University of Chicago Press.

Images

Images are referred to by figure number.

4 La Fontaine de Narcisse/ Brancusi Constantin © Centre Pompidou, MNAM-CCI, Dist. RMN-Grand Palais © Succession Brancusi - All rights reserved. ADAGP, Paris and DACS, London 2023

6 The Metropolitan Museum of Art/Art Resource/Scala, Florence © Center for Creative Photography, The University of Arizona Foundation / DACS 2023

7 Staatliche Kunstsammlung Dresden. Kupferstich-Kabinett, Staatliche Kunstsammlungen Dresden, Photo by Elke Estel/ Hans-Peter Klut

8 Kulturstiftung Sachsen-Anhalt, Kunstmuseum Moritzburg Halle (Saale)Reproduction: Kulturstiftung Sachsen-Anhalt. © Nachlass Hans Finsler/Hans Finsler Estate

9 Magnum Photos

12 Photo Elysée, Lausanne

13 Ullstein bild Dtl / Getty Images

15 Courtesy Werner Bischof Estate / Magnum Photos

19 Kunstmuseum Solothurn / Dübi-Müller-Stiftung, 1980

22 Courtesy Werner Bischof Estate / Magnum Photos

24 Courtesy Werner Bischof Estate / Magnum Photos

29 Skimage / Alamy Stock Photo

32 Ufficia storico, Archivio fotografico, Pontificio Istituto Missioni Estere P.I.M.E., Milano, Italy

33 Wellcome Collection / John Thomson 1871. RGS/National Library of Scotland/Wellcome Institute for the History of Medicine

34 Ufficia storico, Archivio fotografico, Pontificio Istituto Missioni Estere P.I.M.E., Milano, Italy

35 Metropolitan Museum of Art, New York. © Die Photographische Sammlung/SK Stiftung Kultur - August Sander Archiv, Cologne / DACS 2023

37 Ufficia storico, Archivio fotografico, Pontificio Istituto Missioni Estere P.I.M.E., Milano, Italy

Acknowledgments

This volume is the result of an archive research project conducted between 2019 and 2022, and it accompanies the exhibition Tracings first shown at the Kunstmuseum Luzern, Lucerne, Switzerland, 30 September 2023 – 4 February 2024.

The artist owes a debt of gratitude to Fanni Fetzer for her unbiased encouragement regarding the plan to core for the first time his photographic archive and host the exhibition, and to Beat Wismer for his robust enthusiasm and shared wisdom while working with the unknown that awaited him as editor and curator.

For critique and suggestions during the process of ever-changing image editing deliberations I extend profound thanks to Rebekka Steiger, who participated affectionately, scrutinizing individual frames and their pairings with the painter's incorruptible eye; to Philip Blenkinsop, Gary Knight and Carl Stadelhofer, trusted friends of many decades and accomplices both when dreaming up the unthinkable and seeing through tasks that lay ahead. Marco Bischof very generously allowed inclusion of his father Werner Bischof's work in the book. Sophia Remer and Ursula Heidelberger of the Laboratorium, Labor für Fotografie, Zürich, ensured meticulous digitization of my photographic negatives and composite gelatin silver prints.

Tracings. Photography and Thought is the sixth book with Thames & Hudson. Without their faith in my work and foresight I would not have been able to walk my ways. I hope with this present volume available, the five previous acquire additional meaning – my thanks to all who have worked on the project.

Photography is a vagabond among the arts, and it lies in the nature of the craft that a certain something, mechanically or unconsciously netted in the frame at the instant of its creation, emerges much later, and in retrospect appears to be still potent and declarative. The texts written for the book also speak of this occurrence. I am grateful to Giovanna Calvenzi, Carolin Emcke, Fanni Fetzer and Beat Wismer for their findings and interpretations, which complete each other.

I dedicate this book to Tim Page, with fond memories of our lightbox inquiry into the *Mindful Moment*, and with my greatest respect for his lifelong and compassionate devotion to the country that is home to the soul of my grandmother and her ancestors.

Support for the artist's archive research project was granted by the Stanley Thomas Johnson Foundation and by UBS Kulturstiftung.

STANLEY THOMAS
JOHNSON
FOUNDATION

The book was produced with the support of the Swiss Arts Council Pro Helvetia.

swiss arts council
prohelvetia

Additional support from:

kultur
SWISSLOS
Fonds des Kantons Solothurn

N° 105 in the programme of the Binding **Sélection d'Artistes**